GLOBAL
GAME
CHANGE

Thank you for choosing a SAGE product!
If you have any comment, observation or feedback,
I would like to personally hear from you.
Please write to me at **contactceo@sagepub.in**

Vivek Mehra, Managing Director and CEO,
SAGE Publications India Pvt Ltd, New Delhi

Bulk Sales

SAGE India offers special discounts
for purchase of books in bulk.
We also make available special imprints
and excerpts from our books on demand.

For orders and enquiries, write to us at

Marketing Department
SAGE Publications India Pvt Ltd
B1/I-1, Mohan Cooperative Industrial Area
Mathura Road, Post Bag 7
New Delhi 110044, India

E-mail us at **marketing@sagepub.in**

Get to know more about SAGE

Be invited to SAGE events, get on our mailing list.
Write today to **marketing@sagepub.in**

This book is also available as an e-book.

GLOBAL
GAME
CHANGE

How the Global Southern Belt Will Reshape Our World

JOHN NAISBITT
DORIS NAISBITT

SAGE

Response
Business Books

www.sagepublications.com
Los Angeles • London • New Delhi • Singapore • Washington DC

First published in 2016 by

SAGE Publications India Pvt Ltd
B1/I-1 Mohan Cooperative Industrial Area
Mathura Road, New Delhi 110 044, India
www.sagepub.in

SAGE Publications Inc
2455 Teller Road
Thousand Oaks, California 91320, USA

SAGE Publications Ltd
1 Oliver's Yard, 55 City Road
London EC1Y 1SP, United Kingdom

SAGE Publications Asia-Pacific Pte Ltd
3 Church Street
#10-04 Samsung Hub
Singapore 049483

Published by Vivek Mehra for SAGE Publications India Pvt Ltd, typeset in 11/13 pt Berkeley by Diligent Typesetter and printed at Chaman Enterprises, New Delhi.

Library of Congress Cataloging-in-Publication Data

Names: Naisbitt, John, author. | Naisbitt, Doris, author.
Title: Global game change : how the global Southern belt will reshape our
  world / John and Doris Naisbitt.
Description: New Delhi; Thousand Oaks : SAGE, [2016] | Includes
  bibliographical references.
Identifiers: LCCN 2015039140| ISBN 9789351506409 (hardback : alk. paper) |
  ISBN 9789351506416 (ebook) | ISBN 9789351506393 (epub)
Subjects: LCSH: Economic development—Developing countries. | Developing
  countries—Foreign economic relations. | Developing countries—Economic
  conditions—21st century.
Classification: LCC HC59.7 .N2365 2016 | DDC 330.9172/4—dc23 LC record
available at http://lccn.loc.gov/2015039140

ISBN: 987-93-515-0640-9 (HB)

The SAGE Team: Sachin Sharma, Sandhya Gola, and Ritu Chopra

Contents

A Thought about India

America had a dream. China pushes its dream. What about India?
If we think of India, we get a colorful picture in our head: many young talents, entrepreneurs bursting of ideas, the richness and mixture of culture, the beauty and diversity of landscapes, and the richness of its cuisine. We like to envision Indian economy as it could be, not as it is. But what will it be?

For 10 years we have a good friend from India, Manju Yadav, a young woman who left New Delhi with her husband in search for a better life in Austria. Five years ago, their daughter Paani was born. What will India be like when Paani has grown up? By 2022, Prime Minister Modi believes, "it will be clear that this is India's century." Can his promise come true?

India has what it takes. And if we simplify, there are only two indispensable basic ingredients missing: a nourishing environment for entrepreneurs and a climate of hope. Trust in opportunities was the driver of the American dream. To Manju, New York still "is the dream city for most people of the world." On the ground the dream has worn off. The new dreams are built in China, next door to India. And that is India's chance.

The American dream was based on the individual. China's dream is a collective dream. China believes in guanxi, and it is taking guanxi global. China's drive is strong. It has proven that a U-turn from dirt-poor to wealth is possible. In the tailwinds of China's economic power, Asia is moving from a collection of emerging economies to a collection of strong global players passing America and Europe on economic power and technological advancements.

In addition, India has century-old ties to emerging economies in Africa. A new global middle class is being created and new markets can be conquered. How could India miss that chance?

We are optimistic. India will have a bumpy ride, but the dynamics of a young population will prevail. Paani will enter school this year in Austria, but it may well be that she will be among many well-educated young Indians who return home to a country that holds the realistic promise to allow them to make their dreams come true.

Paani's India can be one of the greatest countries in the world.

Prologue

In May 2014, we traveled from Vienna, Austria, to Sydney, Australia. Two flights, 10 and 13 hours with a stop in Beijing, brought us to the other side of the globe. From there the world looks different. Passing through the southern sky, the Sun apparently shows a right–left trajectory unlike the left–right motion when looked at it from the Northern hemisphere. Storms spin clockwise while anticlockwise in the North. And also in geographical matters the world turns upside down. "For us the Far East is the Near East," said Paul Keating, former prime minister of Australia when we sat with him at a dinner table at a conference some years ago in Seoul. His words now ring truer than ever.

Perspectives can turn upside down with changing viewpoints. And often it takes time to get familiar with the unfamiliar, in big and small matters. Even though one would think that an "American–Austrian husband and wife team," as Australia's media called us, do not have too much of a different cultural background, our backgrounds have left their marks. John, a first generation American, grew up on a farm in Glenwood, Utah, a village of about 200 people in America's West. Doris was born in the Austrian Alps in Bad Ischl, summer residence to the Habsburg emperor Franz Josef, most famous for his marriage to empress Sisi. No wonder maybe 80 percent monarchists in town are still yearning for those days.

Until the day we met on September 14, 1994, at a yearly media conference in Villach, a small town in Southern Austria, we had very different paths of life. In the soon-to-follow working relationship as author and publisher, we experienced what makes us different is not dividing, but enriching our relationship, in our private life and in our work together. American optimism often meets European skepticism: "just do it" collides with "what if?"

We could not work together without sharing the curiosity to explore, the drive and joy to learn something new every day. To do global research demands understanding different positions and the willingness to throw old mindsets overboard and replace them with new points of view. To us this is an exciting adventure. We do not invent stories, we report what we see, even if strange to us like storms spinning clockwise in Australia. And we do not have to be right. Others may see a different world evolving. Some might not like the conclusions we come to. We do not always like what we see, but we try to be honest in our reporting.

We do not start our journey in life as a blank sheet.

Change that obviously leads to benefits is easy to embrace. But the more the change interferes with long-term practices and conditions, the harder it gets. In addition, our perception of the present is directed by the experience of the past and greatly influenced by the environment in which we are born and raised. Time, location, and education become the lenses through which we look at the world. Looking back in history we see that it took time until major shifts became anchored in the minds of the people affected.

To a European it seems unusual that some Americans have never left their country. Naturally their country's borders have become the borders of their world. American points of view will differ greatly depending on local environment, level of education, and even the color of their skin. On the other hand, you meet Austrians who look at the world from an Austrian point of view, not really aware that the country's population of 8.5 million is smaller than many districts in many metropolises. It is comparable to the Internet, in which each user is the center, the point at which all strings converge and diverge.

The more extensive a person travels, the more the picture will change as new worlds become accessible. We have especially experienced how radically a picture can change when people visit China for the first time. There is no central point at which a worldview can be created and adjusted. There are millions of different perspectives, rooted in the past, and reaching far into the future. You and we, in our community, our city, our province, and our country are only pieces of a puzzle that make up the world. But the changing positions of the pieces of our common puzzle give clear signals of global game change.

The Ascent of the West

Hegemonies, powerful sovereigns, and leading intellectuals in all continents created spheres of influence within and beyond their borders. The German Book of Civil Law (Buergerliches Gesetzbuch) until today is based on jurisprudence of the 19th century which goes back to Roman law. Think of Socrates, Plato, and Aristotle and the foundation of philosophy, Athens as the cradle of democracy, the Iliad and Odyssey and the art of poetry. Athen's and Rome's political, legal, and cultural influence is still with us today. The Roman Empire in Europe, the Kingdom of Kush and the Egyptians in Africa, the Five Hegemons and the Zhou Dynasty in China, the cultures of the Inca, Maya, and Aztecs in South America, all left their footprints on global cultures.

But none of these cultures gained such comprehensive global influence as did Europe and the United States, the key players of the West. Their political, economic, and cultural influences have spread over the last few centuries, overwhelming local cultures in most continents. Western clothing, Western music, Western business practices, inventions, and innovations spread from the West to the rest of the world. This over time has led to a Western self-perception of superiority over other parts of the world. The West sees itself as the moral authority to set global standards based on a Westerncentric worldview, judging the world by and against Western standards.

This era, we believe, is coming to an end.

From a Westerncentric to a Multicentric World

As we travel the world and do our research, we see the global authority of the West is no longer unchallenged; the Western worldview is no longer accepted as universal. It is increasingly being questioned by emerging economies around the globe that are developing their own standards. If we look at the geographical positions of the emerging economies, it appears that they collectively form a belt around the southern part of the globe: "The Global Southern Belt."

Western hegemony has been diminished from various directions. Reduced by a gradual loss of economic power, its claim to own the global growth formula of democracy and free markets is no longer sustainable. New dynamics are transforming the global community. The Westerncentric world is fading into a multicentric world in which many countries and even more important, "a world of cities" will set the tone in global matters. It is a great opening-up to a mix of opinions, economic and cultural diversity, and, in a longer time frame, new governing models. The game changers will be the countries and cities of the Global Southern Belt, which will reshaping our world in the decades to come.

The Fall of Hegemony in the 15th Century

It was probably not much earlier than the first decade of the 21st century that the West felt the first rumbles to its certainty of authority. In Asia, China began to transform from an emerging economy to a major player in the global economy. In many Latin American countries market reforms and the end of juntas, military dictatorships, and Left-wing authoritarian regimes began to show results. A young generation in Africa, despite corruption and misgovernance, pushed for the long idle qualities of courage and entrepreneurship. From the bottom up the mood was changing, the call for reform in emerging economies got louder and gained momentum. This dynamic was not only against conditions in their own countries, the call for reform shared calls for an end to Western paternalism. The mood was the strongest in China and spread to emerging economies around the globe.

We see many parallels today as we look back to what we know as the Reformation, when the dominance of the ruling Catholic Church was challenged five centuries ago.

In 2017, it will be 500 years since Martin Luther nailed a memorandum of protest on the porch of the Church of Wittenberg Castle. One man's act became an avalanche soon to sweep away old worldviews and to shake the foundation of the most powerful force of the time: the Catholic Church. It was a turning point in history, a true game change. The Catholic geocentric worldview had to give way to the heliocentric worldview and science began to shake off the shackles of religious doctrines that had held it hostage for more than a millennium. The decline of the power of the Catholic Church gained momentum. But the end of its hegemony would not have been possible without the fundamental changes of the time.

The rise of the Catholic Church began 1700 years ago, when the Roman heir to the throne, Constantine, became the ruler of the Roman Empire. Constantine was the first Roman emperor to be baptized as a Christian. It was a U-turn from Roman polytheisms to Christian monotheism. And it allowed Constantine to underscore his authorization by a parallel: God was the sole ruler in heaven, and Constantine was the sole, God-blessed Roman Emperor on earth.

It was the beginning of collaboration of the Catholic Church (the only recognized religion) and the State. Tightly interconnected, each supported the power of the other to achieve mutual benefits. Inequality was God given. Clergy, nobility, citizen, farmer was the social hierarchy. Each rank had its place; each rank had its courts.

In those days epidemics and plagues caused high mortality, and people without worldly prospect were longing for salvation in afterlife. The only place to turn to was the Church. But over time segments of the Catholic Church had degenerated from serving believers to capitalizing on the needs of believers. The door to heaven had a price tag. Until in the 15th century when things began to change.

It was the European Renaissance, with its beginnings in the 14th century in Italy, which started to herald the shift from the dominating theocentric (God in the center) worldview to a much more anthropocentric (mankind in the center) worldview. Humanism as an education movement merged with critical opinions about the theological foundation of Catholicism and gained momentum. The powerful movement spread from northern Italy to most of Europe. Transition started with questions and doubts, a search for alternatives, a shift in mindsets, and different views to once accepted positions. Education supported the interplay of cultural, social, political factors and opened the minds of the people. Paired with a rapid urbanization, it created the opportunity to reach modest wealth for people of various professions and made cities prosperous. Education in the hands of the Church and its economic strength had been strong pillars of the hegemony of the Catholic Church. With the spreading of the Renaissance and Reformation, access to education made its way down the social ladder.

Gutenberg's Printing Press: The Internet in the 15th Century

Until commoners gained access to books, the Church and its clerics were the almost sole readers and interpreters of God's word, the Bible, on which their authority was based. Before Gutenberg's mechanical movable type printing in 1446 revolutionized printing in Europe, books were rare and expensive. Higher education was in the hands of the Church and under the rules of the Church. The spreading of diverse opinions was limited.

Gutenberg's invention opened a door to a new level of communication. It led to an explosion of printing activities and allowed the feeding of the hunger for education. In only a few decades printing spread from only one print shop in Mainz, Germany, to shops in 270 cities in Europe. By 1500, only 50 years after the invention, printing presses around Western Europe produced more than 20 million copies of books. This did not only allow people to read the Bible in their own language, unthinkable only few decades before, but it also led to a media revolution. So-called one-sheet-prints, the forefathers of newspapers, quickly entered the market. Many of them showed caricatures of morally corrupt monks and clerics.

At the same time, continuing urbanization brought people closer to each other and helped thoughts and ideas to reach critical mass. And, as in every transition, there came a tipping point.

The End of Unrestricted Hegemony

Whether Martin Luther did in fact nail his 95 theses of protest on the door of the Church of Wittenberg Castle on October 31, 1517, is controversial among historians. That they were written is unchallenged. Luther's 95 theses were a manifest of discontent with the centuries-old social orders and hierarchies built in Roman Catholic Europe. It was the outcry against corrupt and dysfunctional structures of the Church. Its unintended consequence was the substantial transformation of Europe and the creation of the foundation of what would later be called the Western world: North America, Europe, Australia, and New Zealand.

Today, there is no Martin Luther nailing 95 theses of necessary reforms on a global porch. The calls for reforms reverberate bottom-up. The Internet has raised communication to a new level. Communication is without borders, linking billions of people in the borderless media of our time—social networks. Gutenberg's printing press in the 15th century allowed the spread of different opinions; the Internet in the 21st century allows the spreading of ideas and the uniting of millions of voices around a common message: calls for repair and reform, angry and eager to get their share of economic progress. In an interview with the German magazine *Focus* (21/2015), Henry Kissinger said: "the Internet has much larger social impact than Gutenberg's Bible."

Around 500 years ago, inequality among different classes, aristocrats, clerks, and commoners inhibited equal opportunities for all. The initial success of reforming the Catholic Church resulted in the Church's loss of ultimate authority on education and the interpretation of natural science. The liberation of the restricting grip led to scientific findings, inventions, and innovation. Enlightenment in the 18th century reinforced the surge of ideas, permitted sustainable progress, and prepared the path to the modern age.

The Enablers: "E's"—Education and Economics

Even though less famous than Martin Luther, it was John Calvin, the French theologian and pastor, who gained large influence on the future development of the West. His teachings led to a sea change in moral and working ethics in Europe. Instead of collecting treasures in heaven, diligence and economic success in this life became worthwhile. Education and new learning processes led to growth and allowed advances not only in technology, but also in social life and organization. Ambition and the will to work hard became the driving forces of progress in the old world, and later in the new world, America.

The big "E's" in the 21st century

We are often asked how we judge a country's growth potential. The answer is simple: we look at its education system. It is the foundation of economic progress and the enabler to make independent political choices and decisions.

Once the Church lost its position as the guardian of education, its hegemony was not sustainable.

The lack of education on which to build economic progress is the core problem in most underdeveloped countries. Poverty is not destiny. Today as economic considerations are dwarfing ideologies in importance and impact, education has to be the number one priority for each country. Education is the key to economic progress and social stability. The two key issues of our time are two big E's: Economics and Education.

And while in many developed countries higher education has become as expensive as once handwritten books, this hurdle is being taken down by online education. Free online programs are opening the doors of the best universities to all social classes and people of all continents. Education is the enabler for all nations to emerge as global economic players by their own efforts. The role of governments is to support equal access to education and to create an entrepreneurial friendly environment so that people can take care of themselves.

The Eroding Hegemony of the West

For a while we lived in both Boston and Vienna. It was always interesting to experience how different and at the same time similar they are. Austrians as part of Europe feel a strong moral authority, after all Europe had the Greek philosophers, the Roman Empire, the Renaissance, Reformation, the Enlightenment and humanism, superior values grown over millennia.

Americans have all of this too; the roots of most of its population, and its entrepreneurs, intellectuals, academics, and politicians go back to European countries. And America added a spirit Europe is missing—its drive and optimism. People anywhere are not immune to joining the feeling that their country is, if not superior, then at least a role model in many ways. It just feels good as long as it is true.

After all, the West seemed to have it all: social stability, economic and technological progress, and wealth. But now an increasing number of people feel that what has been achieved over centuries could be gambled away in one or two generations. The call for reform is rumbling the loudest in the most success-spoiled Western countries of Europe and the United States. (And remember, the West is only North America, Europe, Australia, and New Zealand.) The rumble is not questioning Western democracy as such. It is not freedom of speech, human rights, and rule of law that is being challenged. It is the qualification of leaders, governing practices and a loss of trust in politicians that is shaking the 200-year-old Western democracy.

Western democracy is in danger of degenerating to a self-service-store where different groups are seeking to serve only their own best interests. Politicians and voters are creating their own menus. Europeans demand a social welfare net their systems can't afford. Many decry Western democracy as sustainable without reform. But the call for reform quickly falls silent when it comes to any abdication of acquired privilege.

The Global Southern Belt: The Game Changer in the World Community

In our travels to emerging countries in Latin America, Asia, and Africa, we have experienced both anger over current economic and political conditions and optimism for the future. In the meanwhile hungry for change and progress, the emerging economies of the Global Southern Belt will not stand still and wait. Emerging economies around the globe are setting new social economic goals and building new alliances. While some Western countries are sleeping on their glorious past, emerging economies are putting all efforts into creating a brighter future. But between the inglorious past and a promising future for emerging economies the high hurdles of creating the structures for growth have to be taken. The consequence is a bumpy ride with euphoric heights and scary setbacks as the structures for sustainable growth have not yet been established. Nevertheless even large fluctuations do not change the overall trend of the rise of the emerging economies in the Global Southern Belt.

More than 80 percent of world's population is in the process of nation building, learning from the advances and mistakes the West made. In *Mind Set!* we wrote that in China the periphery is the center. What was true for China is now true for the world. What once was pictured the periphery of the West, the countries of Asia, Africa, and Latin America, are transforming to new economic centers in a multicentric world.

Our purpose in this book is to paint a picture of the transition we see evolving in the first half of the 21st century. It is a picture in which we combine trustworthy data and information from various sources, and years, often decades, of travel and personal experience on the ground. While snapshots have their good sides, predictions on day-to-day events are a pointless undertaking as they color the picture in both directions, too optimistic and too pessimistic.

Our discussion here is about profound change in the global community. Its time frame spans over the next decades. We see the opening up of new dynamics, the awaking of new drivers in the global economy, shifts in geopolitical and economic importance. It is about the game change from a Westerncentric to a multicentric world.

1

The Global Southern Belt

From Emerging Economies to Global Players

Megatrends, published in 1982 ended: "My God, what a great time to be alive!" One of the megatrends described was the shift from north to south in the United States, foreshadowing today's Global North–South shift. It said that "although the North South shift sounds like an either or choice, it is not." It was not in the 1980s nor is it now in its new global context. The global game change is a great opening-up of the whole world, with nations in both hemispheres having unprecedented opportunities for renewal and growth.

To the nations of the Global Southern Belt, it is like lifting a curtain revealing a new picture of the global community and their place in it. Many countries are feeling an awakening of self-confidence and trust in their potential. The nations of the Global Northern Belt, where most countries of the West are located, are beginning to anticipate a shift in the economic importance of the South as new opportunities for their faltering futures. Economically and culturally, it can be enrichment for all. Again, what a great time to be alive!

The transition we describe will not happen without bumps on the path and nor will it happen overnight. The time frame in which we will be witnesses and actors in the global game change and the transformation from a Westerncentric to a multicentric world will be the first half of the 21st century. As in any major transitions, this shift will come with the need to correct and adapt to changing conditions. And often changing our mindset will trail behind events. Let us not underestimate how dramatic the change is. The United States has been the world's largest economy since the 1880s. Along with its Western partners America has dominated the world economy during our lifetimes. Western culture celebrated a victorious procession into all continents with Western lifestyle, Western business practices, Western clothes, and Western food. The West represents only 17 percent of the world's population but it holds about 75 percent of the world's wealth.

The West without question has been the global helmsman. This era is coming to an end.

In the coming decades, the way we look at the world will change significantly. It will no longer be "the West and the rest." The world will be watching the rise of the Global Southern Belt (GSB). Emerging nations of the Global Southern Belt will not be under the dominance of the West. They are increasingly aware of their own potential and they are getting aligned to make the most of it. The most dynamic, most influential nation in the Global Southern Belt will of course be China, but it is nonetheless only one country in the three continents.

The Global Sothern Belt

The GBS Encompasses Latin America, Africa, and Asia

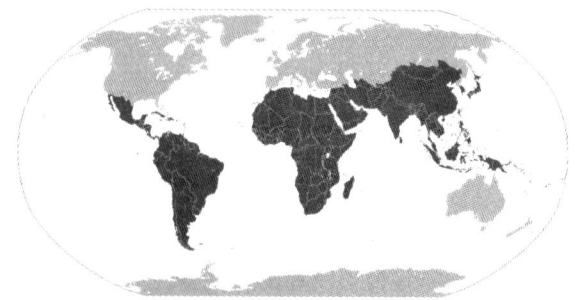

Note: This figure is not to scale. It does not represent any authentic national or international boundaries and is used for illustrative purposes only.

For the West to let go of a Westerncentric worldview will be a highly emotional process. Emotion does not like to listen to reason. The connection between heart and brain is blocked. There is widespread denial about even the possibility of a multicentric 21st century and the rise of the Global Southern Belt.

We are of course also not immune to Westerncentric thinking. That is the spirit in which we grew up. But we cannot have both, a Westerncentric and a multicentric worldview. To let go of the Westerncentric worldview demands a farewell to the Western position of moral and economic superiority. And holding on to the claim is becoming difficult, as more and more cracks have become visible. Whether we look at annual growth rates, stagnation of per capita incomes, high unemployment, declining middle class, rising inequality or an unemployment rate of up to 50 percent among the youth in Spain, Portugal, Greece, and mounting public debts, the West is facing difficult times.

Is there even a path to "dystopia," as Stephen D. King warns? Or is the West entering "a great degeneration," as Niall Ferguson puts it? Is Europe facing "the end of the European dream and the decline of a continent," as Walter Laqueur fears? Or are we actors and witnesses in a great opening-up, the rise of emerging nations of the Global Southern Belt, and a multicentric world from which all nations can benefit?

The Global Southern Belt Will Shape the 21st Century

Our thoughts about the rise of the Global Southern Belt have not evolved one rainy morning when we had nothing to do but think about what we could think about. It started slowly and has grown over years as we experienced the changing mood in countries we visited, the rising self-confidence of many leaders we have met with, their growing optimism despite current problems, increasing nationalism, slow decline of admiration for the West, and pride about their own achievements as emerging economies. An entrepreneurial spirit is awakening with a growing confidence in shaping their own future.

This change has different faces, often small details in the context of the bigger picture gain weight: The start of private home restaurants in Cuba, the strike of hotel employees in Cambodia over the percentage of tips added to bills, the self-organizing entrepreneurial structures in Brazilian slums, the growing art scene in Bogotá, the new entrepreneurial spirit in South Africa, Chinese farmers creating their own private vocational training, high-school students in remote places interviewing us in very good English. Our personal experience is the background against which we measure what we read in international sources available in German and English books, newspapers, magazines, websites publications and data of private and public research firms, global institutions, and organizations.

In the 2011 World Bank report "Multipolarity: The new global economy," for example, we read: "At no time in modern history have so many developing countries been at the forefront of a multipolar economic system. Within the next two decades the rise of emerging economies will inevitably have major implications for the global and geopolitical landscape."

It was after all *Megatrends Asia* that brought us together as an author and publisher team. It was the beginning of our monitoring the shift from Western-established economies to emerging economies first in Asia, and since the turn of the century in Latin America and Africa. And we have watched it gain momentum ever since. During the same period the West began to slow down and to lose ground, and has continued its economic decline. These shifts and the great opening-up of the Global Southern Belt will be the story of the first half of the 21st century.

Arvind Subramanian, Senior Fellow of the Peterson Institutes, goes so far as to call our era "the Golden Age of global growth." He is convinced that "the golden age of global economic growth, which began in mid-to-late 1990s, has mostly survived" and "continues to be the best of economic times."

Already, a brief overview of the economies of the Global Southern Belt gives us a sense of the global game change to a new era of economic shifts, social transformations, and a changing competitive picture.

The long-term dependence of emerging economies on developed economies will increasingly shift to mutual support among developing countries with declining influence of the West.

In this new picture of a multicentric world, China without doubt leads the parade. The West grudgingly registers China's gaining influence in both Western and emerging markets. In only three decades, it has become the world's second largest economy, the biggest manufacturer in the world, and the biggest global trader and soon the biggest consumer market. China has become the largest trading partner of many Asian, African, and Latin American countries as well as many Western countries.

During the next five years China will account for nearly 50 percent of the increase in emerging economies wealth (Credit Suisse Global Wealth Report, 2013). Urbanization and the strategic planning of urban economic clusters have supported its growth. Many Chinese cities have higher global domestic products (GDPs) than some countries in the world.

A World Bank report issued two years ago said that by 2025, a multipolar world will emerge in which economic clout is spread across developed and emerging economies. "Transition to a new world order with more diffuse distribution of economic power is under way," led by three major economic trends:

1. The shift in balance of global growth from developed to emerging economies.
2. The rise of emerging market firms as a force in global business.
3. The evolution of the international monetary system to a multicurrency regime.

In the wake of China's drumbeat, more and more GSB nations are joining the parade.

It does not matter with whom we talk in China, whether they love or hate their government, all are united in the love for their motherland. But that will not result in China returning to the sinocentric world view it held up to the end of the 18th century, when it saw itself as the cultural center of the world. Official China even plays down its incremental influence as an economic success model for emerging economies struggling to follow its path. China represents a multicentric worldview with its own interests as the initial and endpoint of political and economic considerations in which the West continues to play an important role, but not the dominant role. Without the claim to be pulling the strings for other countries, China does rightly claim to be a central player in the transformation to a multicentric global landscape.

When John traveled through China in the 1980s, he would never take a Chinese Airline but fly from one city to another via Hong Kong. Now we see all the new airports, bullet trains, and superhighways not only allowing traveling with great comfort, but also clearing the way for industries to invest. In most Western countries individual rights often collide with investments in the public interest. Emerging markets starting from a low point of democratization and economic development can often operate more efficiently. As long as the promise of economic growth is credible, people hungry for a better life will accept and adapt to necessary changes.

To understand transition processes in emerging economies, the West has to subdue Western thinking and empathize with local conditions and culture. It is not by chance coincidence that China brought forth Peking Opera and Argentina the Tango.

The Role of Digitalization

As part of a generation that grew up without the Internet and only conventional fixed line phones we are very much aware of how the web has opened doors to the world for billions. Especially for the poor and rural population of emerging economies it was a life changer. Digitalization is changing the macro and micro-economics globally. The Internet has already played a big role in accelerating and reinforcing the calls for reform and repair in emerging economies. The rise of China and of IT technologies went hand in hand. It is a powerful medium for economic progress and it increases and enforces transparency. Governments in the Global Southern Belt are increasingly using the Internet as a communication tool; electronic governing is connecting citizens with public services so that this service can become more efficient.

Government Internet service is becoming a tool for creating a nourishing environment for entrepreneurs. But, it will take efforts to cut down on old bureaucratic structures and transform clumsy administration into swiftly operating public services.

It will most likely be the small- and medium-sized companies, which will be faster in applying the next stage of technology. After all, not a single one of the global social networks was created by the innovation center of a large company, but by young and creative students.

Nevertheless, established Internet technologies are opening new doors for small and medium-sized companies as well as creating a new group of entrepreneurs, the micro-globals. Individuals are able to leverage their better knowledge of local conditions in their collaboration with other entrepreneurs globally. John first wrote about this in 1994 in his book, *Global Paradox: The Bigger the World Economy, the More Powerful the Smallest Players*.

Looking back in history the first industrial revolution in the 1880s had profound social economic influence. Mechanical production supported by steam-power transformed economies and raised GDP per capita per year from $694 to $2,753 in the second stage of the industrial revolution. In the third stage at the beginning decade of the 20th century it was mass production by means of electric energy that lifted productivity dramatically. GDP per capita per year made a large jump from $2,753 to $20,042. Now we are about to face the fourth stage: production based on cyber-physical systems. The prognosis is that this industry 4.0, as it is called, will push GDP per capita to the astonishing height of $90,000 by 2020 (Data DB Research/*Der Spiegel*, 2014).

In summer 2012, we gave a talk at a conference in Hangzhou. The days in Hangzhou did not only stay in our memory because of the beauty of the city and the fabulous Chinese food, but also for a visit we paid to an automobile rim factory. The company's chief engineer was a young man in his late 20s. He had developed an automatic production line, which, with only two people overseeing, produces 600 rims per hour. Not hard to imagine that this young engineer could one day program machines to program themselves.

Three-dimensional (3D) printers will enable entrepreneurs to produce anything, anywhere, as long as a digital model is available.

The new industry does not only have the potential to change our economy as profoundly as did the first industrial revolution, but also have the potential to open doors to online platforms, connecting through web meeting software and file sharing sites. Services can operate around the world virtually from any place connected to the web. 3D printers are said to soon be able to produce anything at any location on the planet as long as there is a digital model available: a glass or a cooking pot. It is used in automobile and airplane production, mechanical engineering, and also in architecture and in art and design. Even medical devices such as hip implants will be able to be downloaded and produced. 3D printing transforms physical transportation of goods to transmitting a file.

How often have we thought, "thank God we are healthy" and do not have to worry about what would it be like if we had a medical problem in one of the remote places we visited. In the future that will most likely change. Medical supply in world-class quality will be accessible in poor regions throughout the world. This will no longer be the miracle it seems today.

In 2012, the US Company Proteus received approval for a sensor, not bigger than a grain of sand, which, once swallowed by a human, sends medical data from inside the body to external monitors for diagnosis and tracking. From there it passes the information on to a mobile phone and into the web. The Internet can connect patient and doctor; it enables an automatized and centralized diagnosis and treatment. It is not hard to imagine what tremendous impact telemedicine will have both economically and socially. Countries where medical standards are low and people have to travel for many hours to get medical treatment could revolutionize their health system for a fraction of costs. This is particularly true in Africa, where typically one doctor takes care of 1,000 people.

In contrast to online diagnosis and treatments we remember our visit to a Tibetan hospital in Lhasa. In about one and half hours a doctor explained the Tibetan medical system, which is one of the oldest known medical traditions, in his excellent English. It was a most comprehensive personal approach to keeping people healthy. To answer questions about personal habits alone takes several hours. "But do people always tell the truth?" we wanted to know. "Well," said the doctor, "I did not believe the 93 year old man who said he had sex at least once a day."

Had we had two days available we would both have stayed in the hospital for a checkup. That is what it takes. No rush possible.

Traditions developed over centuries are worth to be held high. At the same time obsolete economic structures are replaced by innovative ideas. Our friend Rowan Gibson, one of the leading global experts on innovation, now travels to African countries on a regular basis to hold workshops on how to create and sustain an innovation capability. He told us, "I see more innovation in the field of mobile apps and services coming out of Kenya these days than out of Finland." In many developing countries young and dynamic IT entrepreneurs are helping millions out of poverty by developing new apps tailored to the needs of the population in regions poor on infrastructure. Online retailers, on average, offer lower prices, thus making their products more available. Small startups can leverage advancements quickly, becoming serious competitors for established companies with less flexibility.

Our business world has become global, and economic flexibility has to merge with cultural flexibility as we face the challenge of moving from local perspectives and biases to encompass broader viewpoints. Our colleague, Stephen Rhinesmith, whose expertise as a cross-cultural management expert we often seek, has for more than 40 years studied how mindsets change. To him "no one is ever born global." The grounds for his observations were laid earlier in his career when for 12 years he was the President of the AFS International Student Exchange Program and oversaw the exchange of 100,000 high-school students from 60 countries. The students lived with families in foreign countries and developed a more global perspective. He says, "while most of these young people may return to their former lifestyle when they get home, but their minds are changed forever."

We agree with Stephen that a basic demand in education is to open young minds to new ideas. But when such education is not available or affordable, a change of environment can lead to truly eye-opening effects. Today, changing the environment often takes place without moving an inch. The Internet and digitalization make it possible. Frontrunners in emerging economies are opening the doors for others to follow.

The digital revolution is leapfrogging in emerging economies creating success stories of champions many in the West never heard of including mPesa, Paga, Konga, Jumia. China's Baidu, Tencent, and of course Alibaba, who have made it into the global limelight. They match the taste and requirements of younger, more global consumers, and they know how to address them. Never in history have there been greater opportunities. Even weaker and unstable areas in Asia, Africa, and Latin America can embrace the new methods if they are willing to let go of old mindsets.

The Changing Consumer Landscape

We are so used to it that we hardly ever think about the fact that in the past decades the vast majority of consumers lived in Western countries and Japan. And many of us are unaware of the impact that will happen in the next 10 years when consumption in emerging markets is estimated to hit $30 trillion per year. The global middle class will more than double its size from 2 billion in 2012 to 4.9 billion by 2030. Asia alone will host 64 percent of the global middle class and make up more than 40 percent of middle-class consumption. During the same period European and American middle class will shrink from 50 percent in 2012 to just 22 percent in 2030 (Davos, 2012; Reuters, by David Rohde).

For the first time a *global* middle class is emerging.

When we talk about a global middle class we must of course differentiate between the various levels of middle class. Brookings Institute defines the US middle class as starting at $41,000. The Department of Health and Human Services defines a family of four living on $23,850 as poor. With the same amount families in all emerging economies would make it to middle class not to mention differences between urban and rural populations.

In addition, consumer behavior in Latin America, Africa, and Asia is not the same. When we are in Latin America, *puravida* (pure life) in almost all countries goes hand in hand with spending money for restaurants, hanging out with friends, and having fun. Brazilians only save around 10 percent of their income while Chinese save almost one-third. While saving money plays a large role in all parts of China, the more southern you go the more easy-going the life style will get. But everywhere in China wealth is rising.

For quite some time we were wondering how the many Chinese high-end shopping malls survive when the number of employees outnumbers the buyers. Thanks to our Hong Kong friend Ronnie Chan, one of the largest real-estate developers in Hong Kong, we know why. Ronnie, who owns several shopping malls in Mainland China, revealed that well-off Chinese do not want to buy in the store. They have a look, and then have the salespeople come to their house to buy in privacy.

There are enough rich Chinese for shopping malls to flourish; Ronnie Chan's Forum 66 in Shanghai or Lane Crawford, the mall right next to our "home away from home" in Beijing, the Ritz

Carlton Financial Street. Since the Ritz Carlton opened its doors in October 2006, we have spent weeks each year at the hotel and have noticed the changes in the origin of guests. At the beginning, about 80 percent of the guests were foreigners, mostly the United States and Europe. Now the percentage has turned around. About 80 percent of the guests are Chinese.

According to a Reuters report the ranks of the world's wealthy will continue to get bigger as the emerging nations create more millionaires. The biggest surge in new members of the middle class over the next 20 years "will come from hundreds of millions of Chinese and Indian's—the percentage of people in India and China below the middle will drop 70 percent by 2030." This will turn the percentage of the poor in the world from rising to shrinking for the first time.

Between 1990 and 2010 global trade among developed countries declined from 54 percent to 28 percent.

The overall flow of global goods will continue to rise, but the direction is changing from developed economies to emerging economies. Our good friend and former long time German language publisher Wolfgang Stock has lived in Peru and Mexico for several years. In a conversation around this book, he was spot on:

We [Germans] used to be the wealthy ones who flew to Latin America for vacation. The direction seems to be reversed. Now they are the ones who fly to Europe and spend quite some money here. Thanks to their many visits by now I know every corner of *Neuschwanstein* [the 19th century Disneyland like Romanesque revival palace of famous King Ludwig of Bayern]. At each visit I feel a little closer to your warning in *MindSet: Europe* without reforms is in danger to become an historic theme park for wealthy international travelers.

We do not believe that tuna covered with ground ants that we ate in Bogota, or grilled scorpions we rejected in Tianhuizhen, or Tortillas filled with fried caterpillars we tried in Mexico will make it into international menus. But in the tailwinds of all the international travel we notice the increasing amount of European food in Asian Supermarkets. Even cheese, while not the favorite of Chinese, is available in various flavors in many Chinese food stores. And our favorite restaurant in Sao Paulo, La Higuera, offers crisp Austrian Veltliner wine to its guests. "The shift in consumer habits has been offset by the increasing participation of emerging economies in global goods trade, both as exporters and importers. Emerging economies now account for 40 percent of goods flows, and 60 percent of those go to other emerging economies" (McKinsey: Global flows in a digital age, May 2014). The Global Southern Belt is participating in global flows at accelerating speed.

In the past decades economic growth was linked to performance in labor-intensive industries. Low wages and increasing productivity contributed to China's rise as the world's soon-to-be largest economy. China, which can easily be taken as a model, will not be able to sustain its economic growth by holding on to yesterday's success formulas. And it is well aware of this. In his 2008 book, *Shanghai Pudong Miracle,* Zhao Qizheng, former minister of the State Council's Information Office, wrote: "Whoever possesses the best of human talents occupies the commanding height in science and technology. Whoever possesses an abundance of intelligent human resources enjoys an advantageous position in the present ever-fiercer international competition." China is very well aware that the future lies in knowledge-intensive industries such as IT technologies, biotech, robotics, and pharmaceuticals. There is a city-to-city competition to have the most innovative, most profitable, and most international high-tech clusters to capitalize on future products and services. "Trade in knowledge intensive goods," writes McKinsey, "is growing around 1.3 times faster than trade in labor-intensive goods."

The blue-collar workers have begun to disappear from the workplace.

The next industrial revolution, the digitalization of industries, holds economic opportunities and social risks. Globally and especially in emerging economies semi-skilled workers are running out of demand. At the same time more and more talent and energy will go into the service sector. Governments will have to reform basic, higher, and vocational education to meet the needs of increasingly digitalized production. Autocratic governments, free of constricting election cycles, will have more flexibility for long-term strategic planning and swift moves if global conditions change, as long as they can deliver on the main demand of their citizens: economic growth and sustainable improvements of living conditions.

The dramatically growing global middle class and rising prosperity will support consumption of high-end technological products in the next decades, holding many opportunities for all nations in the Global Northern Belt.

The United States and Europe have not lost their human potential; they are losing their political potential.

A report in *Huffington Post* on January 21, 2014, was dealing with the "winners and losers of globalization." Branko Milanovic, lead economist at the World Bank's Research Department and professor at the Johns Hopkins University, comes to the somewhat shocking conclusion that the rich and the Chinese middle class will be the winners, the losers: the American middle class. It is sad, but it confirms our experience that optimism that once was so strong in the United States is yielding to resignation. Hope gives drive, even when current conditions are not great. But right now there is little hope among America's middle class. All wake-up calls to reform the Western governing models to match changing global conditions have been washed down by party-political quarrels and internal blockades. The political environment that once created the conditions under which the people could achieve extraordinary goals, is now a brake on adapting and advancing the system.

A new consumer class on the rise

America absolutely has the potential to recover, and the millions of new consumers are good news for many industries. By 2025, a McKinsey study estimates, "1.8 billion people around the world will enter the consuming class, nearly all from emerging markets, and emerging-market consumers will spend $30 trillion annually, up from $12 trillion today." This shift will obviously have great influence on consumption and investment streams. Consumer markets and consumer habits will change significantly. A frontrunner in this shift is the travel industry, where both business and leisure travel will create new demands, new markets, and new beneficiaries. Already visible are the changes in travel streams.

Airlines hubs of the Global Southern Belt will outperform Western airline hubs.

"Next landing in Dubai" was the title of a report in the German newspaper *Die Zeit* in November 2013. Its main message: "Europe for a long time was the junction of air traffic. Now global air traffic streams are shifting."

Airline hubs of the 21st century are moving eastwards. Hubs such as Dubai, Beijing, or Istanbul are attracting more travelers each year, replacing old traditional hubs Paris, London, and Frankfurt.

In the *Airports Council International* top 50 ranking of airports with rising passenger numbers Kuala Lumpur leads with 19.1 percent putting Dubai second at 15.2 percent. Nevertheless, Dubai beats Kuala Lumpur in absolute passenger numbers. And this is not the end of the story. By 2020, Dubai wants to complete the new Al Maktoum International Airport, which will have the capacity to handle 160 million passengers per year, on average almost 440,000 per day. In just one decade Dubai has pushed Heathrow from being the busiest air hub. Oxford Economics estimates aviation to account for 250,000 jobs and 28 percent of Dubai's GDP. No Western Airport has made it into the top ten in rising passenger numbers.

Ten years ago we would not have thought that we would fly to Beijing via Istanbul. The reason we do now is simple. A business class ticket on Lufthansa does not offer flat-bed seats but costs almost twice what we pay on Turkish Airlines, which does have flat-bed seats. In addition, Istanbul Airport lounge offers the great food of Austria's bespoken caterer Do&Co, an entrepreneur of Turkish decent, by the way. As he also owns Demel, one of Austria's most traditional coffeehouses, Austrian deserts add to the pleasure of a meal in the lounge.

And Istanbul's Airport does not plan to sleep on its laurels. In the global competition for the world's largest airports, Istanbul's Yeni Havalimai is reaching for the crown. The driving force of gigantic airport project is the half-state owned Turkish Airlines and the other is Tayyip Erdogan, Turkey's president, who on one hand wants to push Turkey's slowing economy and at the same time elevate Turkey's image. "We have passed by the world, in the air we face no competition," said Lütfi Elvan, Turkey's minister of transport in an interview with *Anadolu News Agency*. Turkish Airlines has not only been awarded as "Best European Airline" three times in a row; its 244 destinations in 105 countries make it the airline with the most destinations worldwide. It is Erdogan's goal to push Turkey to be one of world's 10 largest economies by 2023, the year Turkey celebrates its 100-year centenary as a Republic.

Overflown Rather Than Landed?

Despite the countless opportunities the increasing global middle class offers for tourism in all parts of the world to flourish, it seems that in the next decades the countries of the Northern Belt could be in danger of slipping into the category *overflown* rather than *landed*.

There is still growth potential for all airlines. From 2000 to 2012 North American airlines grew 21 percent, Europe's airlines 51 percent. In the same period Middle East airlines show a rise of 346 percent. Boeing estimates that between 2013 and 2032 the demand for new airplanes in the main Western regions, Europe, and North America will be 14,619 airplanes; Asia Pacific, Latin America, Africa, and the Middle East 19,400 airplanes. Boeing also estimates that the rise of emerging nations will result in fast and efficient transport of goods. This, estimates Boeing, will result in an annual growth rate of air cargo of 5.0 percent through 2032.

By 2016, Asia Pacific passenger traffic will be the largest market for air transport with a 33 percent share of all global travelers.

In the next two years, North America passenger numbers will show a decline of 4.3 percent (IATA, May 2014). The picture does not change when switching from quantity to quality.

In the 2013 Skytrax ranking the best ranking Western airline, the once highly praised Lufthansa, was down to number 11, beaten not only by Singapore and Emirates, but by exotic carriers such as Indonesia's Garuda Airline. "Tourism has shown a remarkable capacity to adjust to changing market conditions," says United Nations World Tourist Organization (UNWTO) Secretary General TalebRifai. Living in Austria we are mostly flying Star Alliance. But, the conditions of redeeming miles are constantly changed to the disadvantage of the members. Airport taxes charged to mileage tickets are elevated to a point that you end up paying the same as if you bought the full ticket. Airfares are high so that if all of this is taken into account a detour with a stopover in an airport that is an attraction by itself, like Dubai, becomes a real option.

The May 2014 McKinsey study on global flows shows that emerging economies will keep gaining shares in global short-term travel. The flow of short-term travelers between emerging economies has risen from 18 percent in 2002 to 23 percent in 2010.

"Also," the study says, "in 2010 emerging economies accounted for 33 percent of all outbound travelers, up from 25 percent in 2000 and 51 percent of all inbound travelers, from 44 percent in 2000."

Destination: Africa

The growing number of entrepreneurs and middle class is opening a door to new business in the hospitality industry: "Hotel groups jostle for position in Africa" is the title of a story in the *Financial Times*, January 11, 2014. And it is not the holiday tourists filling safari lodges and game resorts, even though their number is estimated to rise from 50 million in 2012 to 85 million in 2020 (UNWTO).

In the past 10 years previously unrecognized cities and regions have entered the world map of tourism and business travel.

The new target group of international hotel chains, including Accor, Marriott, Best Western, and Kempinski, is the rapidly rising number of business travelers in Africa's growing number of commercial capitals.

N'Djamena, the capital of Chad, and Luanda, the capital of Angola, may not be well-known cities to many, and yet writes the *Financial Times*, "they are among the five most expensive cities for business travelers and expats when it comes to food, transport, and accommodation costs. It is hard to believe that in Luanda it is difficult to find a hotel room for less than $500 a night." Some countries, one of them Angola, have spotted the investment opportunity and are planning to use its own sovereign wealth fund to invest in the hotel business.

Ghana, Nigeria, Gabon, South Africa, and Kenya are planning to add almost 13,000 rooms to the market. But while the number is high, scattered locations in the fragmented continent limit rational development. In Africa each of the 50 countries has its own rules and regulations. In China, for example, a market 30 percent larger in population, one central government sets the basic rules, while in Africa more than 50 governments decide.

After agriculture, tourism is Kenya's most important industry and according to The World Travel and Tourism Council, responsible for 14 percent of the GDP and 12 percent of employment. Among the foreign investors in Africa's hospitality industry is, no surprise, China. "Kenya," writes *China Daily* "is lauding China's investment as the country is experiencing a revamp in the tourism industry."

Destination: Austria

With 52 million additional people traveling in 2013, international tourism despite stagnating Western economies was well above expectation. In relative terms, China became the largest outbound market in 2012. And that has a positive impact on the West, even on tiny Austria.

A few kilometers east of Vienna, in a Disney-style shopping center, Gucci, Prada, Armani, Escada, Todd's, and Burberry are lined up like sparrows on a wire. The price is right, 20–50 percent reduction on the original price. Soon after the center opened its doors it was flooded not only by Austrians, but much more by neighboring Hungarians, Czechs, and Slovakians.

Now a language hardly heard before seems to be taking over rapidly: Chinese. Large buses are unloading Chinese fashion tourists. They swarm out in streams to return some hours later, each of them carrying bursting bags all with well-known brand names: Gucci, Prada, Armani, Escada, Todd's, Burberry. If the happily exhausted bargain hunters would check the labels on their bags, the hunted shoes, shirts, jackets, and suits would show that most share the same label: "Made in China." Some might be surprised that they just contributed not only to the Austrian, Italian, British, and French economies, but to the Chinese economy as well. A product is made in China, bought in Austria, and in between exists a whole chain of businesses in various countries. All involved are linked and eager to get their share of the cake, including designer, producer, and end user as well as tailors, factory workers, transport industries, trade companies, sales personnel, and last but not the least, airlines and airports.

While brand-hunting global tourists might show some similarity, global companies are already adapting to the difference in local consumer classes in a much more diverse and dispersed customer base. As we said before, the consumers in emerging economies will be different from consumers in saturated markets. The buying patterns of the new middle class will most likely be more cost-conscious. Thousands of new large companies located in many more cities will have to reconfigure their logistic and communication networks. And they will have to adapt to different company and business cultures.

Comparing China's growing GDP per capita growth with consumption habits allows some conclusions of how consumer behavior will change in other emerging economies.

Per capita income in China shows steady growth

1990: $310
2000: $950
2010: $4,450
2013: $6,190

Percentage of consumer goods owned per 100 Chinese households in 1990 and 2011

Goods	1990	2011
Car	0.0	18.6%
Motorcycle	1.9	20.1%
Microwave	0.0	60.0%
Camera	19.2	44.5%
Fixed tel. line	0.0	69.6%
Computer	0.0	81.9%
Washing machine	78.4	97.1%
Warm water	0.0	89.0%

Refrigerator	42.3	97.2%
Color TV	59.0	135.2%
Mobile phone (2000)	19.5	205.3%

Consumer habits in China differ greatly from region to region, from city to city, and in urban and rural areas. While there are similarities in all countries of the Global Southern Belt, each country has its national footprint.

Global Southern Belt: Business Destination

At the World Economic Forum in Davos, 2014, a session was highlighted "BRICS in midlife crisis." Apart from the choice of the BRICS selection, which we question (after all only China has lived up to promises), it is way too early to talk about a midlife crisis when the level of BRICS countries has barely reached puberty. The amount that India is still in an early stage of "maturing" we see in the early wake-up to reality after a short euphoria when Modi was elected. Brazil has not yet been able to shake off stagnation and harness its great potential. And Russia? Lots of energy in its ground, but little in its people. According to an Accenture survey among more than 1,000 executives, 60 percent of firms expect to "shift investments away from BRICS toward other more rapidly growing markets."

There is still a lot of uncertainty. The largest of which is caused by the lack of reform. During the heydays of the resource boom reform attempts were pushed aside gladly. Brazil, Russia, and also South Africa benefitted greatly from resource price peaks. As the boom is fading, reality takes over.

Growing up is a period of constant change, and so is transitioning from an underdeveloped to a develop country.

A number of emerging economies are and will prance sideways. Our focus is on the countries of the Global Southern Belt, which in the next decades will increase economic importance in their overall development.

Europe's top 500 companies have generated a third of their sales in emerging markets in 2013. The direction is set. It is almost three times more than in 1997, according to Morgan Stanley. CEO Wolfgang Eder, head of Austria's steel company Voest Alpine, calls 2014 "the year of the dragon." By 2020 they expect to generate 2.5 billion Euros in Asia, 3 billion Euros in North America. By the end of this decade, Voest Alpine will build 15 new plants in China with the goal to quintuple their revenues. Unilever, the consumer goods titan, generates well over half of its sales in emerging economies.

It was Nissan, the Japanese Partner of Renault, that saved the second largest French carmaker from a loss in 2013. Now a China-offensive is supposed to help in reaching targeted yields. Already in 2017 operational profit is supposed to account for 5 percent of the business volume. The list of enterprises betting on the growing consumer class in the Global Southern Belt is endless.

By 2025, 45 percent of the Fortune 500 companies are estimated to be based in emerging regions, 25 percent more than today.

Despite the shift toward emerging economies the United States in 2013 was still leading in the list of Fortune 500 companies. The number of Chinese companies rose from 79 companies in 2012 to 95 companies in 2013. The ownership structure in Chinese companies differs from American, European, and Japanese companies, as many of the Chinese companies are state-owned.

It will be interesting to see the changes in Forbes list of "The World's Most Innovative Companies." In 2013 among the top 10, six are American, holding the first four in the list in front of number five from the United Kingdom. China's goal to become an innovation nation is not yet reflected even though Baidu made it to number six on the list.

In the next decade 70 percent of the expected new $1 billion companies will be based in emerging markets.

Globally, there are about 8,000 companies with more than $1 billion revenue. Around 6,000 of them are located in developed regions. According to a McKinsey study, rising demand for consumer goods and services will push another 7,000 companies to this size in the next decade and 70 percent of them will be based in emerging markets.

By 2013, there were about 50 companies with revenues of more than $100 billion. They have headquarters in 30 cities. But the rise of emerging economies will add to the number of cities where they need to have a presence. This opens the opportunity for 200–300 cities to host such a large company for the first time. Just think about that. It is not only 200 or 300 new companies. Every new company will create a wake of other new businesses, restaurants, groceries, hairdressers, butchers, lawyers, doctors, and many more.

As we wrote earlier, growth of emerging markets is as good news for the developed world as it is for the GSB nations. It is a win–win, a reciprocal economic stimulus for Western recovery will result in boosting exports to emerging nations. Emerging markets continue to liberalize their economies. Most are models of fiscal rectitude with debt to GDP well below 50 percent, compared with more than 100 percent in the United States and more than 200 percent in Japan and will remain interesting for direct foreign investment. But just as European countries differ strongly in their economic performance, unemployment rate, and growth potential, it is almost impossible to average out risks and opportunities in emerging economies. Even within one country, location is often the decisive factor between success and failure of a project, more so as we see a shift from trade between countries to direct trade city to city.

If you want to understand the reality of the places you are committing your money, read their literature.

We are sure it happens to everyone. In the neighborhood a new store is opening and you just feel this is not going to work. It does not match the demand. And in practically all cases in our neighborhood, we had to watch a slower or fast death. We wonder why people who invest in a store do not begin with studying the neighborhood. It seems a no-brainer to do that even if you think everyone is waiting for your product. We thought of that when we read an interview with Justin Leverenz who manages $37 billion for Oppenheimer Developing Market Funds, in *Fortune Invest*. Oppenheimer's holds on to an optimistic point of view. In an interview of *Fortune Invest* in December 2013, Leverenz rejects the opinion that newer markets are likely to swoon. The 45-year-old funds manager spent 10 years in Asia and speaks Mandarin. More surprising than his language skill might be his advice to investors: "if you want to understand the reality of the places you are committing your money to, then read their literature."

Whatever the secret is, Oppenheimer's Developing Market Fund since 2007 has had a superb rate of 17.3 percent average annual return.

"From a solvency perspective," says Leverenz, "the situation is completely different than in the 1980s and 1990s." The view that "outside capital in emerging markets is only available when global liquidity is good is no longer relevant because by and large, the emerging world is the creditor in the system, not the debtor. The developing world has flexible currencies, limited fiscal debts and relatively healthy banks."

One of the fund's largest holdings is in the Chinese Internet Company Tencent. "I bought it when it was a $6 billion company. It's now $100 billion." Asked how he finds such companies, Leverenz says that he and his two senior analysts spend 70 percent of their time in gaining deep knowledge in one area industry before expanding their knowledge in adjacent things. "It's like the Google idea: Do things that are completely unrelated because that enables you to make connections you otherwise would have missed." Whoever now feels animated to join the fund, it too late; it is closed to new investors.

Emerging markets will grow faster than the developed world for decades to come.

Again, all of this is good news also for the West. "In the past few years relations between developed and developing economies became a two way street, with innovation, investment and competition originating in both developing and emerging markets, and moving across the globe from one to the other," writes Accenture in a 2013 report about the new competitive reality. "In the new competitive reality, companies must develop innovative products specifically for and in emerging markets, and look for opportunities to leverage those products back to the developed world."

No longer locked down by the ties of the West, emerging economies are beginning to build new alliances and partnerships, speeding their development. We are witnessing the shift from a hierarchical world order to an increasing demand for equality among nations. And the gravity of the global business landscape is shifting toward emerging economies.

Gideon Rachman, chief foreign affairs columnist of the *Financial Times*, gives us this summary: "The rise in non-Western economics is a deeply rooted historic shift. Emerging markets will grow faster than the developed world for decades to come."

In 2013, for the first time, the combined GDP of the world's 150 emerging economies, excluding China, was larger than the GDP of all 37 developed countries, excluding the United States (IMF Data). China and the United States each count for more than 30 percent of their groups GDP. If all emerging nations are put into one pot, this is a watershed. But it does not say too much about each single nation. And certainly it does not differentiate between various industry sectors on national or global level.

It is as if looking at the average grade points of a high school. Looking closer you see classes with higher and lower average grade. In each class some students achieve straight As and others barely make it. Statistics lose all intelligence and so does generalizing nations of different economic and social development thrown into one pot. Nevertheless, there is an overall trend in the development of emerging economies despite the vast gaps among them. Just as despite the huge gap between Germany's economic dynamics and Greece's economic disaster they nevertheless are both part of the EU and the West.

Eventually One Economy for the Whole World

The shifting dynamics of economic performances among nations is partly a function of the process of economic globalization, as we are moving from national capitalism to global capitalism. It will take a long time, but eventually we will have one economy for the whole world.

Nevertheless, throughout this book, we have and will use a country's GDP as a measure for comparison. In the competition among emerging and developed economies growth, stagnation or decline of GDP is commonly the measure. It is also currently the only, at least, half-decent measure available. One reason for its relative reliability is that the basic formula of the GDPs of countries has only marginally been adapted to changing conditions since it was established more than 70 years ago.

For years there was almost no GDP growth in Germany, but Germany has many growing and prospering companies whose contributions are wiped out by aggregating them with losing companies and sectors.

Until recently, India had one of the world's highest GDP gains, but this was almost solely because of its growing business information technology (IT) sector. Outsourcing of IT was doing well; but only by fighting the taxing and regulating government every step of the way led to the establishment of that sector.

Opportunities for alliances, mergers, and sales can only be determined by understanding what is happening on the ground in each country, not by bloodless GDPs.

What lies ahead is a process, a time of transition between measures of the past and measures fitting the reality of 21st century. Oppenheimer's Justin Leverenz, who runs the $25 billion Fund, does not invest in GDPs, but in business by business by industries. "Most businesses in the world are like musicians: they aren't that talented. I'm only interested in the virtuosos," he says (*Fortune*, December 9, 2013).

In the following pages, we will highlight some of the Asian, African, and Latin America emerging economies of the Global Southern Belt. The list is by no means complete; facts and stories about each country could fill a book. Our purpose is to give a quick impression of some of the many countries in transition as we move through these early years of the 21st century.

Africa

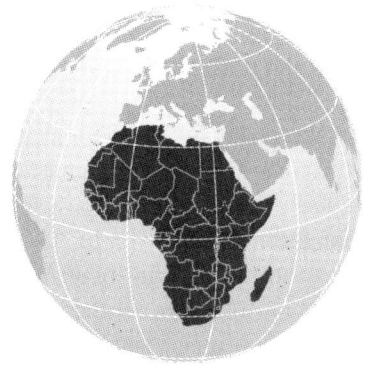

From Hopeless Continent to Myriads of Opportunities in Half a Generation

Of all the parts of the Global Southern Belt we have spent the least time in Africa. We are not Africa specialists, but we are observers of an awakening.

Unfortunately, bad news about Africa finds its way into global media much faster than good news. Africa specialist Laurence Brahm, international lawyer, economist, author, and founder of the Himalayan and African Consensus economic paradigms addresses the problem in the African Consensus Resolution:

> Prevent Extremism at Its Root: Terrorism is not alone the result of fundamental religious beliefs as characterized in certain main-stream media. People turn to extreme measures when they have no

outlet to vent their frustration over conditions of poverty, ethnic marginalization, or both. Often religious beliefs may tragically be used as a rationale or pretext for this extremism. Deep dissatisfaction followed by terrorism are sequential reactions to the same sets of problems. The problems associated with the alienation of ethnic groups must be addressed at its root cause, through economic empowerment, education, health care, and returning to people what is theirs, recognition of their own individual diversity, identity and self-respect. Otherwise dissent and strife will not go away, regardless of how sophisticated the military technology and social re-engineering theories of constituent states.

But with an open mind and a large and diverse enough source the picture changes.

We combine our research with personal experience on the ground, reports of friends and entrepreneurs who spend much more time in Africa than we have in the past few years. To many Africa is less familiar than Asia and Latin America. That is why we spend more time to introduce the "new Africa" we see on the horizon. And there is a lot to report. Our focus is the sub-Sahara regions of Africa and its economic opening-up.

The two big "E's"—economics and education, are the key.

The *Economist* estimates that Africa's collective economy will continue to grow at around 5.5 percent, the average rate over the past decade. This is faster than any other region in the world. Nigeria has Africa's largest population, soon to be 180 million people, and has just passed South Africa as Africa's largest economy.

How quickly things can change was witnessed in China's rise. Problem countries and regions can make surprising improvements and U-turns. In going through old files, we stumbled across a story about Africa, published in the *Economist* in May 2000, the title "The hopeless continent."

In our 2013 files were reports of the opposite kind. The well-regarded German Consulting agency Roland Berger warned investors not to miss the "myriads of opportunities" the African continent offers. And Berger does not stand alone. In the last months of 2013 the German monthly magazine *Der Spiegel* and newspaper *Frankfurter Allgemeine* both dedicated a series to the rise of the Africa. And "Something's moving in Africa" was the title of a several page story in Germany's *Frankfurter Allgemeine Sonntagszeitung*.

The competition for Africa's resources and the purchasing power of its 310 million new middle class consumers is rapidly gaining momentum.

Africa's turnaround is gaining speed. GDP in South Saharan Africa grew an estimated 4.7 percent and 6 percent in South Africa. Many governments are investing in infrastructure projects and export capacity. And while in some countries poverty and unemployment is still high, historians, in comparison with colonialism, are talking about the "second footprint for Africa."

Africa's picture seems familiar and yet so unknown: 1.1 billion people, one-seventh of the world's population, the world's youngest continent with more than 200 million people between 15 and 20 years old. It has the largest dry desert in the world, the Sahara, with a landmass as big as the United States. Niger, according to the United Nations, has the highest birth rate globally with an average of seven births per woman. The saddest record is delivered from the conflict in Congo, where according to the International Rescue Committee in 1998, 5.4 million people were killed in internal conflicts. Congo's oil reserves still do not reach ordinary people. Contrast this with Mali, where the poorest people benefitted the most from economic growth. Or take Lagos, of Nigeria, one of the most populated countries. The city begins to separate itself from the national pattern. Its local government has improved public transportation, advanced business environment, cleaned up streets, and enhanced the lives of its people.

One speaks of "Africa" as if it were a country; nevertheless, each one of its 54 sovereign states shows different faces, from those shaken by conflicts, hopelessness, and poverty to modern, vibrant, with a self-confident middle class.

More than half of Africa's people are still living under the poverty line, but its 29 billionaires, each worth a $1 billion or more, together own a total fortune of $144 billion. Africa's richest man, Aliko Dangote, alone stands at $29 billion. Johannesburg, South Africa has 23,400 millionaires, Lagos in Nigeria 9,800, Kenya's Nairobi 5,000, and Luanda, Angola 2,400. The times Africans were trapped in their now obsolete role as victims of colonization for centuries is over. Africans are slowly waking up to a new self-perception as potential global players. Africa, a huge, contradictive, and fascinating continent, the once lost continent, is getting itself back on the global economic stage; this time not as the recourse for colonial powers, but for its own sake.

Africa's 3 percent share of the global economy holds great potential for growth.

The East African market alone has 140 million people and a relatively stable political situation. East African countries Tanzania, Uganda, Ruanda, Burundi, and Kenya have agreed on a currency union within 10 years. Business is small in absolute numbers but growing significantly.

The common thought that Africa's strong growth is the result of its rich resources of oil and minerals and the hunger for resources in developed economies is not the complete picture any more. Among Africa's 12 countries with the strongest growth since 1995 eight countries are not classical resource countries, including Ruanda, Mozambique, Uganda, Ethiopia, and Tanzania.

Africa's demand on food is growing rapidly. Selling agricultural goods has become a huge business for imports. But with a rising awareness of opportunities across Africa, food imports over time could turn into exporting domestically produced agricultural products (based on data from HIS Economics, GIDD, McKinsey Global Institute, Cityscape 2.2, Business Monitor International, McKinsey Analysis).

African expert Laurence Brahm is convinced that Africa will become the food basket of the world.

In its agriculture sector strategy 2010 to 2014, African Development Bank Group wrote:

> The potential role for agriculture in development is to reduce poverty and drive growth for countries whose economies are agricultural based. This potential has been underexploited. Studies indicate that growth based on agriculture is at least twice as effective than growth based on other sectors in reducing poverty, 3.5 times more for China, and for Latin America 2.7 times more.

On first thought agriculture is not necessarily linked to the Internet. And yet the Internet will also play a decisive role in increasing productivity, value, and social/economic impact. Just as in other industries, Internet offers a learning platform, connecting farmers with experts to get information and advice, connecting farmers to farmers to exchange local experience with new crops, fertilizers, irrigation, trade, and finance. Nigeria, for example, has 95 universities, but an illiteracy rate of 40 percent, mostly in rural regions. Farmers could benefit greatly from agricultural learning materials presented in videos via Internet. In its November 2013 report on the impact of the Internet in Africa, McKinsey estimates that the technology can drive up to $3 billion in annual productivity gains in the sector: "Nigeria has used mobile technology to revamp its system for delivering major savings, eliminated opportunities for corruption, expanding the number of farmers served, and far exceeded its production targets."

For a long time, in many developing countries, the lack of infrastructure has been a high hurdle on the path from the producer to the consumer.

Africa, according to the African Union, will need $93 billion each year to be invested in quality infrastructure. One of the authors of this book (John) in the late 1960s was an advisor to the Royal Government of Thailand on accelerating agricultural development in the country's northeast. He and his Thai colleagues had great success working with the farmers to diversify their crops and increase their yields. But, the farmers refused to follow through because they knew that there did not exist the infrastructure to get increased diversity and yields to the market. It was not an uncommon consideration in those days.

As in Thailand, the lack of good infrastructure constrains productivity. This is as much a hurdle in economic growth as overbearing bureaucracy, widespread corruption, and lack of finance.

Despite their own efforts, Africa's progress will also depend on debt cancellations and foreign aid. It needs further improvements in rural infrastructure, providing cheaper and more reliable power, access to education, better social services, other social systems. Africa's rise will not be a smooth ride but its outlook has changed from decades of stagnation to a high growth potential. The changing climate has become an inspiration to all parts of the society.

The Entrepreneurial Spirit of Africa's Young Generation Has Awakened

"Lions on the move" is the title of the McKinsey 2010 analysis of Africa's progress and potential. McKinsey sees two reasons for Africa's faster economic pulse: better governing and economic reforms including reducing debts and household deficits, inflation under control, privatization of state-owned enterprises, liberalization of trade, and reducing corporate tax.

Africa's story is changing and the signs of Africa's opening-up are getting stronger.

By 2020, McKinsey estimates, Africa's collective GDP will rise from $1.6 trillion to $2.6 trillion, its consumer-spending will rise from $860 billion to $1.4 trillion, and 128 million households will have discretionary income.

In no other region can increases in earnings be higher: "global investors and entrepreneurs cannot afford to miss that opportunity," says McKinsey.

According to CrunchBase, a free database of technology for companies, people, and investors, 2013 was the most active year for technology investment in Africa.

American investors and venture capitalists are increasingly investing in startups across the African continent. IBM launched innovation centers in Lagos and Casablanca. Microsoft announced new goals of the Microsoft 4 Africa Initiative to fuel African innovation. Solomon Assefa, IBM researcher and vice president of Science and technology, sees Africa transforming: "There is increased stability and lot of bandwidth that's come on line, tremendous economic growth, plus a lot of infrastructure being built and a lot of foreign investment."

Only a few of 48 sub-Sahara countries still remain at the lower end of the prosperity index. According to a World Bank study 17 of the 50 fastest economies are coming out of Africa. Africa Experts Robert Kappel and Birte Pfeiffer (GIGA Institute for global studies Hamburg, Germany) are praising progress in single countries, but warning about an overall blind euphoria.

"African entrepreneurs, bankers and investors," says Bartholomäus Grill in his book *Oh Africa*, "have never appeared as sanguine since the end of colonial era."

By 2020, Africa will have a majority of young and urban populations, with an expanding middle class.

Good progress is achieved when investments are tailored to the specifics of a country. African examples are Ruanda's support of tourism and coffee plants, Kenya's IT experts and mobile phone apps, and Ethiopia's flower exports. Or take Botswana, which is dedicated to retrieve the value-added chain for diamonds into the country to not only export raw diamonds, but also process the stones in the country.

The new middle class is the driving force of progress. Africa's 310 million consumer class does not fit the old African cliché of a helpless, poor, and lazy Africa.

The number of mobile phones in Africa has reached 650 million. Better access to information supports civil society and leads to rapid social change. Under the headline "Artists thrive in Africa as freedom grows," *New York Times* wrote about the positive impact "the growth of democratic expectations, the decline of dictatorships, and the explosion of the Internet" have on the flourishing of African artists. New projects and products are creating a colorful art scene: Nigerian's film industry, known as Nollywood, the Rift valley Festival in Kenya, and literary journals like *Kwani?*, the flagship publication founded by some of Kenya's most exciting new writers.

Africa's art scene is increasingly detaching from a European American influence striving for more self-sufficiency. Ginanne Brownell in the *New York Times* in January 2013 writes:

> In Africa, even in the world of art, the road to financial support and recognition has long passed through the West. But the ever shifting landscape of African politics and economics and a protracted financial crisis in the West have led a growing network of artists, curators and nonprofit organizations to seek ways of detaching the continent's art world from its Euro American axis.

The latest data published by World Bank's new *Africa's Pulse* analyzes economic trends and data on the African continent. Its 2014 overall outlook is that sub-Sahara, due to substantial investment in infrastructure, is experiencing a strong recovery in agriculture, expansion of services, electricity capacity, and transport; Africa will remain one of the fastest growing regions with economic growth rising from 4.6 percent in 2014 to 5.2 percent in 2015–2016.

The question whether the continent will manage to change into a bright future remains open. There are as many arguments for it as there are against it. We would not go as far as former president of Nigeria, Olusegun Obansanjo, who predicted the 21st century to be Africa's century and maybe not as far as Berger's myriads of opportunities. We are optimistic. What is needed is entrepreneurial spirit, guts, innovative ideas, and rewards for good efforts.

A Brief Snapshot of Sub-Saharan Africa

Kenya

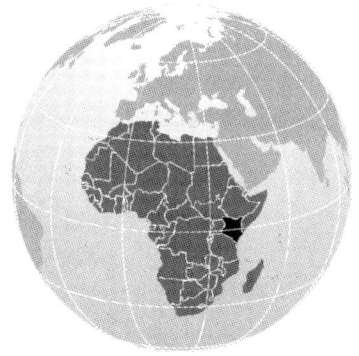

Population: 44,037,656
Urban population 24%
GDP: $45.31 billion
GDP composition: Agriculture 29.3%; industry 17.4%; services 53.3%
Growth rate: 5.1% (World Factbook)
GDP per capita grew from $406.12 in 2000
to $862.23 in 2012 (World Bank)
2014 Index of Economic Freedom: (111 Heritage Foundation)

Kenya's IT technology is leapfrogging ahead in information and communication. Mobile phones and Internet have become Africa's gateway to the world. Young African IT specialists are working on innovations in mobile phone applications.

E-Bay founder Pierre Omidyar sponsored a building in Nairobi, which allows Internet entrepreneurs to work on games for mobile phones, and low-tech games for kids in African markets. The IT and Communication industry in Kenya is responsible for more than 5 percent of Kenya's GDP. Google, IBM, Cisco, and Microsoft do not want to miss out in the fastest growing market for mobile phones, tablets, and laptops and have settled down in the neighborhood. You may not yet have heard of it, but Kenya's Ngong Road now is called Silicon Savannah of Nairobi, and it has become a center for young Africans developing apps for smartphones tailored to the needs of the African markets.

Wireless communication has dramatically changed daily life in Africa. One-third of Kenya's economic activity is processed by mPesa, a payment system that turns a mobile phone into a bank account, credit card, and wallet.

Morocco

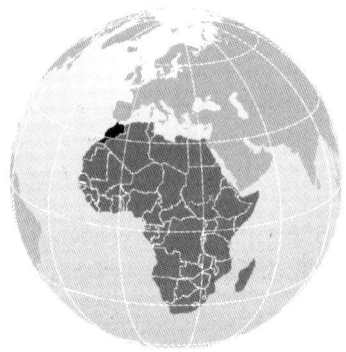

Population: 24,096,669
Urban population: 57% (2011)
GDP: $104.8 billion
GDP composition: Agriculture 15.1%; industry 31.7%; services 53.2% (2012 est.)
Growth rate: 5.1 (World Factbook)
GDP per capita grew from $1,275.88 in 2000 to $3,108-65 in 2013 (World Bank)
2014 Index of Economic Freedom: 103 (Heritage Foundation)

In the midst of the turmoil of Africa's north-Sahara countries Morocco seems to be on the path to a much smoother transition to a modern, moderate Islamic country.

To many Africans who see their future in illegal immigration to Europe, Morocco is the gateway to their promised land. Morocco offers the easiest transit to Spanish cities Ceuta and Melilla. But many do not make it and are stranded in Morocco. Over time the number of illegal refugees has mounted to about 40,000 who now live in the country. Morocco is now the first African country to offer stay permits. Whoever can prove to have lived in the country for five years or more can show a two-year working contract will get the official paper. And Morocco is betting on education to make them valuable members of the society; adults are offered language courses and vocational training and their children are entitled to attend schools. Even health care is part of the program.

Mozambique

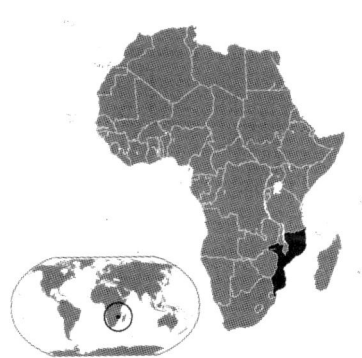

Population: 24,096,669
Urban population: 32.2% (2011)
GDP: $28.15 billion
GDP composition: Agriculture 28.7%; industry 24.9%; services 46.4%
Growth rate: 7% (World Factbook)
GDP per capita grew from $235.82 in 2000 to $578.80 in 2012 (World Bank)
2014 Index of Economic Freedom: 128 (Heritage Foundation)

Mozambique has developed from one of the world's poorest countries to one of Africa's fastest growing countries in just the last decade, growing at a rate of 6–8 percent in the decade up to 2013. Nevertheless, half of Mozambique's population remains below the poverty line. Despite its rich resources in natural gas, coal, and titanium, Mozambique is still depending on donor assistance, debt forgiveness, and rescheduling its debts. But, Mozambique's rich resources are now attracting foreign investment with large projects to fuel economic growth in the coming years.

Mozambique is also only beginning to leverage its potential in agriculture. The government's 2013–2014 agricultural campaign started in November 2013 and supports agriculture and animal husbandry. The expansion of Cahora Bassa dam and building additional dams will allow additional electricity exports and serve the needs in the beginnings of domestic industries.

Nigeria

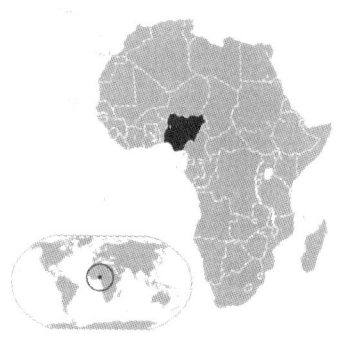

Population: 177,155, 539
Urban population: 49.6% (2011)
GDP: $502 billion
GDP composition: Agriculture 30.9%; industry 43%; services 26%
Growth rate: 6.2% 2013 (The World Factbook)
GDP per capita grew from $374.22 in 200 to $1,555.41 in 2012 (World Bank)
2014 Index of Economic Freedom: (129 Heritage Foundation)

Nigeria is Africa's most populous country. In April 2014, the statistics bureau of Nigeria confirmed that Nigeria's GDP of $502 billion beat South Africa as the largest economy in Africa. Measured by GDP, this statistics puts Nigeria just behind Poland and Norway. Nigeria's growth rate has been an average 7 percent per year over the last five years and the IMF estimates Nigeria's annual growth rate to remain between 6 and 7 percent until 2020. A large GDP, and one of the world's highest growth rates, will result in more investors paying attention to Nigeria.

But while Nigeria's GDP is rising, the majority of the people have not become any richer. Widespread corruption interferes with fighting poverty effectively. The majority of Nigeria's 177 million people still live on less than $1.25 a day. Unemployment rate is 24 percent.

In the northeast of country, radical Islamic sect Boko Haram terrorizes the population, calls for Sharia rule, and destabilizes the region. Since 2012, the conflicts between Muslims in the north and Christians in the south have led to 500,000 people fleeing the region to escape the terror. More than 514 languages and idioms are not helping the country to find common ground.

Nigeria is the world's sixth largest oil exporter but has not managed to bypass oil traders and refine petrol, diesel, and other oil products domestically. Its refineries are old and producing way below capacity. Of the 2.5 million barrels of crude oil Nigeria has to buy 80 percent refined products from traders. In addition, well-organized gangs steal around 150,000 barrels of crude oil each year. Refined oil imports are joined by imports of grain and other crops, even as agronomists confirm Nigeria could be self-sufficient.

Nevertheless, Nigeria is changing. Service industries are booming. Thanks to its rich oil resources, oils and gas industry stands at 14 percent of the economy.

Lagos has begun to peal itself off the national pattern. Its local government has improved public transportation, improved the business environment, cleaned up streets, and enhanced the lives of its people. A Nigerian syndicate is building Eko Atlantic, said to become Nigeria's Manhattan. But shantytowns remain alongside modern skyscrapers. Along Lagunas and channels neighborhoods could be beautiful, but they are filthy and stinky. To make up for the lack of quality stores Internet purchases are in growing demand. In 2014, Lagos could only offer two malls larger than

20,000 square meters. In comparison Johannesburg's population of 4 million can choose among 74 malls.

As wide as the gap is between what Nigeria is today and what it could be in the future, IT offers high growth potential for individuals amidst Nigeria's mess. The telecom industry accounts for more than a quarter of Nigeria's upgrade in GDP (there are now about 115 million mobile phones lines).

Nigeria's daily newspaper *Business Day*, June 13, 2014, tells the story of Jason Njoku, a young Nigerian, who, after failing to start businesses in the UK, took off in Nigeria. He founded iROKOtv, which attracted 500,000 subscribers globally in six months. Now they have around 1 million unique visitors every single month watching from 178 countries in the world. Access to the Internet is still expensive and often out of reach in many sub-Sahara countries. Nevertheless, Jason Njoku says:

> There is unprecedented growth on the continent and we have growing population that will soon see the purchasing of consumer products and services online as an everyday action for all rather than a luxury for a few. In the next three to five years, Africa's tech scene will have turned into a revolution, … in Nigeria from $250 million today to $1 billion in five years.

"The potential is there, but without formal investment, it will not be released—and what a waste that will be." The *Economist* sums it up: "Nigeria now looks like an economy to take seriously."

South Africa

Population: 48,375,645
Urban population: 62% (2010)
GDP: $353.9 billion (2013 est.)
GDP composition: Agriculture 2.6%; industry29%; services 68.4%
Growth rate: 2% (The World Factbook)
GDP per capita grew from $2,638.16 in 2000 to $7,507.65 in 2012 (World Bank)
2014 Index of Economic Freedom: 75 (Heritage Foundation)

Life in Africa has many faces. A few years ago, when we were in Johannesburg, we insisted on visiting downtown Johannesburg, a no-go area for visitors. Never did we experience such latent violence manifest as during our drive through desolate streets, passing former bank buildings, and 5 star hotels: windows broken, trash thrown on crumbled asphalt, buildings occupied by squatters. What a contrast to the Sandton district, where the wealthy are living: shopping malls are connected by underground walkways presenting the best global brands, offering the finest coffee, French croissants, or local Milk Tart. Hardly anyone is as crazy as we are, hiring a car and driver to go to the old center, eager to learn about the many faces the city shows (*Die Welt*, December 15, 2013; *Der Spiegel* 47,48,49/2013; *Frankfurter Allgem. Sonntag*, December15, 2013).

Now we read about Jonathan Liebman, who founded Maboneng precinct in 2008 and has slowly transformed it into an urban neighborhood with galleries, artist's studios, apartments, hotels, and restaurants. Maboneng, which like the rest of downtown Johannesburg, had been turned into a no-go area with a wave of crime during the 1990s period of transition and uncertainty, now has become one of Africa's hippest urban enclaves, drawing life back into downtown Johannesburg, not so long ago written off.

The Internet is the enabler to make various art forms accessible to a greater and even global audience. South Africa's *Chimurenga*, which describes itself as a "project based multiple object, a print magazine, a workplace, and platform for editorial and curatorial activities." Just a Band, Kenyan band, sings to the hearts of young Africans: "Just because I am African with black skin, it doesn't mean I won't win if I try." The refrain evokes the new self-confidence of Africa's new generation: "Don't tell me what I can and can't do. I can change the world."

Tanzania

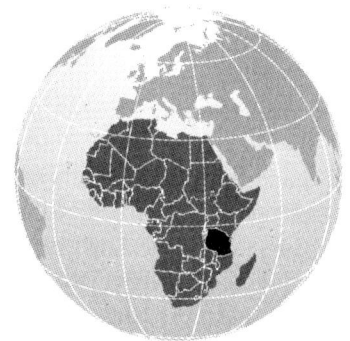

Population: 49,639,138
Urban population: 57% (2011)
GDP: $31.94 billion
GDP composition: Agriculture 27.6%; industry 25%; services 17.4% (2013 est.)
Growth rate: 7.0 (2013 est.) (World Factbook)
GDP per capita grew from $308.14 in 2000 to $608.72 in 2012 (World Bank)
2014 Index of Economic Freedom: 106 (Heritage Foundation)

Two countries became what we today know as Tanzania: Zanzibar and Tanganyika. The two countries merged on April 26, 1964, and adopted the new name Tanzania in October, 1964. Even though Tanzania is East Africa's second largest economy, it is still one of the poorest countries on per capita income and still fighting child labor and international child trafficking. Nevertheless, it shows potential in agriculture, where land suitable for irrigating farming exceeds by far the land actually used. Tanzania is rich in natural resources, coal, natural gas, uranium, nickel, tin, and also gold, platinum, diamonds to name some. But mining only counts for 4 percent of the GDP. Its GDP will be revised in September 2014 and is expected to grow by 20 percent due to rebasing GDP data after factoring in mining industries.

It should not come as a surprise that China in June 23, 2014, opened a "historic" Tanzania China Business Forum in Dar es Salaam (*Tanzania Daily News*, June 22, 2014). Underscored by the six-day visit of China's Vice President Li Yuanchao, its goal is to promote increase cooperation between the two countries. To date, 522 investment projects worth $2.49 billion have been registered (Xinhuanet, June 25, 2014).

In March 2013, a headline in Bloomberg News reads: "Tanzania to grow 10 percent in 2013 with the help of the Chinese." China's $1.4 billion beat US investment of $950 million in 2013 and replaced the United States as the fourth largest investor in the country. By 2013, China's total investment grew to $2.5 billion. Nearly 500 Chinese companies created 150,000 local jobs (Tanzanian *Daily News*, June 25, 2014).

On October 27, 2014, Reuters reported China and Tanzania signing a $1billion deal to build a satellite city and a $500 million financial center in Dar es Salaam. "The satellite city," writes Reuters, "located on the outskirts of Dar es Salaam, will be a self-contained urban zone equipped with water, electricity, roads, banks, schools, and hospitals. It is designed to ease congestion in Dar es Salaam central business district." President JakayaKikwete confirmed a total of five deals, worth more than $1.7 billion formally signed in Beijing.

But it is not the Chinese alone who invest betting on Tanzania's growing markets. Viettel, a Vietnam-based telecom operator, plans to invest $1 billion into a new third-generation mobile phone network in Tanzania. The company will not only offer low-cost smartphones, but will also provide free Internet services to schools, hospitals, and offices (Reuters, October 28, 2014).

North Africa: The Two Big "E's" and an Arab Marshal Plan

All optimism in Africa is directed to sub-Saharan emerging economies. Hope that Arab nations north of the Sahara would be opening up, not to a democratic system by Western understanding, but at least to a gradual improvement of living condition for its people, has vanished. Instead, a decade or decades of instability lay ahead. Revolutions seldom change systems overnight. The ground for stability needs to be laid on which the new government models can be built. Europe did not implement democracy overnight. In a region where borders have been drawn arbitrarily through ethnic groups and tribes, the hurdle to peaceful coexistence is much higher.

Dignity lost

"Nothing more of it, I beg you. Give him food, give him shelter. Have you covered bareness, dignity will come by itself" wrote German poet Friedrich von Schiller in the 19th century. The loss of dignity, being humiliated, and knowing that a better life should be possible was the tipping point for fruit vendor Mohamed Bouazizi in Tunisia. He did not claim welfare or handouts, but only wanted a government that would create conditions that would allow him to care for himself. Sunnite Saddam Hussein discriminated against Shiites; Nuri al-Malaki the Shiite declined to give dignity to Sunnites.

Education is a basic condition to build on unification rather than radicalization. Education is the foundation for political responsibility. But the hope that new governments will invest in the big two "E's"—economic and education—in northern Africa, has mostly vanished. Average youth unemployment is twice as high as the global average. In parts of Egypt and Tunisia half of the young people are without a job. Without hope there can be no dignity.

If the government fails, private initiative has to take over.

On April 3, 2013, *Financial Times* reported that Majid Jafar, CEO of Crescent Petroleum, a privately owned oil and gas company headquartered in the United Arab Emirates, laid out his Arab Stabilization plan to change the dangerous downward spiral.

His private initiative is planting a seed of hope, even though it is still in a very early stage. Majid Jafar: "While each country has its own set of priorities, supporting regional economic growth and reducing the underlying causes of extremism are goals that should be shared by all."

He has proposed a multi-investor trust fund to fight the instability in the region. Its main goals are to fight youth unemployment and integrate women into the working environment. Egypt, Yemen, Jordan, Morocco, and Tunisia are supposed to become main beneficiaries.

The model for Jafar is the Marshal Plan through which the United States invested $12 billion in Europe after the Second World War (WWII). At the end, it was not only to the benefit of Europe, but also to the benefit of the United States. Jafar is convinced that:

1. Entrepreneurs are better equipped to solve global problems than politicians.
2. It is not productive to put money into the budgets of tumbling countries, but better to invest directly into infrastructure, in private and public–private projects.

An investment of $30 billion could create five million jobs in the next five years. An investment of $100 billion would allow building highways, harbor, high-tech communication, and a better supply of water and energy, and create up to 15 million jobs.

Currently, Jafar's strategy paper is in planning stage. Its underlying principles as a result of talks with Arab governments are: respecting sovereignty of donor and receiver countries, improving national investment climate, social progress, regional integration, and transparency. The German weekly newspaper *Die Welt* (March 13, 2014) sees a number of serious problems to the realization of the project; nevertheless, it dedicated a full page to the story that shifts the focus from negative reporting to looking for solutions. "There are too few such forums in Arab countries, which are able to develop large political and economic perspectives, aside from the drama daily politics. If we wait until political stability is achieved, we won't achieve anything," said Jafar. "Imagine the United States after 1945 telling the Germans to first create a stable democracy and voting system, and then receive help."

Will Africa's Rise Be Real This Time?

In its October 2014 issue *Fortune* magazine featured an article entitled "Is Africa's rise for real this time?" *Fortune*'s answer was a solid "yes." Africa's "economies are surging, and foreign investment is exploding. The challenges are immense, but the continent may finally be ready to deliver on its promise."

Even the United States is paying attention. In August 2014, President Barack Obama hosted his first-ever African business summit Washington, attended by dozens of African leaders. The focus was not aiding the poor as such a meeting was in the past, but, as *Fortune* said, "on making multibillion-dollar deals that eclipsed decades of government hand-outs to African states."

The stampede back to Africa began in earnest after the financial crisis hit in 2008 "when countless Africans lost their jobs abroad or simply calculated that their prospects were better at home." *Fortune* quotes one American businessman as saying: "This is Asia 30 years ago. American investors have been the last to acknowledge that Africa is where the action will be for the next 30 years."

Latin America

For millennia the population of what we today know as Latin America was about 30 million people. Indigenous cultures, many of them highly civilized like the Aztec, Inca, and Maya, developed independently of other world cultures. Their cultural development was brutally interrupted in 1492, when Christopher Columbus, the Italian-born explorer, set foot on the "New World" under the flag of the Spanish King Ferdinand. At the turn of the 16th century, Pedro Alvarez Cabral, the Portuguese navigator and explorer, led a fleet of Portuguese ships and claimed the new territory now known as Brazil for the Portuguese King Manuel I. It was the Latin origin of the languages of the conquerors, Spanish and Portuguese, which gave "Latin America" its name. Its population grew to today's 600 million.

Today's Latin America 29 economies make up one of the world's most diverse regions. After rough political and economic times in the 20th century, Latin American countries are mostly democratic and, apart from Venezuela's and Bolivia's extreme socialism (ranking 175 and 158 as repressed in economic freedom), mostly market-driven economies. In May 2008, the Union of South American Nations, now signed by all 12 independent South American countries, was founded. Its goal is economic integration and a common currency, parliament, and passports. American commentators interpreted this move as a pivotal development in the loss of the United States hegemony in the region.

On the western side of the continent the Pacific Alliance (PA) with its members Chile, Colombia, Costa Rica, Mexico, and Peru and, maybe, Panama take a market-oriented approach with the goal of improving transparency and efficiency in capital flows, goods, rule of law, and the protection of intellectual property. In contrast, the Bolivian Alliance (ALBA), Venezuela, Bolivia, Nicaragua, and Ecuador apply a state-centric model, with trade and investments from centralized governments such as China (Venezuela alone $14.7 billion). It is no surprise to us that PA nations have attracted far more direct foreign investment in the past decade (data Heritage Foundation, World Bank).

In 2011, Latin America reached a watershed: for the first time its middle class outnumbered people living in poverty. In the past decade, Latin America's middle class grew 50 percent, which now accounts for 30 percent of the population (World Bank, 2014). Education has improved to an average of eight years from the previous five years. Reforms are partly sluggish, but the continent is on a new and better path, as a stroll through Latin American countries shows. In the competition for growth Paraguay leads: World Bank estimates a growth rate of 11 percent, followed by Panama 9 percent, Peru 6 percent.

A Brief Snapshot of Latin American Countries

Argentina

Population: 42,610,981
Urbanization: 92% (2010)
GDP: $661.8 billion
GDP composition: Agriculture 9.3%; industry 29.7%; services 61%
Growth rate: 3.5% (The Factbook)
GDP per Capita rose from $7,208.81 to $11,557 in 2012 (World Bank)
2014 Index of Economic Freedom: 166 (Heritage Foundation)

When we were in Buenos Aires a few years ago, Argentina was in one of its good years and the atmosphere fairly positive. One hundred years ago, Argentina was one of the richest countries in the world; today, it is one of Latin America's problem countries.

Twelve years after the state bankruptcy in 2002, the world faces a new Argentinian crisis. President Cristina Kirchner's continuous policies of state intervention, nationalization of Repsol's majority stake in Argentina's largest oil company, the Peso crash, and now currency control and restrictions of imports have led to empty shelves in supermarkets, together with abrupt price increases. All this resulted in Kirchner's approval rate dropping to 27 percent in January 2014.

And foreign investments are drying up. "Who invests in a country, in which the government changes private ownership relations like clothes?" asks *La Nation*, the country's leading conservative newspaper. Maybe, Cristina Fernández de Kirchner's second visit to Pope Francis in the Vatican will bring enlightenment to the very much-questioned president.

There is no lack of potential in Argentina. But it has to get out of its mess. There is hope that 2015 elections will be a turning point, at least from an optimistic point of view. But this does not only demand a change in political thinking. Redistribution of wealth and energy subsidies have helped the poorest, but unfortunately have been taken advantage by those who did not really need it. Necessary reforms will be painful. But standing at the abyss Argentina has no choice.

Brazil

Population: 201,009,622
Urban population: 87% (2010)

GDP: $2.422 trillion
GDP composition: Agriculture 5.5%; industry 26,4%; services 68.1%
Growth rate: 2.5% (World Factbook)
GDP per capita rose from 3,694.46 in 2000 to $11,339.52 in 2012 (World Bank)
2014 Index of Economic Freedom: 114 (Heritage Foundation)

A bright future to finally arrive?

Brazil, we confess, is one of our favorite countries. The drive, the dynamics of its people, the music, the food; we love it and luckily we are there quite often. While Brazil has beauty and great potential, it also has entrepreneurs who complain about the lack of reforms and an abundance of bureaucracy.

Despite a considerable economic slowdown in Brazil, the world's seventh largest economy, more than 5 million households will rise to the middle class in this decade, according to an estimate by Boston Consulting Group. But Brazil's middle class has very modest per capita income. The challenge in the coming years will be to deliver higher living standards for the whole population and to bring down barriers to growth. With the country's average age of only 28 years, dynamic, success-hungry entrepreneurs are pushing for better living conditions. And just as in China and Africa urbanization is the main driver of economic growth.

Brazil, despite all obstacles, ranks seventh in the world for attracting direct foreign investment. Sao Paulo ranks number five in hosting large foreign subsidiaries. Foreign investors remain positive in very different consumer markets. Forever21 Inc. produces affordable fashion for young consumers, and BMW, with its luxury automobiles, is in great demand.

Nevertheless, high taxation, high tariffs, an overwhelming bureaucracy, and a lack of infrastructure are high hurdles on the path to increased productivity. Bloomberg calls Brazil's tax system "Byzantine" and, according to World Bank, compliance with 27 tax codes can take businesses 2,600 hours a year, the highest in the world. An underdeveloped infrastructure and an overdeveloped bureaucracy (Bloomberg) do not make a dynamic duo. Brazil's productivity grew 1.2 percent from 1990 to 2012. Brazil was even beaten by India, which in the same period managed to raise its productivity by 4.4 percent (China 8.4 percent).

It is not a lack of potential that makes Brazil go three steps forward and two steps back. Brazil has a lot of unleveraged potential, including a large workforce ready to capitalize on the opportunities of transforming the global economy. And Brazil's entrepreneurs are calling for reforms that will boost competition and create a nourishing business environment that stops Brazil's forward-backward rhythm.

Nevertheless, in the past decade, Brazil has lifted 40 million people out of the slums and poverty into at least the lower middle class. It is this new middle class that now demands sustainable reforms to move further up the social ladder and maintain what they have achieved. The reelection of Rousseff points in the direction of more of the same.

Chile

Population: 17,216,945
Urbanization: 89% (2010)
GDP: $281.7 billion
GDP composition: Agriculture 3.6%; industry 35.4%; services 61%
Growth rate: 4.4%

GDP per capita rose from $5,133.08 in 2000 to $15,363.10 in 2012 (World Factbook)
2014 Index of Economic Freedom: 7 (Heritage Foundation)

Chile, independent from Spain since 1810, has maintained economic growth since the 1980s. In the index of economic freedom, Chile ranks number 7, whereas Brazil, by comparison, ranks 114. No wonder when we spoke at a media conference there some years ago, the mood was very optimistic and engaged.

Chile has been opening its markets unilaterally for several decades. It is the leading South America country in Index of Economic Freedom (Heritage Foundation). Chile's economy relies on the initiative and strength of private enterprises, even in social services. It is hard to believe from a European point of view, but its public services are generally provided by both public and private agencies, so that beneficiaries can have the freedom to choose among different competing alternatives (Heritage Foundation); competition in social services, unthinkable in many countries.

Chile's economic system is boosting entrepreneurship and its taxes are moderate, which makes Chilean products competitive in global markets. Its average growth rate reached almost 5 percent throughout the past 10 years. A key factor in Chile's economic progress is the reduction of educational gaps. Enrollments in higher education have risen from 200,000 students in 1985 to more than one million in 2013.

Like Peru, Chile's bet is on trade liberalization and trade agreements with the West and increasingly with emerging nations around the globe. In 2010, Chile became the first Latin American country to join the Organization for Economic Co-operation and Development (OECD). It is a founding partner in the important free-trade Pacific Alliance (The Latin American trade bloc including Chile, Colombia, Peru, and soon Costa Rica) with the goal of establishing economic integration, free trade, and visa-free travel.

Following Sebastian Pinera, Chile's president from 2010 to March, 2014, Chile again elected President Michelle Bachelet (after her first term from 2006 to 2010). She promised 50 reforms in 100 days to counteract slowing economic growth and to maintain Chile's position as a Latin American success story.

Colombia

Population 45,745,783
Urban population: 75%
GDP $369 billion
GDP composition: Agriculture 6.6%; industry 37.8%, services 55.6%.
Growth rate 4.2%
GDP per capita grew from $2503.55 in 2000 to $7,752.17 in 2012 (World Factbook)
2014 Index of Economic Freedom: no data available

The chances to end the more than half-century conflict with leftist Farc, the largest most active guerilla group in Latin America, have risen as Juan Manuel Santos won re-election in June 2014 with nearly 51 percent. The election was a yes to the peace process President Santos government started in 2012 in an effort to bring an end to the conflict that has killed tens of thousands and forced millions to leave their homes.

For many years hardly anyone would want to spend time in Colombia, including us. But when we landed in Bogota in February 2014, a bright and modern airport welcomed us. Customs clearance was fast and professional. In our hotel security personnel checked everybody at the entrance, and the lobby and restaurant were packed with businessmen and women holding meetings.

Pro-market President Santos has set steps to open the Colombian market. The recent announcement by Colombia's finance minister Mauricio Cardenas to invest $12 billion in infrastructure will open opportunities for business and give growth a boost. Cardenas estimated growth of 4.7 percent in 2014 and a possible annual growth of 7 percent on a sustained basis. With 21.3 percent growth, construction was the biggest driver of Colombia's economy in the third quarter of 2012. Agriculture and mining rose around 6 percent. Assertive promotion of free trade agreements has supported Colombia's ability to cushion economic setbacks in neighboring countries. The free trade agreement with the United States, to whom Colombia is the third largest of Latin American oil exporters, was ratified by the US Congress in 2011 and implemented in 2012. Restaurants with higher price levels reflect the changing consumer habits of a growing middle class, which has expanded by almost 50 percent in the past years. Recovery is still on shaky ground. Drug dealing, underemployment, poor infrastructures remain a challenge. But there is hope and there is ambition.

Costa Rica

Population: 4,695,942
Urban population: 64%

GDP: $61.43 billion
GDP composition: Agriculture 6.2%; industry 21.3%; services 72.5%
Growth rate: 3.5% (World Factbook)
GDP per Capita rose from $4,058.04 in 2000 to $9,386.30 in 2012 (World Bank)
2014 Index of Economic Freedom: 53 Heritage Foundation

On December 1, 1948, Jose Figueres, the then President of Costa Rica, had the guts to steer his country toward an unusual path. He ended the country's military presence with a sledgehammer. In a powerful speech he announced the eliminating of Costa Rica's military, slammed the hammer into the wall, and handed over the keys of the military headquarters to the minister of education while announcing that the military budget would be dedicated to health care, education, and the environment. Today, 25 percent of Costa Rica's land area is either biological reserves or national parks.

Uncertain as such indexes might be, Costa Rica ranks number 1 in the Happy Planet Index and number 1 in the World Data Base of Happiness.

Despite the overall happy population, similar to other Latin American countries, Costa Rica is fighting to reduce unemployment and the poverty rate, which has not been brought down by 20 to 25 percent in the last two decades. Nevertheless, Costa Rica is an attractive working place for neighboring countries. Up to 500,000 Nicaraguans are working legally and illegally in Costa Rica giving reasons for concerns.

The estimated growth rate of 3.8 percent for 2014 and 4.1 percent for 2015 is reason for optimism. The country's political stability and incentives in Costa Rica's free trade zones have attracted the highest level of direct foreign investment per capita in Latin America. Overall living quality is one of the best in Latin America. That at least to a study of the Intelligence Unit of the Economist ranked Costa Rica the second best country in Latin America to be born in 2013, ranking 30 in the global list. It measures health, safety, and prosperous life in the years ahead.

Cuba

Population: 11,047,251 (est. 2014)
Urbanization: 75 percent
GDP: $72.3 billion (est.)
GDP composition: Agriculture 3.8%; industry 22.3%; services 73.9%
Growth rate: 13.1% (2012 est.) (The World Factbook)
GDP per capita rose from $2,744.12 in 2000 to $6,051.22 in 2011 (World Bank)
2014 Index of Economic Freedom: 177 (Heritage Foundation)

If in the book *La View Cachée de Fidel Castro* (The Secret Life of Fidel Castro) Juan Reynaldo Sanchez, a member of Castro's elite inner circle, tells the truth, Fidel Castro ran the country somewhere between being a medieval landlord and Louis XV. Castro's reign ended when a serious disease forced him to hand over power to his brother Raoul, who officially took power in 2008.

Now, there are signs that Cuba's people will slowly be allowed to work to get their share of Cuba's potential. Around 20 percent of Cubans work in the private sector and most land is now farmed by individual farmers, rather than state-owned enterprises. After half a century Cuba's first privately run wholesale market is about to open. Reuters reported Cuba's first independent online newspaper launched by Cuba's best-known dissident Yoani Sanchez on May 21, 2014. Cuba's tolerance for criticism has been rising, but does not yet allow a professional looking website produced on the island. However, there is little danger of disruption from the Internet as most

Cubans will not be able to read a blog and online newspapers. Only 2.6 million of its 11 million population have access to the Internet.

Despite limitations that will only be reduced over time, Cuba is slowly opening up. "China and Cuba: Skip the ideology, let's talk about money" is the title of a report in the *International Business Times* on April 24, 2014. It should not come as a surprise that "Beijing has been pushing Havana on reforms, drawing on its own experience in the last three decades," writes *International Business Times*. "China and Cuba have common goals in their international agendas," said Bruno Rodríguez after his meeting with China's foreign minister Wang Yi when he visited Cuba in April 2014. The Chinese community in Cuba which goes back 150 years, and contributed to Castro's revolution, underlines the ties between the countries.

Cuba's economic opening-up is not limited to trading with China. It is now developing new trading partners including Brazil, and Angola on capitalist terms, but not with America, which is by America's choice.

Mexico

Population: 118,818,228
Urbanization: 78% (2010)
GDP: $1.327 trillion
GDP composition: Agriculture 3.6%; industry 36.6%; services 59.8%
Growth rate: 1.2% (World Factbook)
GDP per capita rose from $6.663.65 in 2000 to $9,748.87 in 2012 (World Bank)
2014 Index of Economic Freedom: 55 (Heritage Foundation)

One of our liveliest private memories of Mexico is when our hosts ordered tortillas stuffed with worms. Eat it or not? The worms were about the size of a child's little finger, white with slight brown spots from the grill. Not so much different from shrimp, we told ourselves, and dug into tortillas. Would they really taste different? We ate it, and we did not notice a difference. But then, why eat it? Our lust for culinary adventures was topped when we were at a speaking engagement in Zambia a little later. We were told that the specialty of the region is a certain worm; this worm the size of a German sausage, eaten unwrapped in its full grilled beauty. Fortunately, they were out of season.

Mexico's worms are smaller, but its GDP per capita at $9,748 beats Zambia's 1,462 almost seven times. And Mexico's economy has been growing faster than Brazil's, its larger rival in the region. According to the *Financial Times* Mexico has signed 44 free trade agreements, more than any other country in the world. "Mexico," says the *Financial Times*, "is no longer a security problem with an economy, but an economy with a security problem."

President Pena Nieto is fighting organized crime by bringing down violence rather than drug kingpins. First results showed homicides dropping in 2013, but it is too early to see whether his new approach is working.

Mexico has established social programs and better access to education to enable more of its population to move up to middle class. Economic mobility within generations is rising and is hungry for new markets. It has become a member of the Pacific Alliance (Latin American trade bloc including Chile, Colombia, Peru, and Costa Rica) with the goal of establishing economic integration, free trade, and visa-free travel.

President Enrique Pena Nieto's ambitious reforms to transform the economy seem to have gained ground. Extraordinarily, Mexico has overturned the 1938 nationalization of its oil industry and opened its energy sector to outside investment. To cover all energy reforms, including the transformational reform of Pemex, the state-owned oil monopoly, more than 20 laws needed to be changed, and a new structure of oil and gas contracts terms is meant to attract international investors.

As in her speech in Mexico City in June 2014, Christine Lagarde, Managing Director of the IMF said:

> Mexico is the only emerging market country that has passed such number of sweeping reforms, in such a short time, and with such broad political support. Perhaps more impressive is that it did not take an economic or financial crisis to invoke these reforms. Instead, it took a great deal of leadership, resilience, and determination on the part of the Mexican people to accomplish this ... Mexico can become the inspiration for the rest of the world.

In an interview for CNN in October 2014, Lagarde called on Europe to finally implement necessary reforms and referred to Mexico: "Apply the Mexican Formula."

Peru

Population: 29,849,303
Urbanization: 77%
GDP: $344 billion
GDP composition: Agriculture 6.2%; industry 37.5%; services 56.3%
Growth rate: 5.1% (2013 est.) (World Factbook)
GDP per capita rose from $2,049.62 in 2000 to $6,573.04 in 2012 (World Bank)
2014 Index of Economic Freedom: 47 (Heritage Foundation)

On January 27, 2014, the dispute over 38,000 sq. km of the Pacific Ocean between Peru and its neighbor Chile finally came to an end, bringing a fight for control over the nitrate industry to a new partnership.

The verdict of the International Court of justice allowed both sides to claim victory. Peru's President Humala called it the beginning of a new stage of cooperation and friendship that will allow a new stage of relations with Chile. South of Peru, Chile is moving itself up the economic growth ladder.

Peru, also Colombia's neighbor, shares the dense rain forests, pacific coast, and excellent fishing grounds. It achieved growth rates above 6.4 percent from 2002 to 2012. It is one of Latin America's best performing economies. Private investment, a free trade policy under President Ollanta Humala's administration, and trade agreements with the United States and Canada, China, Korea, Singapore, Japan, and the European Free Trade Association have opened its export doors. With rich mineral resources Peru's strongest sector is the mining industry, which accounts for more than 60 percent of Peru's exports.

Better infrastructure in its inland has high potential to further boost economic growth. About one fourth of Peruvians live in the capital Lima which has also seen a boom in business due to more enlightened national economic policies.

Venezuela

Population: 28,459,085
Urbanization: 93% (2010)
GDP: $367.5 billion
GDP composition: Agriculture 3.7%; industry 35.5%; services 60.8%
Growth rate: 1.6% (The World Factbook)

GDP per capita rose from $4,799.65 in 2000 to $12,728.73 in 2012 (World Bank)
2014 Index of Economic Freedom: 175 (Heritage Foundation)

Out of control socialist model?

It seems there are two pictures of Venezuela: Nicolas Madura's parallel universe and the picture the world receives. The country with the highest oil reserves seems to be eager to prove that even when you own a goose that lays golden eggs misgoverning can drive a country into disaster. "We have to line up for sugar; we have to line up for rice. The good news is no need to line up for toilet paper because in all of Venezuela there is no toilet paper." That is how Venezuelan friends described daily living conditions when we met them in Costa Rica in February 2014. Venezuela went from extreme inequality, with its rich class living detached from the poor masses, to today's extreme socialism. Venezuela has an out of control misinterpretation of welfare. It also has a housing crisis, electricity shortage, inflation as high as 55 percent, and one of the highest murder rates in the world. Both sides, government and opposition are radicalized.

The country is wasting its high growth trading potential and has a government under Nicolas Maduro with no clear sight to reality. Venezuela in 2014 is one of the two worst problem countries in Latin America, a companion for Argentina.

Latin America: From Backyard of the United States to China's Playground?

Despite Latin America's ups and downs and shortcomings, McKinsey estimates that Latin America together with China is most likely to be a top location for new companies. Sao Paulo alone is estimated to more than triple its number of headquarters by 2025.

Latin American countries emancipated their thinking when breaking loose from the paternalism of the United States. They did not want the United States to do something *for* them, but to do something *with* them. No doubt America is slowly losing ground, even though its $850 billion in combined imports and exports in 2013 is still way ahead of $244 billion of China in 2012. But China is catching up rapidly. Now there is concern whether Latin America is stepping from shower rain into the rain and whether Latin American countries will play their own game or become a ball in the game others play. Former President Fernando Henrique Cardoso worries: "In the past we feared the predominance of the United States. Now it is the opposite."

"As the United States sleeps, China conquers Latin America," was the headline of a guest comment in *Forbes* (October 15, 2014). The author, Michael Fumento, former reporter for *Investor's Business Daily* certainly is very skeptical about China's role. "China sends Latin America junk it wouldn't dare send to the United States or Europe, charging much more," is his take we cannot confirm by our Latin American experience. But any judgment based on subjective opinions, even though backed by local experience, will remain weak.

With the awakening of a new self-confidence, Latin American countries are seeking to integrate their economies to be more competitive and adding weight to their role in the global community. In doing so, Latin American leaders have their preference and make their choice. Whether it will be toward the United States or China, the future of emerging economies will be built on partnerships among all nations, but primarily among each other without interference from the West.

Asia

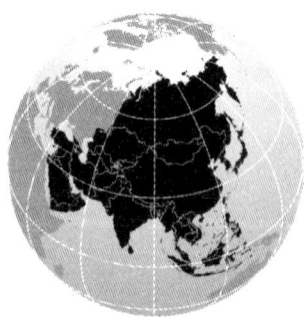

Note: This figure is not to scale. It does not represent any authentic national or international boundaries and is used for illustrative purposes only.

Asia covers about one-third of the landmass of the globe. It is a continent of superlatives: Hosting around four billion people, Asia is the most populated continent with China being the most populated country. Russia is the largest country in the world. The Himalayas are the world's highest mountain chain, Baikal is the deepest and oldest inland lake in the world, Mariana is the deepest part of the world's oceans, and the Dead Sea has the lowest elevation on land and the saltiest body of water. India is known as the world's largest democracy.

Asia has the most intercontinental countries and countries reaching into another continent; among these countries Russia, Kazakhstan, Indonesia, Japan, Egypt, and Turkey. Asia plays an important role as the cradle of many cultures. Most world religions originated in Asia.

In the 20th century, economic growth in Asia started along the coastlines: Japan, South Korea and after its opening-up in the 1980s, in China. The so-called Four Tiger economies, Hong Kong, Taiwan, Singapore, and South Korea, achieved strong growth and rapid industrialization between 1960 and 1990. Since then, China's performance and potential have become overwhelming and a great catalyst for all of Asia.

"By 2030," wrote the *Economist* in its Special Report on Business in Asia, May 31, 2014, "Asia will have surpassed North America and Europe combined in terms of global power, based upon GDP, population size, military spending and technological investment." Some of the world's giant companies are in Asia: Petro China $202 billion; ICBC, China, $215 billion; Samsung Electronics, Korea $186 billion; Toyota, Japan $193 billion; China Construction Bank $174 billion; Alibaba, China $168 billion; tsmc, Taiwan $101 billion, to just mention the companies joining the $100 plus billion club. India's largest enterprise is Reliance Industries $50.9 billion (*Forbes data* and *The Economist*).

In comparison: Apple $483 billion, Siemens, Germany, $114 Billion, Novartis, Switzerland, $227 billion.

The top 10 in the *Forbes* list is half United States, half China. The five Chinese companies are state-owned, and the five US companies are private. But as part of President Xi's rejuvenation of China, China's state-owned enterprises are opening up too.

Asia now accounts for 27 percent of the world's market capitalism; Asia's consumer market is huge, 30 percent of the world's middle class spending; 47 percent of the world's manufacturing takes place in Asia. Almost 55 percent of Asia's trade is within the region.

And China without doubt is Asia's global star.

A Brief Snapshot of Asian Countries

China

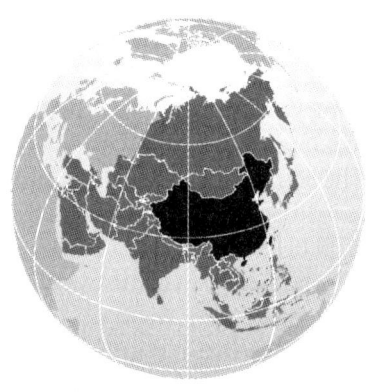

Population: 1,349,585,838
Urbanization: 50.6% (2010)
GDP: $8.939 trillion
GDP composition: Agriculture 9.7%; industry 45.3%; services 45%
Growth rate: 7.6% (World Factbook)
GDP per capita rose from $949.18 in 2000 to $6,091.01 in 2013 (World Bank)
2014 Index of Economic Freedom: 137 (Heritage Foundation)

China can be taken as a global case study of the importance of the two big "E's" (in Chinese, big JJ, Jing Ji and Jiao Yu, the two big "J's"). Chapter 3 will elaborate on China's further opening-up. In the past decade China's "Go West" strategy brought economic growth to former rural and backward regions. Chengdu, the capital of Sichuan province, has become one of China's economic superstars. It is part of China's strategy to revitalize and rejuvenate the country in all regions. Jilin, located in the northeast of China, is one of the provinces eager to catch up with the frontrunners in the parade. When we were visiting Jilin's capital Changchun in April 2013, it was a picture and a mood similar to cities in China's west we have visited earlier over the years. With maybe one difference, Governor Jiang Chaoliang of Jilin Province claims to put emphasis on GDP growth aside and focus on improvements in the quality of living directing efforts toward "what paves the way for future developments and produces long-term benefits."

Changchun is already known as one of China's automobile cities. Nevertheless, we were not surprised to learn that the ambition is to become China's largest automobile producer.

Emission reduction, bolstering agricultural development and service industries, and stimulating the development of private companies by allowing them to enter industries that were previously state industries are key strategies for Jilin. A main focus of the local government is also to improve public welfare, including public housing, social security, and education.

According to *China Daily* January 28, 2014, Jilin province will initiate a three-year campaign to strengthen its service industries, including tourism and health services. Thirty industry clusters will include 700 projects. To fuel innovation research and development the budget will be increased by at least 20 percent. Li Yuanyuan, President of Jilin University, understands the responsibility the university has to provide education fitting China's demands for innovative scientists.

The local government has announced its effort to modernize Jilin, which includes enforcing the rule of law, fighting corruption, and the streamlining of administrative procedures. From an investor's point of view emerging cities offer great opportunities in all spheres of endeavor. But China today is much more selective in foreign investors, acting on eye-level and profit oriented on a national level.

Jilin is just one example of what is happening all over China.

India

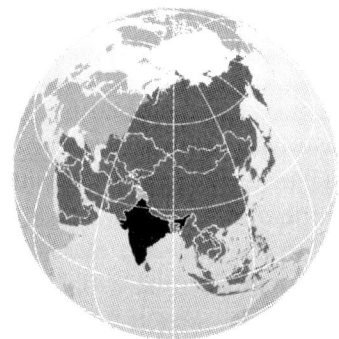

Note: This figure is not to scale. It does not represent any authentic national or international boundaries and is used for illustrative purposes only.

Population: 1,220,800,359
Urbanization: 31.3% (2011)
GDP: $1.758 trillion
GDP composition: Agriculture: 16.9%; industry 17%; services 66.1%
Growth rate: 3.8% (World Factbook)
GDP per capita rose from $455.44 in 2000 to $1,489.24 in 2012 (World Bank)
2014 Index of Economic Freedom: 120 (Heritage Foundation)

In the 1990s India seemed to be on a path of opening-up. On the wings of its significant involvement in the global information sector, India's reputation changed and a annual growth rate of 9 percent in 2007 nourished hope of a China-style economic rise and drew direct foreign investment into the country. Often compared with China, India's GDP per person 30 years ago was the same as China's. Now it is only one-fourth of the size, a dismal record. India's boom stalled, urgently needed reforms did not take place. Not too long ago, when we were waiting to board a plane in Delhi we got into a conversation with an Indian entrepreneur and his family. He said he was moving his family out of India after he had already moved his company to Vietnam. "Bureaucracy was just killing us" he said, "I am not willing up to put up with it any longer."

Socialism and bureaucracy prevailed. "India has become a failing state... too weak and too intrusive," as Gurcharan Das, former CEO of Procter and Gamble India writes in his book *India Grows at Night*. India's growth potential is like *Sleeping Beauty*, the government to wake it with a kiss has not yet arrived.

Despite its reputation as the "world's largest democracy," India's encumbering caste system, is anything but democratic. *Time Magazine* calls this a "tired slogan, true only by the numbers (more than 814 million voters) and undermined by the inequalities and injustices that still stain the nation." India's caste system remains influential in India's society in most aspects of life. Hereditary social stratification is limiting opportunities for a large part of the population. Marriages and occupation are mostly organized within one caste. India's four castes are classified with the highest class, Brahmin, which provides the intellectual elite, scholars, teachers, and religious leaders. The second highest caste is the Kshatriyas, who are traditionally dukes, warriors and high public officials, and law enforcers. The third in the ranking are Vishayas, who are mostly traders, salesmen, landlords, and farmers. The fourth caste is the Sudras, who work as service providers, craftsmen, lease farmers, and blue-color workers.

The worse destiny is to be born classless Dalit, "untouchables" living at the fringe of the society. According to UNICEF and Human Rights Watch, Hindu, Muslim, Buddhist, and Christian untouchables account for one-fourth of the Indian population, around 250 million people.

Inequality, both cultural and social, weighs heavily on India's future but with the elevation of new Prime Minister Narendra Modi, India's prospects and expectations for structural reform and return to serious growth were sky-high. Modi's stunning election victory has put a strong economic growth leader in charge. The year 2014 was expected to become the turning point in India's path to modernity and modest wealth for all. It is, in fact, time to turn the country around.

The outlook in mid-2015, as we update the book, is mixed. After years of questionable growth, a dysfunctional parliament and escalating corruption, for the first time in many years the parliament has a majority of only one party. With Modi and his majority in Parliament, India can play catch-up to the benefits of its citizens. It was said that Modi's ambition is to become one of India's great prime ministers. To turn India into a Chinese-style manufacturing powerhouse and leverage the opportunities Global Game Change offers could become a remarkable victory for a Western-governing model competing with China's efficient, but autocratic governing structures. But there is one significant part in turning a country around. While the vision for a country needs to be communicated top down, the energy for change must be developed bottom up.

Deng Xiaoping's strength was not to give speeches and draft the themes of revival, but to empower the people. While the first approach to escape the iron fist of central planning was taken in pure desperation, next unorthodox steps followed with the tolerance and later with guidance of officials. Gray zones of half-legal trade were built in a country in transition. Trial and error in reforms had proven its value and became a strategy. The most important seed planted was the hope to be able to shape their own future.

Prime Minister Modi is correct when he says: "There are huge global expectations for India." Great expectation can be taken as an encouragement and certainly are a proof of trust the global community has in India. But the promise "to look at a bankruptcy court, a dispute resolution mechanism, at a procurement law" as India's finance minister Arun Jaitley announced, will not be enough. Just as "trying to reform and liberalize" and to "intend to put a huge amount of investment as far as rural infrastructure is concerned," won't do it.

Has Prime Minister Modi really begun to reform India?

"India's leader needs to offer a vision of what he wants to achieve and let others help him," was the headline in an Interview with Mr Modi in the *Economist* (May 23, 2015). Modi says he needs to enhance employment opportunities. But the largest support to entrepreneurs is a business-friendly environment, investment in education and health care. It is to understand how to empower India's young and talented people, give them space to develop, and guide their own creativity toward a path of mutual benefit for themselves and the country. The goal of India becoming "an engine of international growth" is grand and great but it is a marathon, which takes at best around 30,000s single steps to reach the goal. It is easier to relate and connect to the steps than to a far-off target-line.

A valuable asset to China's rise was the know-how and economic power of overseas Chinese, the so-called sea turtles. They brought knowledge, technology, capital, and connections to the country. How attractive is India to around 27 million Indians who live overseas? Abroad living Indians were strong supporters in Prime Minister Modi's election. How much could many of them contribute to a modern India? Worries about the availability of human capital and concerns about the quality in manufacturing are holding many back. "If things would really change in India we would love to return quickly," said the businessman we met at the Delhi airport.

India's goal is to raise its share in the global economy from 2 to 3.5 percent by 2020. This is not an unrealistic goal as such. Especially as wages in China cities are rising and China's centers of economic power, its many high-tech zones, are rapidly moving from cheap labor to high-tech manufacturing, leaving space for India to fill the gap.

Global supply chains have been changing and as we anticipate, the nations of the Global Southern Belt are reshaping our world. India is the second largest and could certainly benefit greatly from shedding off low-cost manufacturing in China. It could bridge the space between the human capital needed in high-tech industries and workers available in India. And certainly it is an important step in reaching the goal for an "Indian century," as new investments are increasingly searching for low-cost locations.

While India and China are founding partners in the new Asian Infrastructure Investment Bank, to find an agreement on China's plans for a Bangladesh–China–India–Myanmar corridor is a much harder task. Nevertheless to be isolated from China's New Silk Road project would have significant implications for India as it will open doors for new trade and capital flows and boost cooperation between Asian and European nations.

In the next decades, India and China will be on a twin path of cooperation and competition, aiming to boost trade and investments. India's urgent need to improve infrastructure and manufacturing meets China's goal of investing $100 billion in the next five years in India. And it seems that the leaders of both countries are seeking to leverage bilateral economic potential not only on economic facts, but supported by an emotional, personal approach.

Improving the China–India relationship and an opening-up to the world are a good part of a rather optimistic one-year resume of Modi's rule. Direct foreign investment is rising as does India's status and gravity in the global community.

A historic deal with Bangladesh will hopefully end border disputes and lead to new trade and transport contracts. At the same time, India is improving its relationship with Iran, as part of its interest in building stronger ties to Central Asia and Eurasia. Mr Modi has assured Afghanistan of India's commitment to build Chabahar port, part of the North–South Corridor passing through Iran to Afghanistan border. We see that in the context of anticipating Iran as opening up economically over the next decades and aiming for a new role as a gateway to new Middle Eastern and African markets. But while in the past decades global trade flows were dominated by large companies, digitalization is now opening countless doors for small and one-person businesses. Consumer demand in emerging economies will differ from the typical Western basket of products. The growing and different demands of the new consumer class work to the advantage for flexible and ambitious Indians. A new era for Indian micromultinationals has begun.

"Good days are here again," Mr Modi wrote in a victory tweet. Maybe for some of the entrepreneurs who left India for a more business-friendly environment India will soon offer reason enough to return. We will take a deep breath on June 21, India's newly installed International Yoga Day, keep hoping for the best and see.

Indonesia

Population: 249.9 million
Urbanization: 50.7% (2011)
GDP: $878 billion
GDP composition: Agriculture 14.3%; industry 46.6%; services 39.1% (World Factbook)
Growth rate: 6.2%
GDP per capita rose from $789.81 in 2000 to $3,556.79 in 2012 (World Bank)
2014 Index of Economic Freedom: 100 (Heritage Foundation)

Indonesia, the world's fourth most populous country, and a founding member of ASEAN, has had a remarkable economic and political recovery since the fall of General Suharto in 1998 and accounts for almost 40 percent of the region's economic output. It is the world's largest exporter of coal, the largest producer of palm oil, and the second largest producer of cocoa and tin. Despite its resources, more than 100 million Indonesians are living on $2 a day or less. Disparity between rich and poor is at record high. A "more people centric" government, as the newly elected President Joko Widodo promised, will include "programs for farmers and fisherman and other traditional laborers, and more spending on health care and social services for the poor." Rising productivity is key to meeting even domestic demand. A 2012 report on Indonesia by McKinsey estimates 90 million Indonesians will have moved to consumer class by 2030, identified three key sectors, in which

Indonesia "could create a $1.8 trillion private sector business opportunity by 2030: Consumer services, agriculture and energy."

In early October of 2013, China's President Xi Jinping made Indonesia his first stop in a Southeast Asian country and Indonesia is one of China's targets in Xi's plan to invest in fast growing economies. China has become Indonesia's largest trading partner, but so far Indonesia's companies have invested more in China than Chinese companies in Indonesia. China has now signaled more activity in Indonesia whose middle class is bumping up against 100 million, although investments at present are still not as high as in Japan, South Korea, and Singapore. Indonesia's young population, half of it younger than 30, is dynamic and there is a lot of ambition.

As we are finishing this book, in October 2014, China is preparing to host the Asia-Pacific Economic Cooperation summit in Beijing, welcoming Indonesia's new President Joko Widodo, sworn in on October 20.

Susilo BambangYuhoyono, president from 2004 to 2014, set the government's goal to achieve 7 percent a year growth by 2030. It will be interesting to see the steps Indonesia's newly elected president will take in his plan to turn Indonesia, the world's largest archipelago, into a "maritime power."

Japan

Population: 127,103,388 million
Urban population: 91.5% (2014)
GDP: $5.007 trillion (2013 est.)

GDP composition: Agriculture 2.6%; industry 39.2%; services 58.2%
Growth rate: 2% (World Factbook)
GDP per capita rose from $37,291.71 in 2000 to $38,492.09 in 2013 (World Bank)
2014 Index of Economic Freedom: 72 (Heritage Foundation)

In 1994, we started our working relationship with *Megatrends Asia, which* said about Japan: "For many years it was the Japanese. The Japanese are coming. It appeared they were going to dominate the world economically. But now a remarkable transformation is taking place. The Chinese are coming. Japanese economic power has reached its peak and is beginning to recede as the Chinese prepare for the year 2000, the year of the Dragon that will usher in the Dragon Century." Of course in 1995, when *Megatrends Asia* was published, Japan did not want to hear that at all.

Japan went from the star performer of the industrial world to the sick economy of Asia. In 1995, for the first time since 1985, Japan lost top ranking as the world's most competitive economy, slipping to fourth (and number nine in the Global Competitive Index 2013–2014). The Economist proclaimed that "this is no economic superpower bent on world domination. It is a hara-kiri economy set to self destruction." Japan has never recovered. There has been almost no real growth for the last two decades. The government continues its unwillingness to allow the economy to organize itself, continuing its deadening, heavy-handed micro-management. This will not change under the current leadership.

Kazakhstan

Population: 17.95 million
Urban population: 53.3% (2014)
GDP: $225.6 billion (2014 est.)
GDP composition: Agriculture 4.9%; industry 29.5%; services 65.6%
Growth rate: 4.6% (World Factbook)
GDP per capita rose from $1,230.81 in 2000 to $13,611.5 in 2013 (World Bank)
2015 Index of Economic Freedom: 63.3 (Heritage Foundation)

Kazakhstan is the world's ninth largest and largest land-bound country in the world. Located in Central Asia 5.4 percent of its landmass reaches into Eastern Europe.

Kazakhstan was the last country to leave the Soviet Union in December 1991. The hangover of the times when decisions for the country were made in Moscow or St Petersburg was over. President Nursultan Nazarbayev was announced as Kazakhstan's president by the Soviet Council in April 1990. In the 1995 election he won with 95 percent of the votes, with a similar result in the last election in 2015.

Kazakhstan has benefited from rich oil resources, but there is strong awareness that without diversification Kazakhstan's economic development will not be sustainable.

At age 74, President Nazarbayev has ambitious plans to modernize Kazakhstan toward a modern society for all. The goal is to become one of the world's top 30 developed nations. Similar to China's 2049 target, Kazakhstan aims to reach the final goal in 2050.

In our visit in May 2015, the mood was optimistic. Astana, the new capital, offers the view of a modern city. The 2017 World Exhibition is a huge construction site.

There is no question that the Silk Road will be a main factor to further boost Kazakhstan's economy. In his first visit to Kazakhstan as President Xi Jinping announced the key project in Nazarbayev University in Astana in 2013. The overland Silk Road, of which Kazakhstan will be a part, will involve energy pipelines, roads, rail links, and telecommunication ties.

The New Silk Road is a key part but not the only tie between Kazakhstan and China. The value of Chinese FDI is now more than $17 billion.

As part of Central Asia, Kazakhstan will benefit greatly from improvements in regional cooperations. In its Scenario for the South Caucasus and Central Asia the World Economic Forum 2014 estimates Kazakhstan's GDP to grow by 20 percent in the next 10 years. Overall trade in Central Asia is estimated to grow by 160 percent, savings in supply chain costs are as high as $1.728 billion and 1.8 million full-time jobs will be added in countries participating in new transport corridors.

South Korea

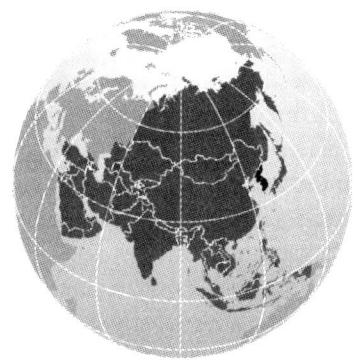

Population: 50.22 million
Urban population: 83.2% (2011)
GDP: $1.198 trillion (2013 est.)
GDP composition: Agriculture 2.6%; industry 39.2%; services 58.2%
Growth rate: 2.8% (World Factbook)
GDP per capita rose from $11,947 in 2000 to $25,976 in 2013 (World Bank)
2014 Index of Economic Freedom: 31 (Heritage Foundation)

Korea is one of the world's great examples of a nation pulling itself out of poverty. Korea moved from the level of poor African and Asian countries to becoming the world's 12th largest economy, setting records in economic development with its GDP tripling in 20 years. Korea has become a leader in IT products such as mobile phones, memory chips. Samsung and LG are the world's top two TV manufacturers and it ranks number five in car production.

Koreas capability in the service sector needs improvement. Its productivity must rise moving from low value to creating high-value jobs is a basic need for advancing its economy. With the rise of the Global Southern Belt, tourism and business services have a lot of room to grow.

Korea's industrial enterprises have been growing steadily and rapidly in emerging markets with the negative impact of low domestic employment. Declining domestic employment in key industries has led to a phenomenon similar to the United States. Korea's middle class is declining, since 1990 from 75 percent to 67 in 2013. Declining personal savings and one of the world's lowest fertility rates (1.30 birth per woman) are the consequences.

Soaring housing and education prizes are increasing the dangerous trend. In our experience Chinese and South Korean parents are very close in the fierce competition to get their child in the best school and university, often under great financial sacrifice for the families. In long conversations with Korean students nothing seemed more important than passing examinations and staying at the top of the rankings of the best. That of course leads to an oversupply of college graduates and a high risk of unemployment and underemployment.

It was no wonder that in our meeting with President Park education was the key theme. Pressure and rote learning is killing creativity. Korea urgently needs to further build on innovation in its already established industries. But, as in many countries, President Park is fighting against institutionalized structures to establish what she calls a "creative economy" to "foster students' talents and dreams."

There is though, little time to dream. We experience the longest working hours in Korea, even longer than in China. E-mails from our Korean publisher and various business partners are often written after midnight and on weekends. There is a limit to diligence and ambition, as desirable as they are.

Korea needs to work toward a more practical education system and a farewell to believing a college degree is the sole door to a successful career and a "face" in the community.

Laos

Population: 6 million
Urban population: 34.3%
GDP: $10.1 billion
GDP composition: Agriculture 24.8%; industry 32%; services 37.5%
Growth rate: 8.3% (World Factbook)
GDP per capita rose from $321.29 in 2000 to $1,645.74 in 2013
(World Bank)
2014 Index of Economic Freedom: 144 (Heritage Foundation)

Laos, a member of ASEAN since 1997, is still one of the poorest countries in the world. Even though its arable land is only four percent, 80 percent of its population practices subsistence agriculture with rice as the main production. Industrial production is limited to micro entities. Laos was approved to join the World Trade Organization in 2013 and in the same year hosted the annual Asian–European meeting.

Shaken by serious economic problems Laos started a program of opening and reform in 1986 with the goal of slowly shifting from planned to market economy.

Laos has growth potential, but faces a lack of infrastructure, lack of education, and financial structures. Its substantial resources of bauxite coal, copper, gold, tin, and other metals are waiting for foreign investments to leverage market potential. Tourism is growing rapidly, yet from a very low point. Nevertheless, Laos has had one of the world's fastest growth rates: from 2002 to 2011 it was never below 6.2 percent and rose to 8.7 percent in 2007.

Surprisingly, Laos's number of patents and published scientific articles is higher than Vietnam. *VietNamNet Bridge* reported that economists warned that Vietnam would fall into the middle-income trap and could fall behind Laos and Cambodia in economic growth.

International Railway Journal on October 16, 2004, reported a new railway that the National Development and Reform Commission approved in October 2014. It will connect Inner Mongolia Laos and Myanmar. The 504-km electrified line will link Yuxi, Kunming Province with Pu'er, Xishuangbanna, and Mohanon at the border to Laos and on to Vientiane. Laos is a landlocked country, new railroad projects would boost tourism, encourage investments and lower transportation costs of exports and consumer goods.

Malaysia

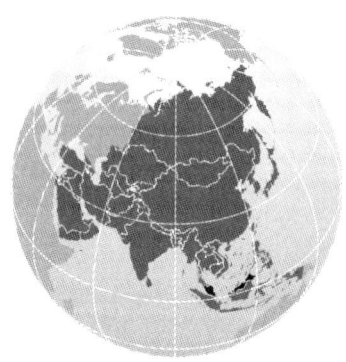

Population: 29.24 million
Urbanization: 72.8% (2011)
GDP: $312.4 billion (2013 est.)
GDP composition: Agriculture: 11.2%; industry 40.6%; services 48.1%
Growth rate: 4.7 percent (World Factbook 2013 est.)
GDP per capita rose from $4004.56 in 2000 to $10.380 in 2012 (World Bank)
2014 Index of Economic Freedom: 37 (Heritage Foundation)

Over recent decades Malaysia has come from producing raw materials to a multisector economy. It is one of the region's economic success stories with high goals for 2020.

In September 2010, Malaysia's government launched an Economic Transformation Program (ETP). Its goal is to lift Malaysia from a mid-income country to a high-income economy with a per capita income of at least $15,000, the World Bank's threshold for high income. The strategic plan to boost the economy expects 92 percent of the investments to come from private sectors. The government sees its role mainly to be the facilitator.

One of the investors, Asia Media, a Malaysian outdoor advertising company, intends to invest $152 million into the ETP program to transform Malaysia into a world-class nation and enhance the country's competitiveness in the ASEAN region. Asia Media's CEO Ricky Wong: "the company supports the development to a knowledge society through infotainment delivery using mobile broadcasting … to elevate communication and infrastructure of Malaysia."

Malaysia is the world's largest issuer of Islamic-compliant financial products, the industry projected to be worth $2 trillion by 2015. Islamic banking has emerged in the past decades as the demand for financial products and services according to Islamic law. Islamic banking wants to offer a credible alternative to traditional banking products.

Myanmar

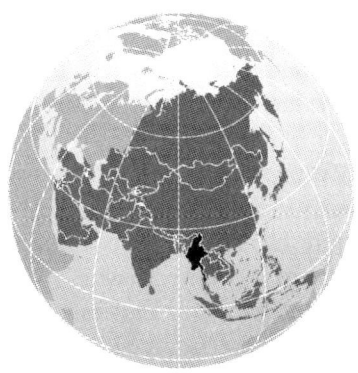

Population: 55,746.253
Urbanization: 32.6 percent (2011)
GDP: $59.43 billion
GDP composition: Agriculture 38%; industry: 20.3%; services: 41.7%
Growth rate: 6.8% (World Factbook)
GDP per capita rose from $194.61 in 2004 to $1,200 in 2012 (World Bank)
2014 Index of Economic Freedom: (–)

Myanmar, long isolated, is now opening up to the world. It is on its path to integrate into the global community. The implementation of reforms and Western ease of sanctions has given the country new opportunities. Microfinance in rural eras is helping to improve living conditions and to lower Myanmar's poverty, still one fourth of the population. Myanmar has a young population, is rich in resources, and has a favorable geographic location that attracts direct foreign investments in food and beverages industry, tourism, garment industry, and IT technologies. With a low rate in Internet users, only 1.1 percent of the population in 2012, the Internet is the most important mechanisms for opening up and connecting globally and is a door wide open for investors. Digitalization is one of the key factors to help the country to advance its development. But, it will take assertive plans to develop high-level IT infrastructure.

"Myanmar's moment: Unique opportunities, major challenges" is the title of a 2013 McKinsey report on Myanmar. And as with many of its Asian neighbor countries, rising productivity is the key to stable growth and achieving economic goals. It estimates Myanmar's growth potential to be 8 percent. But "if current demographic and labor productivity continues Myanmar could grow by less than 4 percent."

During 2014 Myanmar will hold the chairmanship of the Association of South Asian Nations (ASEAN), signifying the country's readmission into the league of respectable states. It will host ASEAN summit in November, which will be attended by President Obama and other world leaders.

Sri Lanka

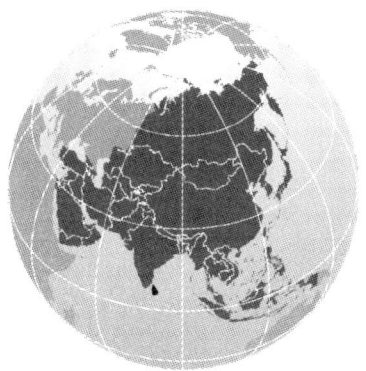

Population: 21.866,445 (July 2014 est.)
GDP: $65.22 billion
Urbanization: 15.1 (2011)
GDP composition: Agriculture 31.8%: industry 25.8%; services 42.4% (World Factbook)
Growth rate: 6.3%
GDP per capita rose from $854.93 in 2000 to $3279 in 2013 (World Bank)
2014 Index of Economic Freedom: 90 (Heritage Foundation)

Sri Lanka has become an exporter of everything from underwear to football shirts for retailers such as Zara of Spain and Britain's Marks and Spencer. According to James Crabtree of the *Financial Times*, Sri Lanka sees an opportunity to establish a garment hub on the corner of the island "just off the coast from the world's busiest east-to-west shipping lane."

New manufacturing, warehousing, and logistic facilities could in time allow Sri Lanka to offer capabilities comparable with competitors in the industrial world. "It is a small example," says Crabtree, "but a telling one demonstrating how companies in Asia continue to find ways to insert themselves into supply chains, mostly with effect of grabbing a greater slice of the global pie."

Thailand

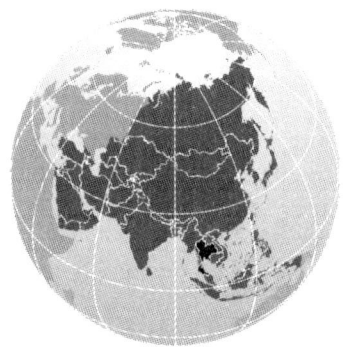

Population: 66.79 million
Urbanization: 34.1 percent (2011)
GDP: $400.9 billion
GDP composition: Agriculture 12.1%; industry 43.6%; services 44.2% (World Factbook)
Growth rate: 3.1% (The Factbook)
GDP per capita rose from $6,500 in 2001 to $8500 in 2013 (World Bank)
2014 Index of Economic Freedom: 72 (Heritage Foundation)

There has been a lot of talk in Asian countries, mainly in Bhutan, about measuring happiness as a meaningful index of people's well-being. Thailand's current military ruler General Prayuth Chan-ocha seems to have picked up on that. He discarded the constitution and demanded that criticism be kept to oneself and replaced with public happiness.

Entrepreneurs can still have a smile when doing business in Thailand; World Bank ranks it as 18 out of 189 countries in its ease of doing business index. Nevertheless, its slow growth around 4 percent on average never recovered after the Asian financial crisis in 1997–1998. Historically built hierarchical structures are still very much in the minds and in place, on top of practically every pyramid the king, at the base peasants living happily. But happiness around its Asian neighbors over the last decades is built on economic progress and flattening hierarchies. And Thailand's performance is not impressive. It remains one of the most unequal societies in the world.

General Prayuth Chan-ocha recently approved a major investment of 120 billion Baht, around $3.7 billion. Thailand reported FDI inflows of $13 billion in 2013 (*Bangkok Post*, June 27, 2014) compared to Singapore's $64 billion, still meager.

Politically polarized, economically behind its Asian neighbors, Thailand faces the uncertainty of an election held under a new constitution, which might have the character of Burma, where military and aristocracy had enough seats to guarantee parliament's ability to block legislation. As of now, the junta has yet to prove its will and ability to push economic reforms, improve rule of law, increase transparency, and restore Thailand's democracy.

Nevertheless, Thailand, a member of ASEAN, has become the automobile manufacturing center of Southeast Asia with the world's second largest producer of hard drives and pick-up trucks. It is the world's largest rubber producer. China's increasing manufacturing costs, low corporate tax, and relatively good infrastructure are holding further opportunities for Thailand.

Turkey

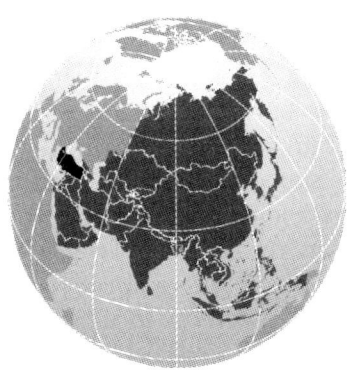

Population: 81,619,392
Urbanization: 71.5 percent
GDP: $821.8 billion (2013 est.)
GDP composition: Agriculture 8.9%; industry 27.3%; services 63.8%

Growth rate: 3.8% (The Factbook)
GDP per capita rose from $4,219.54 in 2000 to $15,300 in 2013 (World Bank)
2014 Index of Economic Freedom: 64 (Heritage Foundation)

In the past decade, Turkey's rapid economic rise, and its modernization and industrialization were a great success story. A new middle class rose, incomes kept climbing. A boom in construction and increase of consumption boosted Turkey as one of the most promising emerging economies, ranking number 17 measured by GDP. *Forbes* listed a $200 billion investment master plan: $29 billion for building the new Yeni Havalimai Airport by 2019, $15 billion for a 26 mile shipping canal to link Marmara to the black sea, $8.4 billion for a public–private estate development for about 5,000 luxury apartments, $1.35 billion for two marinas, two five-star hotels, a massive mall and a 1,000 capacity mosque, $1.4 billion for a new large tunnel under the Bosporus; the list goes on.

Premier Tayyip Erdogan, elected president in August 2014, the man whose name is tightly connected with Turkey's progress is now also very much in question. For many Turks life has become much better. Poverty is not eliminated, but as Germany *Die Zeit* writes under the title "Why do Turks love him?" on April 3, 2014, "almost every Turk can afford a house and a car. Erdogan has turned Turkey into a different, maybe better country, even though his enemies do not want to hear that."

Liberal modern Turks on the other hand do not understand the world of Erdogan's supporters. Liberal Turks do not understand how last year's brutal abolitions of Gezi Protests, recordings of corruption published on YouTube and Twitter, and blocking these websites had no impact on Erdogan's core followers. At the same time, Turkey's growth has shrunk to a disappointing 2.9 percent in 2014, unemployment maintains 11 percent and according to OECD data almost one-third of Turks under 30 years of age have no job. Turkey is on a fork in the road, one road leading backward and the other to move forward.

Turkey's negotiations to become a member of the EU are stuck and suspended since 2006 on eight matters. Given the low growth in the West, Turkey is searching for new markets in emerging economies, but also wants to achieve a more prominent role in Africa. In 2003, Turkish Airlines served four destinations in Africa; today, it connects Turkey with 30 African destinations. Turkish Airline's CEO explained the reason: "Our strategies and activities are in close connection with Turkish foreign and trade politics. To keep growing, we are working closely with the government." The benefits and synergies are obvious; each new destination opens a door to Turkish companies to grab opportunities in new markets. Erdogan's Giant project, a canal connecting the Black Sea with the Sea of Marmara, is supposed to unburden the Bosporus channel. Istanbul's new airport with a capacity of 150 million passengers per year is a representation of the construction boom on one hand, and Turkey's reach to new markets on the other. It will be the largest airport in Europe; even its parking space with 70,000 slots is impressive.

Turkey's opening-up policy for Africa started in 2002. It has established 19 new embassies on the continent. "The aim is to develop ties and close gaps in places we have never been," says a Turkish official. Turkey's enterprises and politicians will continue and increase their Africa policy. Turkey's commerce jumped from $742 million in 2000 to almost $7.5 billion in 2011, still only a fraction of Turkey's overall trade. With an increase of almost 30 percent from 2011, Turkey's exports to Africa reached $13.3 billion in 2012.

Turkey showed its economic potential and is now in danger of an economic downfall with scary implications. Turkey was upgraded to investment grade in 2013, borrowing costs plummeted, middle class grew rapidly, a young population attracted investors, and inflation was under control. In 2014, Turkey has been included on the list of the endangered emerging economies, India, Indonesia, South Africa, and Brazil. With the largest current account deficit and the highest proportion of debt owned by foreigners of the problem countries, Turkey could derail if cheap money is no longer accessible.

Turkey for now remains a contradictive country with a very high potential and a strategically important geographical location as a cultural bridge between Europe and Asia.

Vietnam

Population: 93,421,835 million (July 2014 est.)
Urban population: 34.3%
GDP: $170 billion
GDP composition: Agriculture 19.3%; industry 38.5%; services 42.2%
Growth rate: 5.3% (World Factbook)
GDP per capita rose from $433.33 in 2000 to $1,910.53 in 2013 (World Bank)
2014 Index of Economic Freedom: 147 (Heritage Foundation)

Few who drink coffee in the morning in Europe think that this coffee could have come from Asia, let alone Vietnam. And yet Vietnam is the second largest exporter of coffee after Brazil. The EU is Vietnam's second largest trading partner, with bilateral commerce increasing from 5 billion Euros to 26 billion in 2014. In the past decades Vietnam has gradually shed off the rigid ties of central planning to become a competitive, export-driven economy. It has become Asia's fastest growing economy after China, even though state-owned enterprises still make up 40 percent of the GDP. Overall labor productivity has improved. Vietnam is competing globally in niches from textiles to tourism, from coffee to IT. Compared with ASEAN countries Vietnam's 1 percent share of value-added products is still very low. A rise of 54.9 percent of sales of value-added product in the first quarter of 2014 holds high promise for future gains. Value-added products in seafood saw an especially strong rise.

During his 2014 Europe tour Vietnam's Prime Minister Tan Dung aimed to push EU-Vietnam free trade deal to reduce tariffs, provide legal certainty, and protect investment. The goal is to stimulate economic growth and create jobs for both sides as well as to strengthen ties between Vietnam and the European Union. As tensions with China were rising Vietnam seeks stronger ties with the West and greater integration in global commerce.

We have visited Hanoi and Ho Chi Min City several times in the past years and the great progress Vietnam has made in a very short time is very visible. Even though the colorful pictures of farmers driving oxen-pulling plows through rice fields are still a common sight, the country has transformed from an agricultural base toward manufacturing and services. Building on education, a rising number of university graduates will support Vietnam to leverage its potential to become globally competitive in offering offshore services. Vietnam has a young labor force, an abundance of natural resources, but as in other Asian countries, there is still a lack of qualified engineers and middle management. The coming years hold the challenges to improve labor skills, increase productivity, advance management to increase competitiveness of state-owned enterprises, but they can be overcome.

2

Africa–Asia–Latin America

New Economic Alliances and International Organization Alternatives

In June 2001, we celebrated our first wedding anniversary in Beijing. An American-Chinese friend who was teaching at Beijing University took us to a newly opened restaurant in one of the neighborhoods that at the time were getting very popular after being dormant for some decades. As we were sitting in the little garden we talked about another celebration to come, China joining the World Trade Organization (WTO) later that year. But China's stronger integration into the global economy with some also raised concerns. We remember very well the worry about making too many concessions to America. The big question was: "Does globalization mean Americanization?"

Around 13 years later, on July 6, 2014, the *Financial Times* wrote: "China begins to take great power role in world trade negotiations." By that time China had become the biggest trader of goods, and now the West worries about China's global influence and its intentions in the WTO. "The world of trade is changing and China clearly is changing with it," the article ends.

Game Change in the Global Economic and Financial Architecture

The times when the West was the predominant hub of the global community and the global junction for political and economic connections are coming to an end.

Global governance organizations, launched by the West for the benefit of the West, have dominated the political scene since the end of the Second World War. But the world is not the same as when the UN, IMF, the World Bank were founded.

"I argue that while these institutions may have had some success in dealing with the 20th century problems, they have not been able to adapt to new global challenges that face us today," writes Ian Goldin, former Vice President of the World Bank in his book *Divided Nations: Why Global Governance Is Failing and What We Can Do about It.*

Neither global institutions nor Western governments will be able to continue wielding the baton over an orchestra of emerging economies. There is a new reality in power proportions in which the West no longer plays the center role. The Westerncentric worldview is crumbling. And it started to crumble just as it seemed to be cemented. With the breaking-up of the Soviet Union in 1991 and the implosion of communism in Europe, it seemed only a question of time until Western principles—liberalism, democracy, and free markets would triumph—finally and everywhere. Francis Fukujama's "End of History" was embraced with great satisfaction. But that conceit had a short life.

While the West holds on to celebrating itself as the guardian of universal values and rights, defending its status as ethic and economic hub of the global community, the emerging markets of the Global Southern Belt have gradually opened the door to a new world view. Based on their own history and culture they are laying a new ground for their future. They have discovered that instead of being run by the West they could as well support each other. And they discovered that they were able to stand on their own feet. The proclaimed "End of History" turned into the

"Global Game Change" for new economic alliances in the context of changing worldviews, new geopolitical weighting and new economic arrangements.

The emerging economies of the Global Southern Belt, more than 80 percent of the global population, are increasingly aware of their own rhythms. And more and more organizations, such as the Boao Forum, are tuning up to play as independent orchestras. Admittedly, not without discords.

The Association of Southeast Asia Nations (ASEAN) was formed almost 50 years ago, but for a long time did not have a great presence on the world stage. Over the years their 10 members gained increasing importance: Indonesia, Malaysia, the Philippines, Singapore, Thailand, Brunei, Myanmar, Cambodia, Laos, and Vietnam. With now 600 million people and a combined gross domestic product (GDP) of $2.4 trillion in 2014 ASEAN countries have become an economic powerhouse among the countries of the Global Southern Belt. If it were a single country, its GDP would rank as seventh largest in the world. It is the fourth largest exporting region in the world behind the European Union (EU), North America, and China.

In world affairs, ASEAN is now wide-awake and much of its growth achieved by gains in productivity. It is a very diverse market with different cultures, religions, and ethnicities. HSBC predicts: "it will be one of the fastest growing consumer regions in the next two decades." In 2014, around 67 million ASEAN households are part of the "consuming class" (incomes that allow for significant discretionary purchases). This number is estimated to almost double by 2025 (McKinsey, May 2014).

One Vision—One Identity—One Community

On May 23, 2014, ASEAN labor Ministers and their counterparts from China, Japan, and Korea (not members, but the so called Plus Three Countries of ASEAN) met in Myanmar to strengthen the cooperation among them. Premier Li Keqiang called ASEAN China's priority in outbound investment, and called for active expansion of imports of ASEAN goods into China, and for ASEAN companies to invest and start businesses in China.

"No longer is China the exporting competitor of past decades," writes HSBC in January 2014, "it is an important market for ASEAN." A Singapore scholar and fellow at Nanyan Technology University says: "A deepened economic mutual dependence between China and ASEAN countries is both natural and crucial, not least for maintaining the precious regional peace which is at times challenged. In this respect and at these times of economic uncertainty, it is especially timely to heed Premier Li Keqiang's call to strengthen ties and cooperation for common growth." HSBC hopes "the expected growth in two way trade and investment sets a new more positive tone to relations as these mighty regions become a fully fledged market of 1.9 billion people" (http://www.hsbc.com/news-and-insight/2014/china-and-asean-relations).

The attested bright future of Asia was somewhat clouded at the Boao Forum held in April 2014 in Boao, Hainan. Despite its promising title: "Asia's new future: Identifying new growth drivers."

"Make Asian voice heard," "Promote Asian Cooperation," and "Build Asian Consensus" are the slogans popping up on the Boao Forum website. The Forum, which was established in 2001, has become an important platform for high-end dialogues for Asian countries and emerging economies.

But just one week after the Boao Forum ended, it felt as if the targeted cooperation could run ashore. We were sitting on a wonderful beach in Sanya, not far from Boao, where the Forum was held. As the sun set over the Gulf of Tonkin, flickering lights were lining up at the horizon of the calm ocean. Chinese warships, we were told, were parading in the sea that connects and separates China and Vietnam, both members of the Boao Forum.

A year before, in his address at the 2013 Forum, President Xi Jinping had urged countries to foster "a sense of community of common destiny" to assure that developments in Asia and the rest of the world reach new heights. The ambitious goal is to bring China ASEAN trade to $1 trillion by 2020. In 2013, China's direct investment into ASEAN countries hit $5.74 billion and already $3.56 billion during the first half of 2014.

One hopes that despite political posturing the conflict that brings dissonance to the ASEAN and Boao Forum can be solved peacefully, building on former President Hu's pledge that China would insure that its development brings even greater benefits to its neighbors, underscoring China's commitment to seeking win–win cooperation with other Asian countries and its interest in forging partnerships with its Asian neighbors.

Game Change for the US Dollar?

Between 2002 and 2012, China Asia trade volume grew from $54.8 billion to $400.1 billion in 2012 (Ministry of Commerce China). The slogan on Asean.org tells the goal ASEAN nations have in mind in forming an Economic Community, to be launched in 2015. Within ASEAN, the ASEAN Economic Community (AEC) will be established at the end of 2015. AEC will aim to transform ASEAN into a region with free movement of goods, services, investment, skilled labor, and capital. The goal is regional economic integration, creating one of the world's biggest single markets. And, maybe, a preview of one economy for the whole world, which, we believe, will be the future of global economics in a long-term frame.

"Asean will lead the world in adopting the Yuan as a global currency as it begins using it for trade settlement, financing and investment as the regions faith and dependence in the US dollar weakens," are the closing lines in an article in *Thailand Business News*, October 27, 2014, on China's investment in ASEAN in the light of forming AEC in 2015. Up to now, the deal in Yuan goes through Singapore. According to SWIFT data Yuan deposits in Singapore have reached $220 billion in the first three months of 2014. Yuan loans increased 25 percent to more than $300 billion. SWIFT ranked the Yuan as the seventh global payment currency.

"Yuan claims a bigger share of reserves" was the title of a Reuters report on October 29, 2014. Reuters quotes a survey by Central Banking Publication among 69 central banks in which two-thirds of the respondents said the Yuan "had become more attractive because of the relative strength and growing influence of China's economy … and it is gaining traction among financial institutions and multinational companies."

The Center of Economic Gravity Is Headed Toward the Developing South

Conflicts between strong nations can be overcome for good reasons, as China–India relations show. Ties between China and India, burdened by long-lasting border disputes, have been improving and so are economic connections and trade between them. According to Li Jian, Secretary General of the Delhi-based China Chamber of Commerce and Industry which represents more than 100 Chinese companies, India's huge growth potential is encouraging Chinese companies that are all doing well in India now, to stay on. Arun Jaitley, India's new minister of finance, was not very clear on which reforms will bring India's growth to bounce back to an annual 7–8 percent in the next years, but he did promise to end retrospective taxes that were understandably very much disliked by investors.

Bilateral trade between the two countries reached $66 billion in 2012 and is expected to climb to $100 billion by 2015. India's newly elected leader, business-friendly Narendra Modi, has gotten laurels in advance, but now he has to deliver. Under his leadership some estimates suggest that bilateral trade will hit $300 billion in 2018.

The emerging economies of the Global Southern Belt, with Asia as the currently strongest region, are embarking on a new phase of economic development. An official statement of China's Information Office describes the international situation as: "undergoing profound and intricate changes, newly emerging developing economies have become the major force pushing forward the world's economic development."

Already as early as October 2010, World Bank in its special report on the "rise of the Global South and its impact on South–South cooperation" wrote: "The economic center of gravity is inexorably moving towards the developing South. The remarkable upsurge in cooperation between developing countries characterized as South-South cooperation must be understood as part of this larger story."

Under the headline "The Global South" *Aljazeera* (March 20, 2013) estimated that "by 2020 the combined economic output of Brazil, India, and China will surpass the combined economic output of Canada, France, Germany, Italy, the UK, and the United States together. "By 2030," the report continues, "80 percent of the world's middle class will be living in developing countries."

At that time children born at the turn of the 21st century will be in their early professional years. And the world they live and work in will be very, very different from the one we know today.

China's Vision of an Open World Economy

This book is about the opening-up of the Global Southern Belt and its enormous potential as an economic driver of the 21st century. And yet as global as our research focus is, there is hardly any global issue that we deal with that does not have China in the picture. This in itself is a major statement about China's future role.

China, which as the ancient Empire pictured itself literally as the world's Middle Kingdom, is now marching, jumping, slipping, and sometimes sneaking into a much larger role as the Global Middle Kingdom. Xinhua News Agency, China's official media, presents China's vision of the "Silk Road Economic Belt" and its new role in the center of global trade in the series "New Silk Road, New Dreams." The first article paints a grand picture: "How can the world be win–win? China is answering the question."

The Xinhua May 8, 2014, article presented a map which showed China's ambitions vision for the "New Silk Road" and the "New Maritime Silk Road." The landline Silk Road will begin in Xi'an in Central China and run through Central Asia to Northern Iran and then on to Turkey through the Bosporus Strait, north to Europe, and Rotterdam before turning south ending in Venice.

The Landline and Maritime Silk Roads

········ Landline Silk Road   ---- Maritime Silk Road

Courtesy: Xinhua News Agency.
Note: This figure is not to scale. It does not represent any authentic national or international boundaries and is used for illustrative purposes only.

The Maritime Silk Road begins in Quanzhou, goes through Guangzhou and Hainan, then south to Malacca Strait, Kuala Lumpur, Kolkata, Nairobi around the Horn of Africa through the Red Sea, and through Athens meeting the landline Silk Road in Venice.

The *Diplomat* wrote on May 9, 2014: "The Silk Road and Maritime Silk Road combined will create a massive loop linking three continents. If any single image conveys China's ambitions to reclaim its place as the 'Middle Kingdom', linked to the world by trade and cultural exchanges, the Xinhua map is it. Even the name of the project, the Silk Road, is inextricably linked to China's past as a source of goods and information for the rest of the world."

To the *Diplomat* it is clear that China "believes its principles will be the guiding force in this new community." Xinhua wrote: "China's wisdom for building an open world economy and open international relations is being drawn on more and more each day,"

The vision to create a community with "common interests, fate, and responsibilities" in a new model of "mutual respect and mutual trust," stretching from Asia to Africa and Europe is grand.

How to implement such ambitious plans is a challenge of no small dimension. Mutual Respect and mutual trust among all nations involved does sound like a fairytale. Nonetheless, we should get used to it, because China dreams big.

The Rebirth of Sino–Arab Relations— the Silk Road Spirit

China–Arab relations go back to the days of the first Rashidun Caliphate 632 to 661 BC and remained uninterrupted until the World Wars of the 20th century. In the 21st century, Sino Arab relations have been revitalized as a powerful economic alliance and fortified by the establishment of the China–Arab State Cooperation in 2004. Since then China has become the second largest trading partner of Arab countries; 2012 bilateral trade volume reached $222 billion with an increase of 14 percent in one year.

In the first week of June 2014, the 6th China–Arab States Cooperation Forum was held in Beijing at the same time as the 10th anniversary of its establishment was celebrated. The Forum's aim is to increase trade and investment opportunities for China with the goal of a free trade agreement between the two sides. In the opening session, President Xi Jinping said: "the next decade poses a critical development period for both China and Arab States, which calls us to carry forward the Silk Road spirit and rejuvenate our countries." He encouraged Chinese companies to continue to invest in Arab States in such sectors as energy, petrochemicals, agriculture, manufacturing, and services. The president also announced that the two sides will expand their trade volume to $600 billion in the next 10 years.

The Forum agreed to strengthen efforts to facilitate a free trade agreement between China and the Gulf Cooperation Council, an economic Union of six major oil exporters that border the Gulf: Bahrain, Kuwait, Oman, Qatar, Saudi Arabia, and the United Arab Emirates.

In the next three years, Beijing will train 6,000 people to work in Arab countries and have 10,000 artists visit each other in the coming decade (China Daily, June 6, 2014; CCTV.com, June 4, 2014).

The China–Africa–Latin America Triangle

The Global Southern Belt includes more than 150 of the 196 (the number varies depending on the source) recognized countries of the world. Many of them have limited or poorly developed resources. They are facing challenges of political and economic turmoil but there are strong voices calling for reform, and clear signs for economic growth, with many dynamic economic alliances.

The most consequential of the new interconnectedness among the nations of the Global Southern Belt will be what we call the "China–Africa–Latin America Triangle." Chapter 1 described the strong and growing ties between Africa and China. But China has only set one foot in Africa; the second is put down in Latin America and the Caribbean. "China needs commodities which it cannot and does not want to import just from Asia and Africa anymore," wrote Deutsche Welle (DW) online in October 2013.

As ethnically diverse as are their cultures, as different their histories, China, Africa, and Latin America share the desire to bring hundreds of millions out of poverty. China wants to diversify its markets and commodity sources. Latin American countries want to loosen their ties to their main trading partners the United States and Europe. "Many South American countries benefit from their relationship with China," DW concludes. The *Guardian,* in a report on how US foreign policy leaves an open door for China (January, 2014), quotes Yan Xuetong, Dean of the Institute of Modern International Relations at Tsinghua University, who argues in an article in the *WorldPost* that China is beginning a new foreign policy path of convergence, not conflict. "Deng Xiaoping," Yan writes, "gave first priority to relations with the US under the dictum of keeping a low profile (Tao Guang Yang Hui). President Xi in several recent speeches has articulated a different strategic direction: thriving for achievements (Fen Fa You Wei)."

And Yan Xuetong adds an interesting new aspect:

For more than 20 years, China has operated under a foreign policy framework within which it has neither friends nor enemies.

With a few exceptions, all other countries were essentially treated the same with the maintenance of an external environment most conducive to China's own development as the paramount priority. Under Xi, China will begin to treat friends and enemies differently. For those who are willing to play a constructive role in China's rise, China will seek ways for them to gain greater actual benefits from China's development.

During his first leg of visits in Africa China's Premier Li Keqiang signed 16 deals including loans and agreements for the construction of roads and industrial zones. China is engaged in water and power supply and railways and telecommunication projects (*South Asian Analysis Group*, China a close friend or a neo colonialist, May 12, 2014).

No question that other parties in the China–Africa–Latin America Triangle will benefit from China's new policy. Africa, for example, would like to peel off its old image and benefit from China's skills in developing industry and agricultural business.

The China–Africa–Latin America Triangle will not be an institutional or formal arrangement, but the economic, political, and cultural activities among the nations within the triangle will increase dramatically. A new stream of triangular trade is on the rise. And with all the economic openings, many want a share of the new cake.

China–Africa: "Treasure Voyages" of Our Days

It is a pity we learned so little about China, the explorer. What exciting stories history teachers could tell. China's invention of the compass in the 11th century made much possible. In the 15th century, during the Ming Dynasty, admiral Zheng He guided a fleet of 70 ships and a crew of more than 27,000 to the first of seven so called "treasury voyages." The goal was to increase China's sphere of influence. The treasury fleet sailed the Pacific and Indian oceans, sailing as far as Arabia and East Africa. China's comprehensive, strategic thinking, still in place today, included establishing a linguistic institute in Nanjing to be able to communicate with foreign countries. In 2005, China celebrated the 600th year of Zheng He's first voyage with a smaller replica of a historic ship sailing from Qingdao to Asian and African harbors as Zheng He did centuries ago.

African China relations over the centuries are not well documented in history, but also not burdened by a colonial past. Most likely Maine East High School, where Hilary Clinton attended her first high school years, did not have any more focus on China's maritime history than our high schools in Austria and most parts of the United States. We cannot blame her too much for judging China's current "treasury voyages" to Africa based on the history of the West. It was this background that probably led Hilary Clinton to swipe at China when she visited Zambia in 2011 as she noted, "[w]e saw that during the colonial days, it is easy to come in, take out natural resources, pay off leaders and leave."

China's first documented relations to Africa go back to the 15th century medieval days when Ibn Battuta traveled from Morocco to China. Much closer to China–Africa connections and emotions is the support for African movements against apartheid. Dambisa Moyo, Zambian economist and author of *China's Race for Resources and What It Means for the World*, writes in the *New York Times*, June 29, 2012, that China's investment in Africa is not a new form of imperialism—it is Africa's best hope for economic growth.

Africa's first steps to its economic awakening were to increasingly turn away from the West and seek new alliances. "Politically the model of a liberal democracy is losing its attraction," writes African correspondent Bartholomäus Grill in his book *Oh Africa*. Africa's political elite is looking toward autocratic regimes of emerging economies in Asia. Africans are looking for new role models. The hegemony of the West, its claims of moral and political authority, and the acceptance of the Western universalistic view are eroding. "It is no wonder that the American government is lashing out to its new competitor—while China has made huge investments in Africa, the United States has stood on the sidelines and watched its influence on the continent fade," writes Dambia Moyo.

It can be taken as a symbol that the new headquarters building of the African Union of 54 countries in Addis Ababa, Ethiopia, is a gift from China. China's influence is not limited to investments and trade; it offers information. In January, 2012, China Central Television launched CCTV Africa in Kenya. Its goal is "to provide a platform for its Chinese audience to better understand Africa and promote the China–African friendship so that the real China can be introduced to Africa, and the real Africa can be presented to the world."

The Western opinion monopoly was also cracked by Al Jazeera's ("the island") new TV network based in Qatar. Al Jazeera was founded in April 1996 when the media cooperation between the BBC and Saudi–Arabian Orbit broke on the issue of censorship. The Emir of Qatar, Sheik Hamad bin Chalifa Al Thani, founded Al Jazeera hiring 17 of the dismissed BBC journalists.

China Has No Intention to Export Its Political Model to Africa

"The biggest challenge that Africa confronts is perception," said James Mwangi, chief executive of Kenya's Equity Bank and winner of the Ernst and Young World Entrepreneur of the Year award. "I would like the 50 plus entrepreneurs who were contesting in this competition to look favorably to Africa as their next frontier." But Western perception of a dialog with African countries is hardly on the same eye level. China has a different approach toward Africa. And China has the same problem of a negative perception by the West.

After "100 years of humiliation" by Western powers and Japan, China's example of getting back on its feet and healing the wounds of the past cannot be underestimated as a bonding element with African countries. China is entering Africa's markets communicating on equal eye-level. "China's view of a dynamic Africa also contrasts sharply to the West's doom and gloom analysis of Africa," writes Chen Weihua, deputy editor of *China Daily USA* on May 17, 2013. "China is not perfect, at home and in Africa. But it would be deadly wrong to dismiss China's work in Africa as the selfish grabbing of land and resources or neocolonialism."

Western Double Standards Big Time

On July 12, we were listening to an Austrian radio program "Hörbilder" (audio pictures), in which countries and cities and historical events are portrayed. This time the program was about German South-West Africa, today Namibia, in 1904. It was difficult to listen to the gruesome story of how the Germans under General Lothar von Trotha fought the Hereros, African Nomads, who rebelled against the colonial power. After years of guerilla war the surviving Hereros were deported into concentration camps, their belongings dispossessed, and people subordinated to agricultural labors without rights.

But it took until 2004, a 100 years later, for Germany to admit the historical and moral guilt of Germany's colonial administration. On the other side, Kuaima Riruako, chief of the 100,000 Hereros who today lives in Namibia, has demanded $4 billion for German crimes during colonial era. Joschka Fischer, Germany's minister of finance, gave no excuse saying that he was not willing to "make any comments relevant to compensation claims."

Bartholomäus Grill in his book, *Oh Africa*, describes how the political elites in Africa are welcoming China's engagement, which allows them to increase power, fill their pockets, and live their luxury life. "But," he writes, "chief ideologists in the US and Europe are equal in their double morality: we, the countries of the West, are cooperating with Africa; Chinese are just exploiting it and act in pure self interest. The competitor China is demonized while the West's own goal, unhampered access to Africa's resources and markets, is hidden under a moral veil."

In Its Engagement in Africa China Wants Both: To Benefit and to Bring Benefits

China bets on soft power and investment without any intervention in local politics. And China's soft power campaign combined with its economic engagement may well be more influential in creating sustainable governing models for African countries than Western foreign aid, welfare programs, and lecturing. Dambia Moyo, economist and author of *Dead Aid*, writes:

> Aid servers the link between Africans and their governments, because citizens generally have no say in how the aid dollars are spent and governments too often respond to the needs of the donors rather than those of their citizens. Thankfully, the decrease in the flow of Western aid since the 2008 financial crisis offers a chance to remedy this structural failure so that Africans can finally hold their governments accountable.

African countries like other emerging economies have become aware that Western aid never came without conditions. While direct foreign investment in Africa began to decline in 2009, China's direct investment was increasing. In 2012, African exports to China reached $113.17 billion, an increase of more than 20 percent from 2011; the total volume of China–African trade was estimated at $198.5 billion and is expected to surpass $380 billion by 2015. To Africa's 30 least developed economies China applies a special zero tariff to 60 percent of the exports.

"Africa is now China's major import source, second largest in construction project contracts and fourth largest investment destination," wrote China's State Council Information in August 2013. More than 2,500 Chinese companies have invested in Africa and China's economic offensive and it is gaining speed, reported *China Daily* in January 2014.

Africa Is Going through the Same Industrial Transformation as China But Is Not Copying China

"China's image in Africa," writes the *Economist*, March 23, 2013, "once marred by suspicion, is changing. A growing number of Africans say that the Chinese create jobs, transfer skills, and spend money in local economies. African elites see China as their biggest partner among emerging economies, but by no means the only one."

African countries are not jumping to copy China. They will, just as China did 30 years ago, pick and choose from models that will serve them in achieving economic growth. Building new alliances without the tutelage of the West is part of the new Africa.

As a joint initiative the Chinese Ministry of Commerce and the China Society of Promotion of the Guangcai Program (a program to reduce poverty which counts more than 16,500 Chinese private companies), established the China–Africa Business Council (CABC). The CABC has as its objective to provide practical business tools to ease economic trade and investment links between China and Angola, Cameroon, DRC, Ethiopia, Ghana, Kenya, Liberia, Mozambique, Nigeria, and Tanzania.

To promote Africa's development further, then President Hu Jintao announced the founding of the China–Africa Development (CAD) Fund at the Forum on China–Africa Cooperation in November 2006. China's first equity investment fund run by China Investment Bank focuses on investments and projects in agriculture, manufacturing, infrastructure, and resources.

In the light of the changing global investment environment the CABC and China–Africa Development (CAD) Fund set up two new funds in 2013 to further boost China's investment in Africa. Chi Jianxin, President of the CAD Fund, said that the goal of the fund is to cement the partnership between African countries and China by infusing another $2.4 billion into African projects.

Zheng Yuewen, chairman of CABC, said in an interview on June 6, 2013, with *China Daily:* "The continent can go through the same industrial transformation as China did three decades ago, and in time it will become a major goods producer, rather than just being a shipper of raw materials to different foreign destinations."

Around 80 percent of CABC investors are also private companies. Lifan Group, the Chongqing-based automobile producer, Huajian Group, a shoemakers based in Guangdong and Shenzhen

Energy Corporation, a power supplier, have invested $1.1 billion in 32 African countries and plan to invest additional $5 billion by 2016.

During Premier Li Keqiang's first visits to Ethiopia, Nigeria, Angola, and Kenya, China's Vice Minister of Commerce, Zhang Xiangchen, signed around 60 agreements that "would lay a sound basis for future China African relations. China has the experience and capabilities to contribute to Africa's development."

President Xi's Strategic Direction: "Striving for Achievements"

"China is entering a new era with rapid development of direct investment in African countries," says the CAD website.

> Some are involved in expanding market share, locating closer to the end consumer, or seeking natural resources. CAD Fund seeks to apply its many advantages including identification of policy, risk control, and value added services to make an active contribution to cooperation between Chinese and African enterprises and the establishment of the new strategic partnership between China and Africa.

In 2010, China replaced the United States as Africa's biggest trading partner.

In a key note speech at the sixth Ministerial Conference of the 2012 Forum on China and Africa Cooperation, President Hu Jintao made clear that China was not going to give up its position in African countries: "China wholeheartedly and sincerely supports African countries choosing their own development path, and will whole heartedly and sincerely support them to raise their development abilities."

In March during his visit in Africa 2013 President Xi announced a new series of measures to support Africa's development. Some of the stumbling African countries will need just that, a strong arm to hold on to.

South Africa, for which China is the biggest trading partner, remains in such a turbulent transition period. Nevertheless, Malusi Gigaba, South Africa's Minister of Public Enterprises, in 2012 pronounced "If we can increase investments among ourselves in our different regions, we will establish emerging markets as a powerful economic force in the world."

In May 2014, Premier Li Keqiang visited Ethiopia, Nigeria, Angola, and Kenya in his first visit to Africa. It was most likely no coincidence that this date coincided with the Africa visit of Zhou Enlai in February 1964. Li said China would double its bilateral current trade of $210 billion by 2020. He also announced that China would build a high-speed rail development center in Africa.

George Soros criticized China and Japan and other countries as Africa's new colonialists. Columbia University press published a paper in which Chris Alden, Daniel Large, and Ricardo Soares de Oliveira said, "The overarching driver has been the Chinese government's strategic pursuit of resources and attempts to ensure raw material supplies for growing energy needs within China." And an IMF report attributed 20 percent of Africa's development to China–Africa cooperation. Local governments in China and Africa consider it a win–win partnership. (*South African Analysis Group*, "China in Africa: A close friend or a neo colonialist?" May 12, 2014).

To further growth Africa must move up the value added chain.

Around 80 percent of Africa's exports to China are mineral products. Kenya's president, Uhuru Kenyatta, defended China, which is often blamed as only interested in exploiting African resources, in *China Daily* August 13, 2013, by saying that China's and Kenya's relationship is not based on mineral resources exploitation, but "on investment, manufacturing, and infrastructure development."

Africa's bilateral trade with China in about a dozen years grew 20 times, from $10 billion to $210 billion in 2013. This is 2,000 times that of 1960. In 2013, more than 1.4 million Chinese visited Africa, thus adding to Africa's exchange revenues. More than 2,000 Chinese companies, around one million Chinese, from engineers to workers to chefs, are working throughout the continent. More added value and workplaces are created in other countries. Africa is still too much at the beginning of the value-added chain.

China's political policy of noninterference does serve question-able autocratic leaders, but its direct investments in infrastructure and state-owned enterprises also open business opportunities for the local population. At the same time, China's low-price exports have hurt local industries in many African countries. Brenthouse Trust estimates that in the textile industry alone 750,000 jobs were lost in the last decade. Even in South Africa 40 percent of shoes and textiles are coming from China.

The more important other emerging economies become for Africa the more dependent it will be on them. Africa needs to break through the circle of old problems returning: corruption, unemployment, gap between urban and rural, office palaces, and rotten villages without electricity. Chinese direct foreign invest-ment in power supply science and technology services is a bridge in reaching that goal. China's goal to further integrate small and medium-size investors into local African societies is in the interest of China and Africa.

On a global sideshow it will be interesting to follow the con-sequences "stronger ties" to China will have on Taiwan. Gambia dropped Taiwan in November 2013 in favor of bigger China, leav-ing only three African countries, Swaziland, Sao Tomé and Principe and Burkina Faso, diplomatically attached to Taiwan.

China Leads, India Seeks to Catch Up

As we wrote earlier, Chinese ships crossed the Indian Ocean to reach Africa's east coast in seven treasury voyages. And it is not by chance that the world's third largest ocean is called the Indian

Ocean. During the early 20th century many Indians came to build railways, their descendants still living in African countries. Mahatma Ghandi lived in South Africa for two decades. Africa's national movement was backed by Jawaharlal Nehru, India's first prime minister from 1947 to 1964. His socialist legacy still weighs heavily on India. And while India's overbearing bureaucracy and economic slowdown leads to a rather gloomy outlook, Indian businessmen keep their enthusiasm for the African markets. In an article titled "A burgeoning commercial axis on India–Africa," the *Financial Times* quotes Temi Ofong, head of corporate banking for Barclays Africa: "The relationship between India and Africa is a very long and a very deep one. The interest for the African continent is not waning ... For me, Africa is not a five year story. For the next 20 to 30 years, it is going to be growing."

All can turn positive under India's new Prime Minister Narendra Modi who has announced that Africa will play an important role in his international economic plans. The significant Indian diaspora in Africa will be useful to Modi's primary target of a more active structure internationally. According to a McKinsey 2014 report on India–Africa relations, "India can look to quadruple its revenues from Africa to $160 billion by 2025. It can aspire to capture almost 7 percent of the IT services market, 5 percent of the fast moving consumer goods, 10 percent of the power sector, and 2–5 percent of the agri-allied services."

The *Economist* (October 26, 2013) sees India and China as "Elephants and Tigers" and believes that "in many ways Africa is a test how India intends to behave as arising power." Maybe, China will give India some opportunity to catch up. In our experience, it is true what Zhang Xiping, director of the National Research Center of Overseas Sinology, wrote in *China Daily* on April 13, 2014: "Chinese undergraduates can easily talk about Western intellectuals and tell stories related to Western culture, but they know little about Cambodia and Laos." This was, of course, a result of Western dominance in almost all regards. As the picture is changing and Asia becomes the economically most dynamic region, to get more familiar with Asian cultures can have economic side effects. Especially with Justin Leverenz advice in mind, which we quote in the introduction: "If you want to understand the reality of the places you are committing your money to, then read their literature."

"During the last hundred years," wrote Zhang, "we have devoted a lot more attention to Europe and the US than to our neighbors." This is now changing.

China–Latin America

"Latin America is the clear trade winner from Chinese global integration" was the bottom line already in 2006 in a study of the OECD. In 2010, during his visit in South America, the then Chinese Premier Wen Jiabao proposed a $5 billion investment and $10 billion line of credit to support infrastructure industries in Latin America. By that time China's loans to Latin America had reached $37 billion, and Chinese investments had surged to more than $10 billion, up 50 percent from 2009. Between 2005 and 2013, China's commitment to Latin America reached almost $100 billion. Its investment grew from $621 million in 2001 to $44 billion in 2010. In addition by 2011 loan credits had reached $75 billion since 2005.

Perhaps nothing has contributed more to a changing Latin America over the past decade than Chinese engagement with the region.

Under the title "Flexible friends," the *Economist*, April 12, 2014, wrote: "The rise of China has changed every region." China's economic presence in Latin America and the Caribbean keeps growing and investment in Latin America has and will continue under the new Chinese leadership. Not to the greatest pleasure of Latin America's previous best friend, the United States.

Already on his first Latin America trip President Xi Jinping visited four free-trade partners of China, Trinidad, Tobago, Mexico, and Costa Rica. *International Business Times* in its December 30, 2013, issue wrote: "The economic advancement of the Asian giant into Latin America appears unstoppable, and it does not show any signs of slowdown."

Xi Jinping's 2013 trip across the region was a highly symbolic gesture and he was welcomed with open arms. No wonder, when visiting Trinidad and Tobago President Xi's pockets were filled with some $3 billion in development loans. Since he began in office, he has also led a strategic effort to develop closer ties with Mexico, which had been strained for several years previously. He has traveled to Brazil in July 2014 for the World Cup and a meeting of BRICS leaders. In anticipation of that visit, Chinese Foreign Minister Wang Yi traveled to Argentina, Brazil, Cuba, and Venezuela from April 18–27, 2014. This is a significant amount of time for the Chinese Foreign Minister to be in the region, and shows the importance that Beijing places on developing regional ties.

"Does this put China in competition with the United States for the hearts and minds of Latin America and the Caribbean?" asks Eric Farnsworth, Vice President of the Americas Society in Washington DC. His answer is that both governments "are taking steps based on their own internal calculations and priorities and not in competition with each other or at the expense of the other." That is the fairy tale view.

China's Strategy in Building Latin American Alliances

Rush Doshi and David Walter have a different view in their comment in the *Wall Street Journal*, October 2, 2013: "The best way to understand China's Caribbean courtship is to consider the last distant power to have designs on the region: the Soviet Union. Today the Caribbean is regarded as a strategic and economic backwater by Washington. But the Soviets saw—and Beijing sees—something different: an American vulnerability."

Financial Times on December 12, 2013, titles a report "Checkbook diplomacy" and assumes that "in entering the Caribbean region, China does not really care about the United States' feelings. With the United States becoming an absentee superpower in the region, China is moving to fill the vacuum and is underpinning its overtures with infrastructure investment." Cheng Li, a senior fellow of the Brookings Institute, says "the US should pay more attention to China in the Caribbean, even if it is only at an early stage."

A recent UN Economic Commission study of Latin America and the Caribbean said that it was most likely that China will outstrip the EU as second-largest economic partner (first is United States) in 2016, with some predicting it will eventually eclipse its trade with the United States.

In October 2012, the annual China Latin America and Caribbean (LAC) Business Summit was held for the sixth time, this time in Hangzhou. Attendees on both sides had good reasons to be optimistic about the multilateral economic relationship and the "great deal of room for companies in China and Latin America to create new partnerships that not only boost two-way trade, but also spur reciprocal investments."

During the 7th Summit held in Costa Rica in November 2013, China signed more than 50 bilateral agreements with Latin American and Caribbean countries. Economic development has made progress in Chile, Colombia, and Mexico, where China invested a total of $55 billion in 2012. To further promote logistics services and capital flows the Commerce and Trade Chambers of Chile, Colombia, Mexico, and Peru signed an agreement to create the China Pacific Alliance Multi-Chamber Union. Future investments will be diversified to include manufacturing, agribusiness, and small and medium-sized enterprises. China is also the largest lender to Latin American countries with Venezuela leading at $50 billion.

China–Latin America Relations Are Getting Closer and Closer

Mexico though is still tightly connected with its neighbor, the United States, selling more to America in one week than it sells to China in a year. Nevertheless, trade between Mexico and China grew 7.6 percent to $62.66 billion. Mexico imported $56.94 billion of goods and exported $5.72 billion in 2012, according to official Mexican data. Mexico as a low-cost manufacturer is as much a competitor as it could become an export platform for Chinese commodities targeting the US market. It also wants to break the formula of exporting raw materials mainly copper, iron ore, and soybeans and import inexpensive manufacturing products and basic technologies. Several trade agreements were signed between the two countries as Beijing promised to invest more in the Latin American region.

China's largest trading partner in Latin America is Brazil. Trade between China and Brazil reached $75 billion in 2012 and hit $83.3 billion in 2013. In only two years, Chinese carmakers have conquered two percent of Brazil's car market. "Central to the new reality is China's relationship with Brazil, the largest Latin American economy by far. At the same time, the relationship between these two giants is changing, moving beyond its initial phase to a more mature understanding of the nature of each respective country and what can reasonably be expected from the other," writes China US Focus online. Clodoaldo Hugueney, former Ambassador of Brazil in China, said that "China and Latin America have complimentary roles—they need raw materials, we have them in buckets. China is not only important for Latin America, it is important for the whole world."

According to the IMF, "Trade between China and Latin America grew 8 percent to $255.5 billion in 2012, faster than the 6 percent growth of the continent's trade with the United States, China's investment in the continent's energy and infrastructure is rising rapidly, with more than $500 billion of infrastructure projects in the Latin American market," writes *South China Morning Post*, March 17, 2014. Latin American companies, in just the last 5 years, invested more than $200 billion in foreign deals, many with China. China's exports to Latin America surged from $3.9 billion in 2000 to $86 billion in 2011 (Inter-American Development Bank).

Nevertheless, China's trade with Latin America has still plenty of space to grow, and plenty of reason to work on its new image as a global power.

China's Media Move to Latin America

There is no doubt that China wants to increase its influence in Latin America. If Rogerio in Chile wants to learn more about China and Chinese politics, he does not need to go to China's English TV channel. Since 2007, he can watch China Central Television (CCTV) news in his mother tongue, Spanish. Or he can watch CCTVs *Americas Now*, a weekly magazine program focusing on Central and South American issues. If information on TV is not enough, Rogerio can read China's official media voice *People's Daily*, which started its Spanish website in 2011.

China and Latin America are moving closer together. And while China does not yet have any private global TV network like America's CNN, CCTV has made progress in reporting to the world. In its beginnings in 2000 CCTV International (then called CCTV9) was not much different from China's opening-up to the world economically. China first copied and then, to our opinion, advanced the international TV network CNN making its first steps on the stage of the global media. We have been watching the CCTV news programs from their early stages to its very good global reporting today.

It is part of often-quoted soft power to address Latin Americans in their mother tongue. In addition, more than 30 Confucius Institutes in Latin America are contributing their share to a better understanding of China.

Cuba's Opening-up

A recent World Bank outlook is positive. It estimates growth in Latin America and the Caribbean to be 3.7 percent by 2016, with some countries, such as Colombia, above 4 percent. Christopher Sabatini, in *Foreign Affairs*, March 2012, wrote: "US scholars and policymakers need a reminder that development does not mean the end of politics and that 21st century Latin America has its own, autonomous dynamics. A little realism would go a long way."

Neither Europe nor the United States were present when 33 countries met at the Summit of the Community of Latin American and Caribbean States (Spanish: Comunidad de Estados Lationoamericanos y CELAC) in Havana in 2013 with its focus was on regional integration. Julia Sweig, from the Washington Council of Foreign Relation's, believes that this second summit could be a turning point: "I can't imagine a return to the old pattern of Washington dominating the Inter-American system," she said. "I'd like to imagine that the Obama administration has the imagination and creativity and confidence to adjust to the new Latin America of foreign policy independence."

Christopher Sabatini in *Foreign Affairs*: "Washington's regional agenda has been driven by the belief that democratic political development and multilateral economic liberalization would reinforce each other and benefit both local and the United States. Unfortunately, this approach has largely ignored local economic logic and the persistence of competition between states, not to mention the diversity of market economies … Beijing has also stepped into the void, using its growing economic strength to weaken Washington's economic leverage in the hemisphere"

China confirmed its efforts to actively support the forum as an important platform for the further development of China–Latin America cooperative partnership. President Xi Jinping, who sent his congratulations and welcomed the plan to establish a China-CELAC forum, said that the partnership should be of equal mutual benefit and serve common development.

According to a report in *Inside Costa Rica* on February 1, 2014, "[b]esides integration among its 33 members, a primary objective of CELAC is to decrease U.S. influence in Latin America and the Caribbean. Even countries that are close allies of Washington are now approaching China for commercial opportunities."

"Washington is so out of touch with the continental reality that it is the US policy that ended up isolated."

For Cuba, whose presidency of the organization came to a close, it was an opportunity "to show a country in reform, with a significant expansion of the private sector, increasing freedom of travel, and in the process opening up for foreign investment. The Summit is a blow to Washington … so out of touch with the continental reality that it is the U.S. policy that ended up isolated" (*HuffPost*, Latinovoices, February 3, 2014).

The large number of heads of states of Latin America present in Havana shed light on the gap between Washington's Cuba politics and the Cuba politics with the rest of the region. Latin American and Caribbean countries are betting on reconciliation through economic reform and a slow opening-up of Cuba and the hope that it will have some influence on Cuba's lip service to "more democracy and human rights" (*HuffPost*).

The summit of the Community of Latin American and Caribbean States is one of many. Waving the flag for Latin American integration will need to act beyond pledges to "continue advancing," a formulation that sounds all too familiar from many summits of the EU, producing nothing but lip service.

Free Trade Breakthrough among Latin American Economies

Latin American nations are not only tightening their economic connections with China, various efforts are being made to strengthen free trade including boosting intercontinental trade. Many of these efforts are rarely reported in Western media.

However, greater attention was given to presidents Enrique Pena Nieto of Mexico, Juan Manuel Santos of Colombia, Sebastian Pinera of Chile, and Ollanta Humala of Peru in May 2013, when they finalized a trade integration pact, The Pacific Alliance, which was signed in June 2012, *Wall Street Journal* (July 7, 2013) called it "likely to be the most effective catalyst for growth in the region since the North American Free Trade Agreement in 1994." The Pacific Alliance Agreement encompasses 210 million people, which amounts to 36 percent of Latin America's population. The aim of the alliance is also to create certainty and stability for foreign investors. Seen as a single region, it would be the eighth largest economy and the seventh largest exporter in the global community.

From the year 2011, when the idea was born, it took seven meetings of the four presidents to work out how the region will implement free movement of goods, services, investment, capital, and people. By Western standards it is a record time. Colombia's media celebrated it as eliminating tariffs on 92 percent of trade in goods.

Latin America–Africa

Many headlines focus on China's strong economic presence in the African countries. Less so for Brazil's growing engagement in Africa, especially in Portuguese speaking countries, Guinea-Bissau, Cap Verde, Angola, and Mozambique. In the coming decade, Latin America, China, and Africa will be in the role of competitors as well as alliance partners.

Latin America and the Caribbean are not only intensifying the ties among each other and China, but also at the same time improving economic relations with African countries. Around 75 million of Brazil's almost 200 million people are of African descent. Besides sharing the sad part of history of exploitation by Western colonial powers, many countries in both continents share massive challenges: misgovernment, the gap between poor and rich, corruption, to name some. Both regions have the advantage of a young population, vast natural resources, and good prospect for growth. Despite different historical, cultural, and ethnic backgrounds, efforts to boost biregional relations and to develop institutional mechanisms to support relations and share long-term visions are increasing. Political dialogue is needed to raise the still relatively modest level of cooperation to be able to leverage the opportunities for cooperation in science and technology, education, environment, energy, infrastructure, and tourism.

The door is wide open to greater interaction between Latin American and African countries.

Conferences and summits, if they go beyond lip service, are ways to clear problems and build on common interests. The third Africa–South America Summit (ASA), held on February, 2013 in Malabo, Equatorial Guinea, had the goal to explore "strategies and mechanisms to promote South–South cooperation." Trade between South America and Africa increased from $7 billion to $39 billion in 2011. Africa and South America share a history of colonialism, said Ecuador's foreign minister Ricardo Patino, but still "we do not know each other well, we don't have experience in joint work … there is so much we can offer each other, and not only in terms of commerce."

Marco Hausiki, Deputy Prime Minister of Namibia, said: "the peoples of South America and Africa share a common historical background of waging the struggle for freedom and self-determination. We must speak with one voice to advance the common interests of our people" (*Global Research*, March 4, 2013).

Brazil and Nigeria, each with the largest population in their continent, are still functioning way below their potential.

Finding and building on common ground across cultural, political, and economic backgrounds, serving current domestic demands while keeping long-term interests of all participants in mind is challenging. This is the goal between the two countries with the largest population in their continents, Brazil and Nigeria. Growing from $1.5 billion to $9 billion from 2002 to 2012, trade volume has increased by 500 percent. Petrobras, Brazil's Oil Company, invested hundreds of millions in Nigeria's energy sectors. Visiting diplomacy followed the South African Summit when President Dilma Rousseff visited Nigeria's President Goodluck Jonathan. The very ambitious memorandum of agreement covers "agriculture and food security, petroleum, power, bio-fuel, trade and investment, mining, education, aviation, infrastructure management, finance, and culture."

While the United States gave lip service, China went into action.

We remember the first time we became aware of Barack Obama. We were in our hotel room in Singapore and CNN was reporting live from the July 2004 Democratic convention announcing John Kerry as their candidate for presidency. A young Obama had been the convention's keynote speaker. We were impressed and remember it to this day. How much must any African hearing him been surprised. And it was only the beginning of the story.

No one was surprised about the excitement that swept through Africa's countries when in 2008 this man, one of their sons, Barack Obama, was elected president of the United States. It encouraged the vision of a new relationship between the two continents. President Obama's words, "I have the blood of Africa within me, and my family's own story encompasses both the tragedy and triumphs of the larger African story," were truly touching. But it was President Xi Jinping who was courting Africa with "sincere friendship" during his first foreign tour after becoming China's new leader.

Africa's expectations were encouraged when the White House said President Obama's 2013 trip to Senegal, South Africa, and Tanzania was to "reinforce U.S. commitment to expending economic growth, investment, and trade." But on top of the US agenda was the old requirement to "strengthen democratic institutions and invest in the next generation of African leaders."

A wakeup call to the United States on Africa came from Senator Chris Coons, chairman of the Senate Foreign Relations Subcommittee on Africa Affairs: "America is losing ground and ceding on economic opportunities in Africa to competitors. China, which has made dramatic inroads across the continent in recent years, may undermine or even counter value-driven U.S. goals in the region, and should serve as a wake-up call for enhanced American trade and investment."

In May 2014, the *Financial Times* reported big news: "US prepares African trade push." After more than a decade of various China–Africa Forums "the US has announced that in August it would hold the first US Africa business Forum to 'strengthen trade and financial ties.'" Maybe, there is some awareness that the United States is not exactly a front runner in this "push." A senior US government official anyhow asked for FT for anonymity when he said: "There is clearly a sense of opportunity in Africa and the US government is embracing that. We see Africa as a real source of opportunity."

To compare, in the last decade, while the US Africa trade doubled to $110 billion, China–Africa trade in 2013 climbed to more than $200 billion.

The reality is that America is losing influence in the emerging economies of the Global Southern Belt.

"The US is losing leverage in Latin America," was Eric Johnson's warning at the Inter-American Dialogue (*Financial Times*, August 7, 2013): "How will China's involvement in the region alter Latin America's international position? … Latin America will no longer be the backyard (of the US), but can increasingly pursue its own interest abroad." Johnson worries that China is increasingly slipping into the role the United States used to play, supplying Latin America with economic market and military equipment, thus reducing America's political and economic influence in the region.

Kevin Gallagher, professor of international relations at Boston University blames the United States as "blind to Latin America" (*China Daily*, June 3, 2013). While the offer for America's Trans Pacific Partnership is attached to heavy conditions, he writes, President Xi's offer to invest more than $3 billion has only few conditions attached.

Since 2003, Gallagher continues, "China's policy banks provided $86 billion of finance to Latin America, more than their counterparts at the World Bank, the Inter-American Development Bank and the US Export-Import Bank combined." It seems that Obama's goal in "redefining relationships" when he visited Latin America in March 2011 is still on hold.

President Obama's picture of the United States is still one of the glory days: "In fact, by most measures America has rarely been stronger relative to the rest of the world. Those who argue—who suggest that America is in decline or has seen its global leadership slip away—are either misreading history or engaged in partisan politics."

Game Changers on the Rise: Five Opportunities for US Growth and Renewal

The United States has often proven its ability to get back on its feet. With a positive and hands on approach rather than whining Americans have the ability to change course and turn the ship around. In a report in June 2013, McKinsey spots five opportunities for the United States to grow. There are increasing positive signals for a US recovery. Claims for jobless benefits have fallen to a 14-year low of 264,000 (Reuters, October 2014), production in factories, mines and utilities advanced by 1.0 percent in September, the biggest gain since November 2012.

Shale gas and oil production has become the a major driver which is estimated to add as much as $690 billion a year to the US GDP, and in addition create 1.7 million jobs by 2020. It could eliminate America's energy imports make it energy independent, but it faces challenges environmental risks. Anyone who travels the United States will confirm the high potential of investments in infrastructure McKinsey lists as one of the US growth opportunities with a potential of creating 1.8 million jobs by 2030 and boost annual GDP by up to $320 billion.

To raise competiveness in knowledge-intensive goods, increase operational efficiency by using big data as a productivity tool and a more effective US system of talent development are the additional US "game changers" McKinsey lists. But each of them is connect with "if" and "could." McKinsey closes: "Taking action now could mark a turning point for the US economy and drive growth and prosperity for decades to come."

Hope and gloom clash in global outlook is the title of the *Financial Times* analysis of the IMF annual meeting on October 10, 2014. While the IMF outlook for the United States and Europe is rather gloomy, this picture is not shared by emerging economies. "In their eyes," writes the *Financial Times*, "global growth is faster than its average over the past 30 years and the outlook is changing rapidly with China now the largest economy in the world. Inequality is falling and though reform is difficult and some countries are struggling badly, most are striding toward prosperity."

All of these statements are based on what we believe is an obsolete Westerncentric worldview. The economic awakening of two-thirds of the globe holds great opportunities also for the developed world, as examples show in this book. But we also have to admit that some of the achievements we praise, shorter working hours, early retirement, and disproportionate social welfare have become unaffordable in stagnating and declining economies. That is the reality. And all efforts to turn the economic performance of the West around have to take realty into account.

Game Change in the Global Financial Architecture: A New Roadmap?

Among the nations of the Global Southern Belt, the development of BRICS (Brazil, Russia, India, China, and South Africa) has been in the focus of global markets. Whether one agrees with O'Neill's 2001 selection or not, over time BRICS was adopted by the BRIC States themselves with an initial meeting in New York in September 2006 and a first formal BRIC summit in Yekaterinburg, Russia, in June 2009. In December 2010, China officially invited South Africa to join the group and with the agreement of the other members South Africa added the S and made it BRICS. We believe that the transformation of the global economy will be driven not only by BRICS (with Russia and India adding very little to its dynamics anyway) but by the much larger number of emerging economies of the Global Southern Belt.

Nevertheless, BRICS states, which represent 43 percent of the world's population in four continents, have taken a leading role among emerging economies within the increasing self-assured and confident participation in the global community.

As Laurence Brahm, with wide experience as international lawyer, economist, author, and founder of the Himalayan and African Consensus economic paradigms, put it: "BRICS are shifting the tectonic plates beneath our existing global financial order. They have the answer to their own challenges. Their voice and influence will grow with the changing flows of global capital. It is only a logical consequence that BRICS countries are now taking the leading role in creating their own bilateral trade agreements outside the WTO laying the road map for a new development bank, currency stabilization fund, and trade dispute mechanism that can parallel the functions once only held by the World Bank, IMF, and WTO."

For now BRICS is the voice for emerging economies of the Global Southern Belt, which is part of the dynamics that are already working on replacing the old financial architecture, sharing the Chinese philosophy "all insight arouses out of practice." GSB countries do not believe in green table theories, but in what has proven to work in practice based on common sense. There is a lot that divides Russia, India, China, South Africa, and Brazil, but there is even more coming between them, Washington and Brussels.

Step by step emerging economies are emancipating from Western tutelage.

Sharing the common interests of a new global consensus the leaders of the BRICS nations met in India on March 20, 2012, and agreed on issuing a call for a new global financial architecture in what they called the "Delhi Declaration." It established the principle that an alternative financial architecture is necessary to parallel the old one—in short the democratization of our global financial system.

"We call for a more representative international financial architecture, with an increase in the voice and representation of developing countries and the establishment and improvement of a just international monetary system that can serve the interests of all countries and support the development of emerging and developing economies. Moreover, these economies having experienced broad-based growth are now significant contributors to global recovery."

In March 2013, President Xi Jinping and President Putin signed some 30 agreements, followed by the two countries attending the fifth BRICS Summit on March 26–27 in Durban, South Africa. BRICS heads-of-state laid out a clear roadmap for a BRICS development bank as an alternative to the World Bank and established the BRICS Business Council during the BRICS Heads of State Summit in March 2013 to act as an administrative body envisioning a free trade zone established under the BRICS mechanism, working in parallel with WTO. On October 24, 2014, China and 20 other countries signed a memorandum to start the international development bank. The bank, which will focus on financing infrastructure projects in underdeveloped countries in the region, is a reasonable consequence to the increasing frustration building up in China and other emerging economies. In addition, there is a growing disproportion between China's global economic position (now as the largest economy by PPP measures) and its voting strength in operations of the World Bank, which is 5.3 percent versus the US 16 percent.

Among the countries signed are large economies such as India and China, wealthy countries such as Brunei, Qatar, and Singapore, and emerging economies such as Bangladesh, Laos, Myanmar, and Thailand. Australia, Indonesia, and Korea, despite China's importance as a trading partner, have not yet decided to sign. The reaction, no surprise, was mixed. While officially the World Bank and the Asian Developing Bank welcomed the new bank, the United States raised concern characterizing it "as an attempt to undercut the World Bank and the Asian development Bank," which are dominated by the United States and Japan (*New York Times*, October 25, 2014).

As another step to bypass global financial institutions BRICS nations approved a $100 billion currency stabilization fund as an alternative IMF in September 2013. China committed $41 billion, Brazil, Russia, and India each $18 billion, and South Africa $5 billion (Reuters, September 5, 2013). A BRICS currency stabilization fund, Contingent Reserve Arrangement (CRA), could pool together an estimated $240 billion in foreign exchange reserves, making it larger than the combined GDP of about 150 countries. BRICS nations aspire to become less dependent on the dollar as global reserve currency. A basket of Pesos, Ruble, Rupee, Yuan, and Rand, as internationally traded currencies, will possibly be positioned as an alternative. The leaders of BRICS nations believe in conducting trade between the five BRICS nations in their own currencies, an idea that has wide acceptance among other emerging market nations. Two agreements signed among the development banks of Brazil, Russia, India, China, and South Africa say that local currency loans will be made available for trade between these countries. Easy cross-country convertibility among the five will offer a de facto alternative to Dollars as settlement currency, and moreover shield their economies from dislocations in the West.

Moved to a BRICS currency stabilization fund, Contingent Reserve Arrangement (CRA) could pool together an estimated $240 billion in foreign exchange reserves, making it larger than the combined GDP of about 150 countries. Joint efforts are made to enhance the stature of BRICS not only as regional power centers of the developing world, but as a force for pulling their neighbors out from underdevelopment. *WallAfrica* concludes that "much is unknown about BRICS Development Bank, but few can doubt the potential it can offer ... the chance to transform the powerful symbolism of the group into a source of action, by empowering BRICS with the real capacity to apply to their vision."

Andrew Kenningham, economist at Capital Economics LTD in London, has a more skeptical view: "It will not be easy to reach an agreement on the banks capital contributions and governance structures. If and when it gets up and running, it may simply duplicate or substitute for funds led by the Chinese Development Bank" (Bloomberg, March 27, 2013).

"BRICS participants have made significant progress in the formation of joint institutions, which in the future should strengthen cooperation," writes *Russia & India Report* in the run-up to the BRICS meeting in Fortaleza, Brazil in July 14, 2014.

Laurence Brahm: "A BRICS currency stabilization fund could effectively replace the IMF as lender of last resort to the developing world (and maybe parts of the developed world). And with these developments, the post-Bretton Woods arrangement that we have all come to know and accept haplessly will have changed forever."

3

China

The Game Changer

About half a year after this book was published first in China in January 2015, a headline in the *Financial Times* (May 29, 2015) read: "Now China makes the rules." What has been overlooked in the past three decades is that China's plan has not changed, it has just become more and more visible until even the most Western-oriented could not negate the role China will be playing.

> US failure to prevent much of the global community from joining the China-proposed Asian Infrastructure Bank (AIIB) marks not just a setback for US efforts to dominate global financial affairs. It also provides the precedent whereby would-be US allies can begin to dissent from US hegemonistic demands. (*Financial Times*, April 8, 2015)

China remains a polarizing country. Much more so as it has a significant attribute that makes it stand out in the global community: it is a game changer; first in its own territory and now on global grounds. In the last 10 years, we have traveled the country intensively experiencing it first-hand resulting in five books on China. We have also spoken to many audiences outside China about what we have experienced and observed. We have found

Western audiences in particular are very sensitive to our being too China-friendly. Maybe we are. But there is more than one way to look at China, and there is hardly only one China. China has many faces and facets. To do research on China is an exciting and forever unfinished task, as the country changes at unprecedented speed.

We have found that the way one looks at China differs depending on the angle of the observer. We the American–Austrian husband and wife team carry a mixture of two cultures: the American independent, optimistic "just do it" spirit and Austrian caution with a predisposition to preemptive conformity. As much as we can, we slip into the Chinese mindset that sees the individual as part of the whole with loyalty to the country's 5,000 years of history of respect to superiors and citizens listening to rather than opposing authorities.

China: More Global and More Chinese

Our goal is to draw a picture of how China changes, what role it will play as the leader of the Global Southern Belt and as a game changer in the global community. We have found disequilibrium in the world that focuses on China's faults and shortcomings. We stress the right to focus on China's potential and strengths. But most of all we focus on its economic development and global impact.

President Xi Jinping and the new leadership are determined to lead China into the next stage: to rejuvenate China and reposition it on a global level. How China changes and how it will change the framework in the global community will be based on its history, culture, self-perception, visions, and dreams, never by allowing the West to press it into Western-made molds. In other words, expect China to become more Chinese domestically and more global internationally.

On a global level China will expand its position as a major global investor. Its investments are geographically well distributed and China's entrepreneurs and enterprises have gained experience, improving flexibility to operate in various environments.

To become more cosmopolitan on global playgrounds while acting more Chinese domestically is, nevertheless, a balancing act. To reach steadiness will demand work in both regards. China's economic strength resulted in increasing weightage in the global community, but it is still a lightweight as an authority in the global community. Global appreciation is tightly linked to accepting or dismissing China's domestic development that, we believe, is becoming more Chinese.

Xi Jinping's rejuvenation of China will have different interpretations. It is a process, not one act. It will include economic as well as political reforms. China is a game changer in the global community. How much China will change domestically cannot yet be anticipated, but the Chinese dream should not be taken lightly.

China's Domestic Game Change

Do not underestimate China's ability for rapid change. The most significant characteristic and strength in China's rise was and is its will to radical change. In 1978, China moved from acting ideologically driven to results-driven. Deng Xiaoping's U-turn to reform and opening-up changed the country's direction from a downward to an upward spiral. China's opening-up was based on opening-up to mistakes of the past combined with the will to analyze, regroup, and change course. The corrections under Deng were sharp, but they were within China's long-term strategic plan: to create modest wealth for all Chinese by the year 2020. It was within the frame of Chinese thinking that if conditions change, entirely different and unforeseen paths could be taken to reach the goal.

Many of China's reform steps took boldness. In 1999, the National People's Congress (NPC) declared that the private sector was no longer just a supplement to the state economy, but was now a key part of the national economy, a breakthrough in China's economic policy. What to Western ears might sound like the next logical step was another U-turn in China. It allowed private enterprises to become the locomotives in competing effectively in global markets and the engines of industrial growth. Global competitors under the umbrella of the WTO would gain greater access to the Chinese domestic markets, necessitating more flexibility of Chinese firms. The course had been set in1993 under Vice-Premier Zhu Rongji, one of the great architects of a new, more global China.

Many signs are pointing in the direction that President Xi Jinping and Premier Li Keqiang are taking in the next bold moves to increase China's role as the leader of the Global Southern Belt and as a key player in the global community. One cannot straight-line extrapolate China's conversion from the past to China's future, but one can conclude that China's leadership has the will and ability to change course in order to keep China on course. Premier Li has been talking about the need for a "self-composed" revolution to reduce his government's power and promote "market mechanisms" for growth. To our experience, "self-composed" is the key.

China's Role as a Global Game Changer

Already in the beginning of China's reform and opening-up, it was clear that China wanted to open up to the world. From the beginning the emphasis was on *the world*. The West's interpreta-tion of *the world* nevertheless was *the West*. When the West finally welcomed China in joining the WTO in 2001 by Western under-standing China was moving closer to the West.

From China's point of view to become a member of the WTO meant what the title of the organization says: *World Trade Organization*, an organization bringing together members from all over the world. Among them are countries that for decades had hardly ever been in the focus of Western economic reporting. But they were already on the screen of China's long-term strategic planning.

In its first years of China's rebirth learning from developed countries to build up China's capacities was paramount. The next strategic step was to move closer to what the West called the underdeveloped world. Engagement grew fast. From 2005 to mid 2013 China's global overseas investment was $688 billion. A very strong focus and the largest part of the investment and contracts went to nations of the Global Southern Belt.

South America	$77.0 billion
East Asia	$157.2 billion
West Asia	$84.9 billion
Sub-Saharan Africa	$119.7 billion
Arab World	$60.2 billion

Source: Derek Scissors, "China's steady Global Investment: American Choices," Heritage Foundation Issue Brief, July 22, 2013.

On a global scale, China was the world's third largest investor for the second year in 2013. Outbound investment reached a record high of $108 billion. A record that is most likely to rise. *Financial Times*, October 6, 2014, quotes Liao Qun, chief economist and head of Citic Bank research who predicts China's total outbound investment to hit $200 billion by 2017 with a growing share invested in Europe. Xinhua referred to a statement of the ministry of commerce saying that the new procedures for domestic companies were "aimed to allowing more freedom for outbound investment." A hint is that the current rule that any overseas investment that exceeds $100 million needs to be approved by the ministry will fall (Xinhua, September 10, 2014).

Just to put China's starting point in perspective: "In 1978, when China started its historic change, total reserves of the country were RMB 108.99 billion, including state-owned enterprises and the central treasury. All of it was deposited in one bank, making up 83 percent of the country's total sum of money," as Wu Xiaobo writes in his book, *China Emerging*.

China's current total investment of $499 billion in the GSB does not only have economic impact. China gained, as we describe in Chapter 2, strong influence in helping to develop self-confidence and detach itself from the Western dependence and influence of emerging economies. The intense travel diplomacy of the new leadership underscores the global scale of China's strategic consideration and the further important role of the nations of the GSB. During 2013, President Xi made trips to Russia, Switzerland, Germany, Romania, Kazakhstan, Uzbekistan, Kyrgyzstan, Turkmenistan, People's Republic of Congo, Tanzania, South Africa, Malaysia, and Indonesia.

By far not as visible and by far not much spoken is China's influence on future developments in the efforts to reduce climate change. China has been blamed for its role as the largest emitter of carbon dioxide. But now the picture has changed and China is also said to be the carrier of hope in fighting pollution. The German Potsdam Institute for Climate Impact Research attributes China "enormous drive" and *Germanwatch*, a German NGO praises: "fascinating in what dimension China is beginning to turn the unwieldy ship around."

With an investment of $56 billion China in 2013 put more money into green energy than any other country. China is well on its way to become the game changer in international climate negotiations.

In all of this, China has not been operating in the dark. Anyone interested can get a rather clear picture of China's strategies today and tomorrow. This is true for the global picture, as well as in its relationship with different regions and countries.

For readers interested in more details about China's further plans, we have added a summary about China's Third Plenum at the end of the book.

China: A Game Changer for Africa

In 2006, Beijing published an official paper on its future African Policy in *People's Daily Online*:

> The first years of the new century witness a continuation of complex and profound changes in the international situation and further advance of globalization … China, the largest developing country in the world follows the path of peaceful development … The African continent, which encompasses the largest number of

developing countries is an important force for world peace and development. China–Africa traditionally friendly relations face fresh opportunities under the new circumstances.

The document laid out a general frame in which China–Africa relations should develop. Part I describes Africa's position and role, part II China's relation with Africa, part III China–Africa policy, and in part IV the paper included a 14-paragraph outline of "Enhancing All-round Cooperation Between Africa and China." The outline of the cooperation includes political, economic, education, science, culture, and social aspects. And it fits very well into China's approach of an active, independent, and expanding position in the global community.

In the global context China never saw and does not see itself as the East. It was the Middle Kingdom for millennia. The economic focus toward the West in the first decades of reform and opening-up was not driven by the intention to become like the West, but to learn from the West. Today, China is opening to all directions with a strong presence in Africa.

No surprise that the West did not pay much attention when in 2000 another multinational organization The Forum on China–Africa Cooperation was founded. Its purpose: "to create a platform for a new type of China–Africa partnership featuring long-term stability, equality, and mutual benefit."

While China–Africa relations are very much in the limelight, China's latest advances in the coldest regions of the globe get less attention.

No Region Overlooked: China and the Arctic and Antarctica

Global media intensely covered the rescue efforts of the Chinese vessel Xue Long (Snow Dragon) when the Russian ship MV Akademik Shokalskiy was stranded in frozen seas of the Arctic in the globe's coldest environment. Much less attention has been paid to China's overall presence in Antarctica and Arctic. After building three Antarctic research stations: Great Wall, Zhongshan, and Kunlun, China unveiled its fourth Antarctic research base, Taishan, in February 2014. A fifth is planned for 2015.

Even though China's current missions are scientific research, the growing presence is a significant sign of China's future geopolitical role. In a few decades, when in 2048 the Antarctic treaty is up for review, regulations on using resources will be renegotiated. Chen Lianzeng, deputy director of China's State Oceanic Administration, said in an interview with *China Daily* "peaceful use of Antarctica in the future will be a blessing for all humankind." Of what kind this use will be was not revealed.

In fact, Antarctica's resources hold great potential to cause geopolitical conflicts. The continent's oil reserves are estimated to be up to 203 million barrels, the largest in the world (Ellie Fogarty, Lowy Institute Policy Brief 2011). By 2030, global water demand will exceed current sustainable supplies by as much as 40 percent. A "water war" in the Antarctica, which holds 90 percent of the world's fresh water, could be a risk, says a US National Intelligence office report in 2012. China is catching up fast. In the context of the full potential of the Antarctic, it is most likely that China will increase its presence on the continent to ensure a favorable position when 2048 comes.

China's new geopolitical role will not stop at icy waters. It will also play a bigger role in the increasingly ice-free Arctic, a region believed to hold rich mineral and energy resources as well as shipping opportunities.

In December 2013, as the China-Nordic Arctic Research Center was established in Shanghai, 10 research institutes, including China, Iceland, Denmark, Finland, Norway, and Sweden, signed an agreement to boost cooperation in Arctic research. Zhang Xia, deputy chief of the new China-Nordic Arctic Research Center said: "as a latecomer, China has a lot of homework to do to learn more about the rapidly changing region."

The high potential in the Arctic global natural resources was underscored when Swedish Lundin Petroleum made what could be the biggest oil discovery in the Norwegian Arctic. Lundin's executives and analysts are hailing the 400 million barrels of oil and 125 million barrels of natural gas and call it a possible game changer (*Financial Times*, October 15, 2014).

China's Positioning in East Asia and Indian Ocean Countries

From a Golden to a Diamond Decade?

China's maritime Silk Road underscores its interests and role in the East Asian region. As the world's largest exporter and second largest importer, China has a vast interest in building and expanding its maritime infrastructure. China is the world's largest ship builder, it controls 20 percent of the world's container fleet, and it has many of the world's largest container ports. President Xi Jinping first presented the idea of maritime Silk Road in an address to the Indonesian Parliament in October 2013. The goal is to increase maritime cooperation between China and the ASEAN countries, to run ports and establish free trade zones in Indian Ocean countries, reinforcing China's economic and diplomatic interests in the Indian Ocean region.

To boost the Maritime Silk Road, China in May 2014 put up a budget of $1.6 billion to build ports and improve infrastructure to connect with Southeast Asian and Indian Ocean coastal countries. Gwadar Port, Pakistan, located between oil-rich western Asia, highly populated South Asia and Central Asia with its rich on resources, is strategically important. In Malaysia, China plans to invest $2 billion to upgrade Kuantan port. It will also put up $480 million into a China–ASEAN Maritime Cooperation Fund to support common maritime interests. Expectations are so high that Premier Li Keqiang spoke of upgrading the Golden Decade 2000–2010 to a Diamond Decade.

It appears that one focus of China's diplomacy in the next years will be on neighboring countries as the new leadership aims to forge the nation also as a strong regional power. For economic reasons alone, this makes a lot of sense. President Xi Jinping is attributed to have said: "A nearby neighbor is better than a distant relative."

Yang Baoyun, professor of Southeast Asian Studies at Peking University, said: "the new Maritime Silk Road will bring tangible benefits to neighbors along the route and will be a driving force for the prosperity of the entire East Asian region."

India does not share that opinion. Even though China–India relations have improved in general, Prime Minister Modi's answer to China's growing influence and role in the region is "Project Mausam," a symbolic name. In many Asian languages *Mausam* means weather or season, with the seasonal monsoon to sail across the Indian Ocean. India's goal is to reestablish its ties with ancient trade partners and reestablish an Indian Ocean world along the shoreline of the Indian Ocean stretching from East Africa, Arabian Peninsula, Iran, South Asia Sri Lanka, and Southeast Asia (*The Diplomat,* September18, 2014). "It is," writes the *Diplomat*, "the most significant foreign policy initiative designed to counter China." Details of the project are yet to be announced.

In the context of China's role as the leading nation of the Global Southern Belt, its maritime expansion plans are one step to stronger economic ties and easier access to markets. Disputes [hopefully] will appear as bumps in the road.

China's investment in South East Asia has been growing at double-digit speed. In 2011 and 2012, the top six investment destinations were Indonesia, Vietnam, Philippines, Malaysia, Thailand, and Singapore (*The Guardian*, March, 2012). During an October 2013 visit to Thailand, Premier Li promoted China's high-speed trains, persuading Thailand's congress to approve a bullet train railway system cooperation project with China, which will help to secure more infrastructure deals in Southeast Asia.

Associated Press of Pakistan on May 28, 2014, reported "the China–Pakistan Economic Corner will expand the depth and breadth of their bilateral relations by mutual support and cooperation." China's approach is to "engage neighboring countries for common development and economic integration." *Dawn. com*, June 2, 2014, reported that China has invested around

$52 billion in major projects in Pakistan. Pakistan's President, Mamnoon Hussain, called the largest project, the Hydropower, "to be a monument of the century. It will benefit not only Pakistan and China, but also the whole region with billions of people" (*The Diplomat*, February 20, 2014).

Investments are not a one-way road. In 2013, foreign direct investment of the top 10 Asian economies in China rose 7.1 percent reaching a total of $102.5 billion. In 2013, investment in financial and nonfinancial sectors in China rose to an estimated $127 billion, only $32 billion less than the investment in the United States (UN report, January 2014). China is now closing the gap as number two after the United States in inflow of investment.

The neighboring country Russia is being used to counterbalance Washington's global influence. China's $400 billion gas deal with Russia was an important step in that direction. Meanwhile, being encouraged by the EU and US sanctions, Russia and China have tightened their bonds in mutual interests.

China's "New Silk Road"

The increasing economic ties of the Asian nations of the Global Southern Belt have led China to revitalize ancient landline trade routes. The new Silk Road Railway, also called Yu Xin Europe Railway, and the Silk Road Economic Belt, is part of China's Western development initiative. It will expand China's policy of "opening to the West," as part of its new global economic strategy. In China, the project will link provinces and regions including Xingjiang, Tibet, Sichuan, Shaanxi, Gansu, and Chongqing. It will cut through Kazakhstan, pass through Russia, Belarus, and Poland, and cut the five-week shipping time of the past to only two weeks (*China Daily*, March 27, 2014).

China's "New Silk Road" that connects China, Asian countries, and Europe opens new opportunities. "Duisburg now is located along the Silk Road" was the headline of a report on President Xi's visit in Duisburg, Germany. Germany's Vice Chancellor Sigmar Gabriel and Hannelore Kraft, Prime Minister of Germany's province Nordrhein Westfalen (NWR), which generates 22 percent of Germany's GDP. The New Silk Road supports the structural transformation the region had to go through after the decline of steel and coal industries. In the past decade, NWR experienced a boom in Chinese investments. From 2003 to 2014, the number of Chinese companies, including multinational corporations, climbed from 300 to 800, creating 8,000 jobs. China's trade minister Gao Hucheng praised the collaboration of economy, science, and culture between Germany and China. The freight train, connecting Chongqing and Duisburg since 2001, is 750 meter long and has 50 containers, each equipped with a *Global Positioning System*. Freight costs are 10,000 Euros per container. It takes the train 16 days, one-third of the previous shipping time, and it is significantly cheaper than airfreight.

Despite China's strong investment in the Global Southern Belt, economic partnership with Europe is still on its agenda. The rate at which China is buying European assets was rising sharply during the crisis in the Eurozone, including buying shares in Club Méditerranée, mostly called Club Med, Greek retailer FolliFollie, Germany's concrete pump maker Putzmeister, and Energias of Portugal, the country's dominant power utility.

Xinhuanet commented on Premier Li's March 2014 visit in several cities of Germany as injecting new vitality into China–European relations. Cui Hongjian, director for European Studies of the China Institute of International Studies, commented on The Asia–Europe Summit (ASEM) in Milan in October 2014: "the summit has offered a good opportunity to bring Silk Road Economic Zone and the 21st century Maritime Silk Road conceptions into Asia Europe cooperation."

China's investments in Europe might have been underestimated for some time. Virtually unnoticed during the worst days of Europe's debt crisis, China-based companies made their move to snap up hard-hit European companies. According to Deutsche Bank by the year 2012, Chinese investment stock had nearly quadrupled to nearly 27 billion Euros.

On October 7, 2014, in a front-page article published in the *Financial Times* titled "China changes course with a huge bet on European assets," it wrote: "The buying spree, analysts say, was nothing short of a transformation of the model of Chinese outbound investment. It is expected to increase steadily over the next decade." Also, it pointed out: "This was partly opportunistic buying because assets were cheap and partly it was a structural secular shift in Chinese outbound investment, from securing natural resources in developing countries to acquiring brands and technology in developed countries."

China's impressive investments and contracts in Europe:

Britain	$23.6 billion
France	$10.6 billion
Italy	$6.9 billion
Germany	$5.9 billion
Greece	$5.5 billion
Portugal	$5.4 billion
Spain	$2.4 billion

Including Switzerland, China's investments and contracts in Europe expanded to $82 billion (Derek Scissors, Heritage Foundation Issue Brief, July 22, 2013).

China–Europe: Trade for a Billion a Day

"EU-China let it flow," was the headline in *European Parliament/News* (October 8, 2013). The EU is China's largest trading partner, and for the EU, China is the second largest trading partner (behind the US). The EU's foreign direct investment (FDI) in China is €25.5 billion and China's FDI in Europe in 2012 hit a new record of $6.5 billion (*International Business Times*, February 27, 2014)—a good reason for Premier Li Keqiang to set out on a whirlwind economic tour to spur overseas deals, shortly after he had taken office in March 2013. He resolved the solar trade dispute with the EU. He signed several cooperative deals to build infrastructure, and pushed for providing large-scale energy projects, including nuclear power plants in Central and Eastern Europe.

In November 2013, Premier Li achieved agreement on a cooperative deal to build a high-speed railway in Romania. Several of the deals he has made have been backed by Chinese loans of up to

$10 billion for countries to update their infrastructure. Along the way, China is focusing on building relations, resolving difficulties, and promoting China's economic transformation and reforms and its position as a global investor. During a visit to China in early December 2013, England's Prime Minister David Cameron said that China's investment in the UK over the previous 18 months exceeded everything in the past three decades, covering sectors ranging from telecom and infrastructure to nuclear power and high-speed trains.

To provide a simpler and more secure legal framework for investors and of both sides the EU and China started to negotiate a comprehensive EU–China Investment Agreement at the EU–China Summit in November 2013. The Agreement is supposed to progressively liberalize investment and eliminate restrictions for investors to each other's market—a good timing as Germany, Europe's powerhouse, had to face a decline in exports by 5.8 percent in August 2014. The forecast on Germany's 2015 GDP was reviewed and decreased from 2 percent to 1.2 percent, all the more reason to look for leveraging new export markets especially in Asia.

China and Germany share mutual interests. China wants support for its New Silk Road and Germany among others sees an opportunity in China's demands in its car market.

Deals worth more than $18 billion were signed in the third top-level talks between China and Germany in October 2014. Besides signing for China to buy 70 A320 airbuses the deals included agriculture, automobile, telecoms, healthcare, and education. Li Keqiang could not have embraced the goal of boosting trade and investment and deepening Germany–China innovation relationships with warmer words: "The two sides have deeply engaged, like gearwheels meshing with each other, to form an interwoven interest group" (*China Daily*, October 10, 2014).

China's New Assertiveness

The continuing weakness of the Western economies, the rise of the Global Southern Belt, and China's economic ties to many of its emerging economies give increasing weight to China's future foreign policy and, last but not least to the question whether China's rise will take place peacefully. China has been setting foot into America's backyard, South America and the Caribbean, while at the same time increasing its effort to get America out of its own backyard, the Asia Pacific. Conflicts with Japan in the East China Sea over Diaoyu Island, confrontations with the Philippines and Vietnam in the South China Sea, and a unilateral declaration of an Air Defense Identification Zone are seen by many as provocative.

We quoted Yan Xuetong, the Dean of the Institute of Modern International Relations at Tsinghua University, in Chapter 2 which we want to repeat in this chapter because of the importance and relevance of the statement:

> For more than twenty years, China has operated under a foreign policy framework within which it has neither friends nor enemies. With a few exceptions, all other countries were essentially treated the same with the maintenance of an external environment most conductive to China's own development the paramount priority. Under Xi, China will begin to treat friends and enemies differently. For those who are willing to play a constructive role in China's rise, China will seek ways for them to gain greater actual benefits from China's development.

China will favor those who side with it and penalize those who are hostile to it.

It is not likely that any Chinese officially would confirm such politics. It just does not fit the Chinese communication style. Nevertheless, the classification of people, movements, and countries into friends and enemies cannot be disclaimed. Taiwan, Hong Kong, conflicts in Tibet, and Uyghur are on hold to be solved in one way or another. For now, it seems to us they are kind of gray zones in which a messy ending would lead to destabilization and economic setbacks. Not to mention the loss of any authority in the global community. But the innovative solution is yet to be found.

China and the United States: Getting Acquainted in New Roles

China's new role and self-confident presence in the global community raises questions about future relations between the two largest economies, the United States and China. While President Xi Jinping's official visit to Latin American countries can be interpreted as a statement for China's alignments with the Global Southern Belt, his unprecedented informal meeting with US President Barack Obama in California in early June 2013, two months after he took office, allowed at least a hint of interpretation about thoughts China's new president has about the character of the relationship between the two globally most influential nations.

There is no doubt that domestic and global interests can be in contradiction. Rising nationalism domestically and the demand for an adjustment to international conditions have yet to be solved. China's progress resulted in global recognition of its economic achievements, but certainly not in the appreciation China aspires to.

The United States finds itself in a role it had not anticipated only a decade ago: its economic and leadership authority in question. China, which even in its most glorious times had very limited global influence, can very well handle a gradual rise of recognition. To step down from the throne of the world's only superpower, lately nevertheless proven toothless, is much harder. China is the game changer, but despite all hassle we believe it was easier to achieve current status than to maintain economic and political stability in a domestically transforming society.

There is no question that China and the United States will be the most influential nations of the first half of the 21st century. How they will play their roles is yet to be sorted out. Verbally, the two leaders of the world's largest economies have committed to build a new type of relationship and leave the historic rivalries behind. Nevertheless, it will have to be on eye-level. China's Foreign Minister Wang Yi told US Secretary of State John Kerry that even though Beijing is committed to settle disputes over the

East and South China Sea: "Nobody can shake China's resolve in safeguarding sovereignty. Yet, uncertainty remains pending." In his fifth trip to Asia since taking office last year Secretary Kerry assured the Chinese officials and leaders that the United States does not intend to contain China, and that China matters greatly to the United States.

On February 20, 2013, Secretary Kerry said in his first speech about foreign policy: "We create 5,000 jobs for every billion dollars of goods and services that we export." This leads to the conclusion that "in 2012, US$148.45 billion worth of commodities exported to China could have created more than 740,000 jobs for the US," writes Zhou Shijian, senior fellow, Tsinghua Center for US–China Relations, in *China US Focus* on January 7, 2014.

Game Change in Global Economics

From 1980 to the end of October 2013, US investment in China amounted to US$72.78 billion, ranking fourth. From January to October 2013, US exports to China were valued at US$131.3 billion, accounting for 10 percent of the US total export over the same period. China and the United States invested in each other on an increasingly large scale.

In 2013, China's direct investment in the United States grew faster than US investment in China. In the first 11 months it rose 28.3 percent, amounting to more than $80 billion. China's Investment in the United States jumped 232 percent; in the EU it was up almost 90 percent, and in Australia 109 percent.

China's opening to global markets does not stop at its currency. In the past eight years, since 2005, the RMB has appreciated by 35 percent and increased its internationalization process. At the G20 Summit on September 5, 2013, President Xi Jinping said that China will

> build a stable and anti-risk international monetary system, conduct reform on the basket of currencies for Special Drawing Rights. China will strive to deepen the reform on the marketization of

interest and exchange rates, to increase the elasticity of the RMB exchange range, and to gradually make the RMB capital account convertible.

The Shanghai Free Trade Zone, with its aim to turn Shanghai into a world financial center, sets another signal in this direction by speeding up financial reform and opening up. On May 17, 2011, the World Bank released a report "Global Development Horizons: The New Global Economy," which estimates that the current leading position of the US dollar will come to an end before 2025 and be replaced by a multicurrency regime based on the US dollar, Euro, and RMB.

The Largest-ever Chinese Acquisition of a US Company

China's presence on global markets in all fields is impressive. In 2012 Chinese buyers spent $11.57 billion in 49 deals to acquire U.S. companies or stakes in US firms, reports *Dialogic*. After China's Cnooc LTD was thwarted in its attempt to acquire Unocal Corp for $18.5 billion in 2005, China's Shuanghui International in 2013 succeeded in taking over US pork giant Smithfield Foods for $7.1 billion. It was the largest ever Chinese acquisition of a US company.

In the US finance is the leading target of Chinese investment. Investments and contracts have reached $57 billion, with a total of $106.9 billion including Canada. William Wilson, senior research fellow of the Heritage Foundation's Asian Studies Center, sees a significant change in the US and China's investment patterns from the developing to the developed world, with the prime target the United States in the first half of 2014. He expects China to transform from a net recipient of FDI to become a net exporter of capital within the next few years. Until a few years ago, Chinese outbound foreign investment was dominated by large state-owned enterprises, but now private firms are dominating investment of Chinese capital in the US "accounting for more than 80 percent of transactions and more than 70 percent of total transaction values, with China investing more in the United States than the United States in China."

In its 2011 report "Multipolarity: The new global economy," the World Bank writes: "The world economy is in the midst of a transformative change. One of the most visible outcomes of this transformation is the rise of a number of dynamic emerging market countries to the realm of the global economy."

China's negotiations to establish an internationally funded bank, the Asian Infrastructure Investment bank, to finance projects in underdeveloped countries (with China contributing $50 billion) to rival World Bank have been opposed by the United States. *New York Times* on October 9, 2014, quotes a senior administration official, who wants to stay anonymous:

> the Treasury Department had concluded that the new bank would fail to meet environmental standards, procurement requirements and other safeguard adopted by the World Bank and the Asian Development bank. How would the new institution add value? How would the Asian Infrastructure Investment Bank be structured so that it doesn't undercut the standards with a race to the bottom?

Clay Lowery, a senior US Treasury official 2005 to 2009, in the same report calls Obama's objections not entirely well founded and argues that the Chinese plan "could be a positive development—potentially a great way to get Asian countries to work together on significant financial needs in the region."

Changing Positions

The 5,000 year Middle Kingdom of China and the 500 year "new world" America will go through a decade of successes and failures to find their positions in a multicentric world. Zbigniew Brezinski, best known as the national security advisor to US president Jimmy Carter, in an extraordinary column in the *New York Times* in February 2013 shows both concern and a positive outlook about future China–US relations. He laid out the following guidelines:

1. Wars for global domination are not a serious prospect in what is now the Post-hegemonic Age.

2. There is no need for conflict between America and China now that global dominance is no longer achievable.
3. One-sided national economic triumphs cannot be achieved in the increasingly interwoven global economy without participation calamites consequences for everyone.
4. Neither the United States nor China is driven by hostile ideologies.
5. Despite our very different political systems, both our societies are, in different ways, open.

In the February 2014 meeting of president Xi Jinping and US secretary of State John Kerry, each side defended its own stand on controversial issues, each with the domestic and the global context in mind. In US–China relations as well as in China's role as a model and driver of the emerging economies of the Global Southern Belt, stability is of key importance.

Economically, as China is retooling its growth model, investors seem to be confident that the economy will keep growing at a solid pace. President Xi Jinping and premier Li Keqiang keep renewing their goal: "We will foster a new open economic system."

On the opening of China's legislative session on March 5, 2014, Premier Li Keqiang made a strong policy speech to kick off the next level of reforms in China. *China Daily* reported that Premier Li used the word "reform" a record 77 times in his 100-minute speech. "Reform," he said, "has brought us the greatest benefits. Reform is the top priority for the government. We must rely fully on people and break mental shackles and vested interests to deepen reforms on all fronts."

Into Global Limelight: China's Entrepreneurs

China at first was a domestic game changer. Then it gradually became a game changer in the global community. Individual entrepreneurs became millionaires and billionaires, but seldom gained global attention and impact. Alibaba's sensational IPO to some was the latest wake-up call to the game change challenging the long undisputed leading role of US innovators.

We will have to get used to the emergence of Chinese star economic performers. Are China's young entrepreneurs different from American or European entrepreneurs? Yes and no. Yes because despite all cultural differences all young people we met in China, the US, Europe, Africa, or Latin America have a simple goal: a satisfying career and the perfect partner for life. No because the way Chinese do business differs from the Western way. Very often when we spend time in the Club Lounge of our hotel where many business talks are taking place, we can watch the body language of the Western and Chinese businessmen. Western business people keep talking top down, often lecturing the Chinese how this and that needs to be done. The Chinese close up, quietly and friendly, and we know the game is over.

This is not a how to do business in China book. But one thing is quickly said: build up trust and show respect. Chinese are warmhearted, but focused on what they want to achieve. If you have something to offer that serves them and you, great. Otherwise forget it. No nonsense; it's business.

It is often said that China is still waiting for the first contemporary breakthroughs in inventions and innovations spreading from China to the world. Thus, to many Western observers and commentators it came as a surprise when the *Financial Times* announced Jack Ma as their 2013 "Person of the Year." China's billionaire entrepreneur is the founder of the world's most successful and largest e-commerce company, Alibaba, founded in 2003. Alibaba's Internet markets are dealing with more transactions than E-Bay and Amazon put together. Jack Ma now ranks number 1 on China's rich list.

Alibaba went public on the New York Stock Exchange in 2014. *Forbes*, September 22, 2014, carried out a report titled: "Alibaba's claims title for largest global IPO ever with extra share sales." With $25 billion it surpassed Agricultural Bank of China, which raised $22.1 billion in its IPO on Hong Kong Stock Exchange. To compare, number one "Alibaba processed more than $248 billion of online transactions in 2013, and handled 70 percent of all packages delivered in that time, all in China; number two, Amazon, processed $100 billion and number three e-Bay $76 billion online transactions" (*Forbes*, June 27, 2014). Alibaba's a growth potential is expected to hit $600 billion by 2018–2019. No wonder that Ma is seen by the *Financial Times* as "godfather of China's scrappy entrepreneurial spirit. He epitomizes the new entrepreneurial China where a poor person can become huge through perseverance."

Just before Alibaba made its debut on September 19, 2014, on the New York Stock Exchange, Jack Ma said it would be a "life changing day" for its 20,000 employees. That evening, given the time difference, Alibaba employees and other citizens of Hangzhou witnessed the "life changing" event on gigantic television screens in multiple locations. Stock incentives Alibaba offers its employees meant that there was $44.8 billion to divide among 11,000 of them. Each one has more than 100 million Yuan ($16.3 million). Ma himself is now worth about 250 billion. Ten years ago, there was only one Chinese individual worth more than $10 billion. Today there are 176. "What is more amazing," said Rupert Hoogewerf, Chairman of *Hurun Report*, a monthly magazine best known for its Chinese rich list, "is that the entrepreneurial spirit that have enveloped China shows no sign of abating, with eight self-made individuals born in the 1980s making the list. Any country would be proud of that."

Choosing Jack Ma as "Person of the Year" to the *Financial Times* was: "his decision in May to step down as Alibaba's chief executive (handing the reins to successor Jonathan Lu) at the age of 48 to devote himself to tackling some of China's biggest problems—in particular its looming environmental disaster."

A second focus Ma told the FT "is people's culture and education—if we don't do this then young Chinese people will grow up with deep pockets but shallow minds."

Ma was born in Hangzhou, located in Zhejiang province, said to be the center of entrepreneurship in China. As a child Ma was bad at mathematics but fascinated with English, so he devoted himself to learn the language. Well known in China is his story of getting up early every morning for nine years and riding his bike to a nearby hotel in his town of Hangzhou where he offered himself for free as a tour guide to foreign tourists in order to practice

English. Even though he failed entrance examinations twice, he finally made it and attended Hangzhou Teacher's Institute, graduating in 1988 with a bachelor degree and teaching English and international trade at the Hangzhou Dianzi University for some time.

Later, Ma started to build websites for Chinese companies with the help of American friends. It was at a time when he had to convince the companies first that the Internet does indeed exist. In 1999, Ma and 17 of his friends founded what turned out to be the Alibaba we know today.

Be in love with the government, but never marry it.

When asked by the *Financial Times* about the challenges of dealing with the Chinese government, Ma pointed out that there had never been an organization in China or perhaps anywhere that is as large as Alibaba. It has more than 600 million registered accounts and has around 100 million shoppers a day. "At the beginning I thought the government would worry. But we focus on business and the creation of jobs. The government seems to feel more comfortable now." To his employees he has often said that Alibaba should "be in love with the government but never marry it." He has repeatedly turned down offers to establish joint ventures with state companies.

In a letter Ma wrote to his employees in the run-up of Alibaba going public he said: "We must allow time and the results of our work will speak for themselves." That in many ways is also true for China.

China, a Game Changer in Global Research and Development (R&D)

Developed in the United States or Germany, made in China, is still common thinking. But as many things in China also this has been changing for years. One example of such change we got to know about some years ago was, of all places, at the Vienna Café

Brewer Ball. By the way, it is said to be the most joyful ball of all Viennese balls. There we got to know the man who is behind the fresh coffee one can buy in newly built highway rest stations, Gerald Steger, CEO of café+co International. The group now operates 70,000 vending and espresso machines, which made them market leader in machine catering in central and Eastern Europe.

The interesting story to us was when we learned café+co's cooperation and R&D partner Ad Maas has turned the China workshop picture around: "For the money I have to pay one R&D engineer in Europe in China you can hire several." So he hired the R&D team in China and moved the completion of the machines to Germany. The result was developing a special energy-saving technology in China, which is used in premium café+co machines in Central and Eastern Europe.

For sure only one of many examples of the chain of economic value added, developed in China produced in Germany, is turned around even by small and medium-sized enterprises. A fact that *Wall Street Journal*, January 16, 2014, wrote about under the title: "The Rise of China's Innovation Machine." WSJ concludes that in the years ahead "China's technology sector is reaching a critical mass of expertise, talent and financial firepower that could realign the power structure of the global technology industry in the years ahead." *Computerworld* already in December 24, 2012, warned that by 2023 the United States might have lost its R&D leadership.

China is at the brink to make the step from visionary entrepreneurs who are innovative to visionaries who are inventive. A giant step was announced in late July 2014. China is racing to complete the plan to build a 52 km super particle collider which will "dwarf every other accelerator on the planet" (aljazeera.com, September 20, 2014). Aljazeera quotes Gerard 'tHooft who was awarded the Nobel Prize in Physics in 1999, who believes China's collider project "will bring hundreds, probably thousands of top class scientists with different specializations, from pure theory to experimental physics and engineering from abroad to China."

Scientists at the CERN complex have also begun to explore the potential to construct a super collider. But their deadline for a preliminary conceptual design is scheduled for 2018, four years later than China's deadline.

Professor Arkani Hamed, Princeton Institute for Advanced Study: "China without question will become the leader in the field of physics."

China: A Nightmare for American Internet Companies?

"Why China is a nightmare for American Internet companies" was the title of a report in February 27, 2014. "Global domination is more or less the goal big American Internet companies are aiming for," wrote *Time*. From a US perspective, entering the world's largest Internet market is a hard task. Censorship, human rights, logistics and Chinese rules create hurdles. LinkedIn, whose mission is "to connect all the world's professionals" was one of the few to launch a local Chinese website.

While American companies are still working on a manageable entrance to China's web users, China has already set foot in the United States: Sina Weibo has been testing an English version of its Chinese social network and WeChat, used by almost all our Chinese friends wherever they are in the world, is courting for global users.

We find it amusing and also a little sarcastic when in China we hear CCTV America encouraging its audience: "Follow us on Twitter and Facebook."

Despite all latent conflicts, China's Internet companies are going global. Sina Weibo is planning a US IPO for the end of 2014. China's most used Internet portal Tencent, founded in 1998 with its social networks QQ and WeChat, serves one billion users and is about to pass Facebook. Tencent and Alibaba have issued virtual credit cards and are intensifying competition in China's e-commerce markets.

A number of Chinese entrepreneurs who have already come in global limelights, few in the Western world, are familiar with the name GuZicheng. And yet the now 28-year-old man is a multimillionaire. His company Kanbox is the leading cloud storage and sharing service provider in China. His success story sounds like one of the stories one usually associates with America. At 15 he set up BBS, after one year his site received more than 200,000 hits per day. Only four years later he developed the Storm Player, one of China's most popular multimedia players, with a friend he had met online and only met in person several years later after Storm Player had become a national hit. "The Internet is one of the few business arenas where we can start from zero and still achieve success at an early age," said Gu. The simple secret behind his success besides talent is the ambition he still has. "The other day we had a discussion whether we should work 14 or 16 hours a day. Everyone adopts an around the clock work-style as second nature. We're happy to be pioneers in the cloud storage service" (*China Daily*, August 12, 2013).

Leo Chen, known as Chen Ou, created one of China's top cosmetic e-traders. The good-looking guy made himself his company's public face. His strategy of budgeted personal branding saved him about 100 million Yuan in advertising costs, he said. Before Chen established the site in 2010, he and two other cofounders had no experience in e-commerce, or selling women's cosmetics.

Another name hardly heard outside China is Jiang Lei. As an exceptional talent he skipped grades at school and enrolled at Tsinghua University when he was 16 years old. At 20 years of age he founded his own company, Tiexue Technology. Tiexue.net. became China's largest military affairs e-commerce site with 30 million hits in 2012. Not much different than US super talented, he quit his PhD studies at Tsinghua, hiding it from his parents for two years. In 2012, the company revenues were over 100 million Yuan, as sales keep increasing. "The internet has a lower threshold for young entrepreneurs to start their own business. Tiexue. net keeps attracting people who have interest in military-inspired casual wear," he says.

Reversing the direction business models travel

For a long time the publishing world would say that books only travel from the United States to Europe. A one-way road of success also seemed to be true for business models. Designed by the United States, copied in China. "Copying China Business Models in the US catches on as a new Tech Start-up trend—quite the reverse," was the title of a *Forbes* report in August 7, 2014. Hubert Thieblot, CEO of business Curse, was seeking inspiration to Chinese startup YY. "It was YY's social entertainment that got Thieblots's attention" and made him launch Curse Voice, his new communication platform, which by June 2014 has reached one million active users.

Many young Chinese do not have to dream of becoming the new Zuckerberg; they can dream of becoming the new Chen, Guo, or Jiang. Outstanding Chinese established entrepreneurs and sports champions have entered the global stage. Chinese companies are climbing up the Fortune 500 list, with the success of Chinese companies such as Alibaba, Baidu, Tencent, and Xiaomi. It is interesting to hear what during the Interactive Advertising Bureau conference in New York in September 2013, Martin Sorrell, CEO of the world's leading marketing and communications services WPP said: "The trite answer to what's the next big thing would be mobile and data, but I would say it's Chinese business models. We in the West think we have a monopoly on this wisdom, but we don't."

The Chinese Dream: A National Vision and Individual Dreams

Already today China offers favorable conditions for young Chinese entrepreneurs. In the thousands of e-mails we received in reaction to our columns in *China Youth Daily* and *Youth Digest*, only one person complained about the government. All others who wrote e-mails worried about their personal growth and success in the competitive environment. To be the best at the best high school and university and then to be the best in their endeavor is the goal, wish, and dream. And the demand on the government is to create the conditions that enable them to move upward.

President Xi Jinping's call for further opening-up and a rejuvenation of the nation rings out in the context of a rising China, but it will also play in the context of a stronger and rising middle class and a success-hungry youth. China's next level of reform and rejuvenation is orchestrated top down, but at the same time there is a rejuvenation of the people bottom-up. Better-educated, increasingly sophisticated Chinese citizens, youth-linked and open to the world, demand more respect for individual rights. The individual dream, for millennia subordinated to the well-being of the nation, is gaining momentum. As we wrote in *China's Megatrends*, stability in China will depend on keeping the equilibrium between top-down directions and bottom-up demands and initiatives. Xi Jinping's call for rejuvenation is addressed to a patriotic, but more global-thinking generation. The Chinese dream as a national vision is growing parallel to the liberation of the individual.

Not every Chinese is happy with the government, "but" that does not keep them away from living the life they want, doing business and enjoying the many things they now can afford. We very much agree with the advice Maria Pinelli, Global Vice Chair of Strategic growth Markets for Ernst & Young offers for dealing with Chinese business people in *Forbes*, May 21, 2014: "Most of us sound off about government policies that we dislike. But Chinese entrepreneurs don't waste their energy whining about things they can't change. They just get on with it. Billionaires in the making are natural optimists; they don't let politicians spoil their day."

China's New Role in the Global Community

Economics play the decisive role—whether it is Tibet, Xingjiang province, or any other region in China. In China's development, domestic considerations are always in the foreground. Nevertheless, China's further opening-up is not taking place in a vacuum, but in the context of a transformation in global relationships.

No matter how you measure it, China is becoming the world's biggest economy. After reporting that the International Monetary Fund (IMF) had just declared that China already ranks as the world's biggest economy in purchasing-power-parity terms, the *Economist* (October 11, 2014) said that "historically China is merely regaining a title it has held for much of recorded history. In 1820, it probably produced one-third of global economic output. The brief interlude in which America overshadowed it is now over."

CHAPTER 4

Governance

Performing under Changing Conditions

What is good governing? Our very simple answer is when the government trusts the people and people trust the government, that is the measure. The vast majority of people measure their government by the effect its governance has on their own well-being. In a simplified way governing can be compared to employer–employee relationships. Employees, in general, are judging their bosses depending on the impact their behavior and performance has on them: the economic success of the company, the freedom to contribute, the ability to grow in the company, the working environment to name some criteria. To achieve that goal managing a company over time has undergone severe changes. Leadership 50 years ago was interpreted in a different way and so was the relation of employees and superior authority in the company.

In addition, the context in which companies do whatever they do has changed significantly. All internal and external changes resulted in a constant process of correcting, adapting, and reinventing. What is true for enterprises is true for countries. Domestic and international conditions have changed. To govern a country successfully has to take that into account. But while in the business world reinventing is acknowledged as part of economic survival, the economic, political, and social necessity to reinvent governing quickly hits resistance from the political establishment. Nevertheless in the context global game change neither well-established democracies nor countries at various stages of developing new governing models will be able to afford persisting in a status quo.

While there is wide consensus that democracy delivers the best foundation of how to govern a country, interpretation of how democracy should be implemented is stretched to the extreme diverging as far as the interpretation by the Democratic People's Republic of Korea and that of United States of America. It is worth taking a brief look back to the roots of democracy.

Democracy as the model for good governance goes back to ancient Greece. In the sixth century BC Athens was caught in a social/economic crisis. To overcome it Athenians established an institutionally backed participation of citizens in the interest of the community. Even though limited to only part of its population (women, slaves and foreigners were precluded), Athenian democracy became the forerunner of Western democracy. In Greek the words *demos* (people) and *kratia* (rule) mean "rule of the people."

The days of evangelizing ideologies are over.

In the authors' upbringing in rural communities, religion played a strong role in life. Even if our parents would not know what misdoings we had in mind, God would. He set the rules against which our behavior was measured.

But while an almighty God in most religions set a framework of highest authority, there has never been an ultimate authority for democracy to refer to. Nevertheless, the supremacy of the West has been linked to the dominance of the Catholic Church, backed by its self-determination as God's representative on earth. The Church did not only give its blessings to worldly rulers, its "God given" order to evangelize delivered emperors and kings the entitlement to invade and convert countries and convert "infidels" fully to Catholic beliefs, principles, and values.

Holy Roman Empire (Latin sacrum Romanum Imperium) was the official denomination for the rulership of Roman–German emperors from the Middle Ages to 1806. It was based on the claim to pursue traditions of the Roman Empire and it legitimized sovereignty as in accordance with God's will. "In God we trust" up to this day is the official motto of the United States. "In God we trust" is on US dollar bills and it is in the mindset of the leading nation of the West that God is on its side, and therefore in God's America we trust, should be a global motto.

The West has made it its mission to convert "infidels" to its principles and values. But the reality is that just as not everyone wants to be Catholic, not everyone wants to be proselytized to be "Western "or "American." This is not about diminishing the accomplishments of Western democracy, which in our personal opinion is to value high, but about understanding that in different cultures different underlying principles are integrated in governing processes. Recent experience in Iraq and Afghanistan has awakened many Americans to this realization.

The Painful Farewell to Western Superiority

The mindset of Western superiority is deeply rooted in history and anchored emotionality. It is the foundation on which Western democracy defines itself. In this regard, the West understands itself to be the highest authority on democracy and how it should be implemented in national governing models.

It began in good old Europe when in the light of the enlightenment, the Eurocentric worldview, Europe as the sole center of thinking and acting, began to establish itself. All cultures should be based on European ideals, values, and norms. The most comprehensive German encyclopedia in 1741 describes Europe as "the smallest continent of the world," but for "various reasons the most preferable."

Little more than 100 years later highly regarded *Brockhaus*, the German-language encyclopedia, explained Europe as the "culturally, historically, and politically most important of all five continents with highly influential sovereignty on the tangible and even more so, on the intellectual world."

The Eurocentric Worldview and the Claim of Western Supremacy

Measuring the world by a Eurocentric worldview has been adopted by what we today call the West: North America, Europe, Australia, and New Zealand. America, the new world of European descent, is attributed to have established the first sustainable democracy in the 18th century. The United States rose to the most powerful military and economic country and thus underscored the comprehensive supremacy of the West. The ideological conflicts in the second half of the 20th century ended with the victory of democracy as the economically and socially most successful governing model, with America as the main model.

Backed by a century of economic, military, and cultural dominance the West measured any country and any governing model from a Western perspective and with an outside-in view. But it is at least questionable whether the Western model is a one-fits-all mold. Not even within the Western world, does applying the same norms work, as the growing gap between northern and southern European nations demonstrates. Emerging nations with tribally and ethnically divided societies have different foundations for developing governing models to provide sustainable economic growth and stable social arrangements.

In addition to the cultural and historical background of each nation, good governance now needs to be measured against the changing demands of the 21st century. Today's world is much more split by social/economic gaps and inequality than by ideologies.

The Underlying Principle of Democracy: The People Are in Charge

The majority decides. The problem is that the majority does not always vote for what turns out to be best for all citizens. And the majority in many cases is bribable. In Western democracy justification for governing is to be elected. Consequently election-driven thinking prevails. That holds the danger that, as in Europe, people who benefit from the system are increasingly outnumbering those who finance the system.

The people in charge have become a challenge to the system. The stimulus to vote is: who promises what is best for *me now*. Decisions are not put in the context of strategies that work best including long-term considerations. Measures inflicting temporary pain are hard to sell even if beneficial in the longer run. In ancient Greece, Plato who refused Athen's democracy, worried about the competence of the people as "citizens live from day to day, indulging the pleasures of the moment."

To be elected, as well as to stay in power, politicians have to court for every vote. Once elected rising debts and shrinking budgets make it hard to keep the promises made. Necessary reforms are not enforceable without losing the favor of the voters who then blame the government they first blackmail for failing to deliver. Lately, since the 2008 financial crisis we have known that debt-financed democracies are not sustainable in the long run. Nevertheless, borrowing to satisfy short-term demands at the expense of long-term investments has become a habit in many democracies.

At the same time inequality is rising. Inequality means different things to different people. To US Republicans schemes to correct inequality smell of class welfare and redistribution of wealth. Democrats talk about the inequality of opportunity. To socialists it is the redistribution of wealth. But if good governing means to create equal opportunities for all (talented at the same level and equally ambitious one would have to add), what are the key points for any governing model to reach that goal?

Abraham Lincoln, 16th president of the United States from 1861 to 1865 said: "You will not strengthen the weak by weakening the strong. You will not help those who have to earn their living by ruining those who pay them. You will not create fraternalism by fueling class hatred. You will not help the poor by annihilating the rich. You will never be able to sustainably help people if you do for them what they should and can do for themselves."

Global Dynamics and Missed Opportunities

A German saying goes: The one who pays decides. Global game change is fed by the twin path of the decline of the West and the rise of the emerging economies of the Global Southern Belt. China, the frontrunner in this development, has serious challenges to manage, but the often-anticipated crash has not come. Instead its economic importance is rising. The frontrunner of the West, the United States, certainly often has proven its ability to recover. So how serious is the situation really? Is the United States in systemic decline? Peggy Noonan, former presidential speech writer and author of seven books on politics, religion, and culture and weekly columnist in the *Wall Street Journal*, asked former Singapore Prime Minister Lee Kuan Yew in an interview: "Is the United States in systemic decline?" His answer must be music to any American ear: "Absolutely not. America faces tremendously difficult times," but "for the next two to three decades" it "will remain the sole superpower" (*Wall Street Journal*, April 8, 2013).

Nevertheless, Lee warns America:

> If you follow the ideological direction of Europe, you are done for. American and European governments believed that they could always afford to support the poor and the needy: widows, orphans, the old and the homeless, unwed mothers. Their sociologists expounded the theory that hardship and failure were due … to flaws in the economic system. So charity became entitlement. The stigma on charity disappeared. Welfare costs grew faster than the government's willingness to raise taxes. They took the easy way out by borrowing to give higher benefits to the current generation of voters. The result: deficits and dangerously high public debt.

The Largest Economic Deal of All Time or Much Ado about Nothing?

Europe and the United States are anything but toothless remnants of once glorious days. Economic alliances among the still strong economies of Europe and the United States could result in economic boosts for both. Nevertheless since the initial decision to negotiate a free trade zone between Europe and the United States went through several unsuccessful stages of negotiations in 1990, 1998, and 2005. With the recent sagging of economic growth in both the United States and the EU, interest in a grand trade agreement has been rising again, especially on the part of the United States. Members of the European Commission and representatives of the United States have started the next stage of negotiating details of the agreement in July 2013.

But the EU is not so sure. The EU could drop controversial investor protection rules from its free-trade talks with the United States, the *Wall Street Journal* wrote on September 29, 2014. In the US social networks call the Trans Atlantic Trade and Investment Partnership "the biggest corporate power gab in a decade." *Russia Today* on October 11, 2014 wrote that "the main aim of the protests is to 'reclaim democracy,' which in this case stands for an end to the negotiations on three major trade agreements."

"What are we bringing upon us?" *Die Zeit* (June 26, 2014) asked in a several-page report. "On one side," the article concludes, "profitability and economic growth, on the other side the question whether there are things that are more important than growth, for example that a government, a parliament, a country can decide autonomously whether it considers hormone meat as dangerous, and certain banking transactions as dangerous in public safety." Genetic modified crop is allowed in the United States, but forbidden in the EU. The United States is using growth hormones in breeding pigs and cows, using widespread hormone Ractopamin which is forbidden in 160 countries, including China that so often is blamed for its lack of safety in food. European markets close their door to such hormone meat; the agreement would open those doors. The list could go on to car parts, pharmaceuticals, and chemicals.

Revitalizing SMEs or Toothless Pleasantries?

America's self-confidence does have impact on the free trade agreement, which is supposed to eliminate customs and reduce bureaucracy. But while for economists that all sounds good, representatives have to deal with a United States that seems to know that Europe, with all its doubts, needs the deal much more than the United States. Negotiations are cumbersome and slow. A final agreement in 2014 is out of reach. It would not come as a surprise if after a few years not too much more than friendly words and declarations of intent would still be the result.

Steve Forbes believes "the US and Europe have gratuitously weakened themselves with idiotic economic policies of excessive taxation, unstable money, stifling regulations, and bloated public sectors." He believes that a turning point to recovery will begin with the US 2014 November elections and that Europe reluctantly will follow (June 2014, *Forbes Asia*). It is a great achievement of the 20th century to not leave those who cannot care for themselves behind. But many Europeans are counting too much on social welfare and too little on their own diligence, forcing politics to ever more promises of indulgence the system cannot afford.

The European Welfare System Was Established Under Bismarck, When Life Expectancy Was around 50 Years

Since Duke Otto Eduard Leopold von Bismarck's reign as the chancellor of the German empire in the second half of the 19th century, life expectancy has improved to 80 years, and we expect the same benefits could be paid three times more. In judging a system the questions "What is rewarded?" and "What is punished?" often add to clarity. When stagnating wages, inflation, and bracket creep lessen spending power, motivation to accomplish is declining as well. Europe has a great welfare system that aims to protect people who cannot care for themselves to be helped out by the state. But what was created as a social net is also corrupted as a self-service outlet by social parasites. In many countries social welfare offers too much space for a very generous interpretation of the right for social support. If you demand necessary reforms, you lose votes, even if the benefits for the voters would prevail in the longer run.

"Is it time to risk less democracy" was the title of a report in German newspaper *Die Welt* in July 2012. "At its core, history is teaching us that the Western welfare state can only be stable if it accomplishes more than it actually can afford. There may well be good social reasons. But one does not have to be an economic sage to see that it cannot go well in the long run."

Western Governance Practice: Kicking the Can Down the Road

In Western countries the call for reinventing democracy is getting louder and louder. As in the days of Martin Luther, there is growing protest against misgoverning and growing inequality. Resentment is mounting against the dominance of financial markets, against exploitation of the environment, against corruption, all rooted in paralyzed, dysfunctional structures feeding into the widespread lack of trust of politicians and political parties. The unwillingness to move from lip service to implementing reforms results in the lack of economic growth in almost all Western nations. "Kicking the can down the road" (leaving importance issues for future generations to solve) has become standard procedure. "Do not get to the core of the problem it might cause you to lose votes," has become the watchword of many Western politicians.

In his column in the *New York Times*, David Brooks wrote on May 21, 2014: "It is now clear that the end of the Soviet Union heralded an era of democratic complacency. Without a rival to test them, democratic governments have decayed across the globe. In the United States, Washington is polarized, stagnant, and dysfunctional; a pathetic 26 percent of Americans trust their government to do the right thing. In Europe, elected officials have grown remote from voters, responding poorly to the Euro crisis and contributing to massive unemployment."

Western Democracies in Search of Painless Solutions

The *Economist* in its March 1, 2014, issue dedicated a six-page essay to the question "What's gone wrong with democracy?" It reported "more than half of the voters in seven European countries have no trust whatsoever in government." German's *Die Zeit* in November 2013 published a discussion about "Ways out of (Europe's) crisis" between Helmut Schmidt, former German chancellor and Joschka Fischer, former German minister of foreign affairs. The title: "Europe needs a coup."

Under the headline: "Block Juncker (Jean Claude Juncker, now President of the European Parliament) to save real democracy in Europe," Gideon Rachmann wrote after the election of the European parliament: "It is above all nations that democracy can live and breathe. That is why in the EU you end up with the absurd situation in which voters are said to have 'chosen' a leader they have never heard of" (*Financial Times*, June 7, 2014).

CNN commentator Fareed Zakaria, in an interview on Amazon: "America's economy and society remain dynamic. Its political system is broken. First recognize the problem. Stop mouthing slogans about how we have the greatest democracy. Our system is now highly dysfunctional and corrupt. We need to fix it."

The bottom-up demand for reform is not to question Western democracy as such. It is not freedom of speech, human rights, and rule of law that is being challenged. It is the qualification of leaders, governing practices, and a loss of trust in politicians that is shaking the Western democracies. "What is needed is not so much a vision of the proper role of the state as a strategy to make democracy dynamic again," wrote David Brooks in his column in the *New York Times*. "Western democracy needs to reinvent itself."

Half Time: Can the Game Be Turned around?

Can you starve in front of a full serving plate? Yes you can—literarily and metaphorically. The leading countries of the West are doing exactly that. They are sitting in front of full serving plates, but are starving. The serving plates offer nourishing dishes: a leading position in technological progress, a long history of invention and innovation, a high level of productivity, a reservoir of natural recourses, the benefits of population diversity, an abundance of talent, the best universities in the world, and the highest levels of per capita income. And most of all, the political structures of the West are resting on the pillars of matured democracies.

So—what is the problem?

The rise of the West was built on strong work ethics, diligence, and ambition, but we are losing ground fighting for fewer working hours, greater social benefits while ignoring the rising competition of a well-educated, forceful, and hard-working youth in emerging economies, especially in Asia. We might not like it, it might not be great, but we have to face reality.

A very strong call to face the reality came from the absolute sovereign of the Vatican City State, better known as Pope Francis when he spoke to the European Parliament in November 2014 in Strasbourg. Europe, he declared has lost its way, its energy sapped by economic crisis, and a remote, technocratic bureaucracy. It is increasingly a by-stander in a world that has become "less and less Eurocentric" (*International New York Times*, November 26, 2014).

In an unusually blunt language his verdict on Europe was, "that it is now a grandmother, no longer fertile and vibrant." Europe frequently looks at the continent "with aloofness, mistrust and even, at times, suspicion. The time has come to for us to abandon the idea of a Europe which is fearful and self absorbed."

Facing the Facts

In his book *When the Money Runs Out: The End Of Western Affluence*, Steven D. King warns that the West has an economic expectation of the future that does not match the reality of stagnation. In his view, stringent steps are necessary to avoid massive political and economic upheaval.

It does not give too much comfort when Oliver J. Blanchard, chief economist of the IMF after years of dealing with the crisis says: "We don't have a sense of the final destination. Where we end, I really don't have much of a clue" (*New York Times*, April 25, 2013).

In his book *Divided Nations: Why Global Governance Is Failing and What We Can Do about It*, Ian Goldin, former World Bank policy director and adviser to Nelson Mandela, concludes "the picture of global governance today is one of duplication, ambiguity, overlap and confusion."

"What is in the head of European top politicians, this lazy club, which keeps making wrong diagnosis and after each meeting presents solutions that are too little too late" wrote Netherland's famous publicist and historian Geert Mak in his book *What if Europe fails?* Up to 27 percent unemployment, 50 percent among the young "lost generation" in Spain, Greece, and Portugal and no growth is the grim reality. The promise of "becoming the most dynamic and most competitive knowledge-driven economy by 2010" as proclaimed by the EU heads of state at the Lisbon Conference in March 2000, has long vanished. Banknotes picturing imaginary buildings and bridges, lacking heart and soul, the Euro, starry-eyed anticipated as a bonding element. Europe did not only stumble into a debt crisis, it has lost its credibility and never achieved a real common identity. Having their own interests in mind, 28 member countries are pulling in different directions, clumsily bound together by an unloved, undemocratic, overbearing Brussels bureaucracy.

The EU has 28 mindsets and two hearts beating in the different rhythms of socialism and market economy.

Europe is dealing with a ramshackle banking sector, a rising gap between Northern and Southern countries with youth (under 25) unemployment unchanged at 53.7 since it peaked in February 2013 in Spain and 51.5 in Greece. While the Greek president at the beginning of fifth Hellenic Presidency of the Council of the European Union presented Greek's reform course as a guarantee for success, its unemployment rate in January 2014 hit a new high of 27.8 percent. Economic data does not allow too much optimism. Greek industry production shrank by 6.1 percent in November 2013. German newspaper *Die Welt* calculated that financial loss of young unemployed people in Europe between 2010 and 2011 mounted up to 76 billion Euros.

"Europe sacrifices a generation with 17-year unemployment impasse frustration is not only amongst Europe's youth," was the title of a Bloomberg report on October 8, 2014. Not much has changed since former French Resistance hero Stéphane Hessel, 93 years old at the time, when he published a 21-page pocket book *Time for Outrage* in 2010. He criticized various aspects of Europe's political development and called for political resistance. It became a huge bestseller, selling millions of copies in Europe. Movements in Spain, France, Greece and the Occupy Wall Street movement embraced Hessel's work as a source for inspiration.

In 2014 the situation has not improved. Growth rate in France was estimated to reach a plus of 3.6 percent; France's audit court in June 2014 fears a minus 4 percent. French President Hollande's approval rate dropped to 18 percent in April 2014. One fourth of the French gave their vote to Front National, the nationalist party, in the European Parliament elections. It is another wake-up call. President Hollande demands the EU to increase its growth politics. But Paris will need to help itself. Without the guts for effective measures, for example raise weekly working hours from current 35 to 37 hours, which is estimated to raise GDP by 3 percent, talk about reform will remain toothless.

French historian, anthropologist, and former presidential adviser Emmanuel Todd in *Die Zeit*, May 22, 2014, speaks of an "inability to self-criticism" and warns of "Germany's efficiency madness." He believes that Europe is moving toward disaster. He believes that "the Euro and austerity policy are destroying Europe's southern societies. Industries and elites have emigrated and the young are unemployed and stopped having children." To Todd, from a demographical point of view, their immigration to Germany is almost as bad as war and just as siphoning of talent.

There is increasing outrage against the "corrupted political class" characterized by Spain's leading daily *El País*, a strong call for breaking today's questionable ties between the banking system and politics. "The lost generation" was the title of an article in *Die Zeit* in June 2014. It dealt with the frustration of youth in southern Europe, who do not only face high unemployment rates, but can only expect much lower income than the previous generation.

"French, Spanish and Italian generations, who have been born beginning 1960, will no longer benefit from economic growth of their countries, all wealth gains acquired go to the generation born before them."

And on October 6, 2014, French Prime Minister Manuel Valls admitted to business leaders in London: "I'm worried how the euro zone has detached itself from the rest of the world economy. If there is no strategy to support growth at the euro zone, we will be in even greater trouble."

Grim, But Not Hopeless

Latest headlines about a coming recession in the EU have once more clouded the picture. Nevertheless, one member country of the EU has shown that despite unfavorable conditions in the EU good economic performance is possible: Poland. For decades under the grip and rule of the Soviet Union, Poland in 1989 used its chance. Three weeks after the fall of the Soviet Union the first noncommunist government took over. Galloping inflation and high federal deficits urged action. Lech Walesa chose Tadeusz Mazowiecki, a member of Solidarity movement, to head the government. Balcerowicz, the appointed minister of economics, had drafted a concept for economic liberalization and reforms already in the 1980s. Favored by the enormous popularity of the Party and the support of Solidarność movement, tough reforms were implemented. Closing unproductive state companies, rising living costs at first resulted in high social costs, the demise of agricultural cooperatives and high unemployment. But since the 1990s, Poland's economy has been improving and since it became a member of the EU in 2004, Poland became a star performer, avoiding a recession even in 2008. Its GDP per capita rose from $1,900 in 1990 to $13,400 in 2013. Life expectancy rose from 70 years in 2009 to almost 79 years in 2012.

Poland still needs to improve infrastructure, business environment, reform its tax system, and loosen a rather rigid labor code. Poland's current growth rate of 1.6 percent is not too exciting, but good in contrast to its powerful neighbor Germany with its economy shrinking 0.6 percent in the second quarter of 2014. Most of all, despite being hit by the EU sanctions on Russia, the mood of Polish people is upbeat.

Poland is not the only positive spike. Another European country has proven that economic stability and sustainable progress is possible even when located like an island amidst the tumbling EU: Switzerland. We remember the years when the EU was still euphoric about a bright future as the economic driver of the global economy, adding pressure to join the club. Switzerland aligned its economic practices to a greater degree with the EU; after all, half of its exports go into the EU, but it resisted becoming a member. Asked for our opinion on membership our answer stayed the same: "Why would you join the EU when you can join the world?" Such questions are not asked any more.

Switzerland suffers from a strong Franc and the pressure of neighboring EU to revise its corporate tax system that allows each canton to offer special tax rates to companies trading outside Switzerland. But different than the EU, which praised the peaking Euro (up to 1:64 against the US$) as a confirmation for its glory, Switzerland fought the rapid rise of its currency by putting a lid of 1:20 to Euro Franc exchange rate in 2011 to keep Swiss industries and services competitive. The United States and international institutions forced Switzerland to change its banking secrecy laws and tax evasion.

Nevertheless, Switzerland keeps walking its own path. On July 1, 2014, a free trade agreement with China came into force. After Iceland it was the second European country to sign such a pact. China's rapidly growing middle class has become a key market for luxury goods, boosting the value of Swiss watch exports to Swiss franc 1.45 billion in 2013. Reductions of Chinese import tariffs and greater protections of intellectual property of the Swiss Made labels are positive results. While some analysts question a large impact on selling luxury watches in China, the agreement is a signal and step in the plan for deals with other BRIC countries, said Jean-Daniel Pasche, President of the Federation of the Swiss Watch Industry.

In its overall performance Switzerland is the global star performer, ranked number one as the most competitive economy of the world for the sixth time in the World Economic Forum ranking in September 2014. Attracting talent from all parts of the world and efficient hiring and firing practices led to highly skilled work force, high level of innovation, and high productivity, one of the most stable macroeconomic environments and a GDP per capita of $47,303. Switzerland, hit by shrinking exports to the EU, cannot detach from a slowing global economy, but it does leverage its potential.

Number two in the world's most competitive nations is Singapore, another small country. Number three, the US has moved up two spots from the last year.

The competitiveness of a country is not a verdict or an indicator how single companies are doing. Much is depending on visionary thinking and an open mind to anticipate changing conditions. Germany certainly is an innovation-driven nation. But in the context of the global game change with shrinking and emerging markets, changing consumer behavior and new competitors no company can afford to rest on laurels of the past.

Certainly not untouched by its own business interests in Africa, German Commerzbank published a wake-up call to the German corporate world in December 2013 and presented itself as a partner for investment: "Renaissance in South Sahara." Commerzbank refers to the emergence of a middle class, with an increasing demand on higher quality and products and services and believes that the service sector, with the financial services in particular will benefit from this trend. "The construction sector is set for dynamic growth driven by an infrastructure expansion and housing construction. Technological leapfrogging offers opportunities in renewable energy and information and communication technologies." (*Commerzbank, Renaissance in Sub-Saharan Africa*, 2nd edition, December 2013)

The German Investment and Development society (DEG) recommends two regions as promising: Indonesia and the five east African countries. BASF's Kurt Bock, CEO of the world's largest chemical maker by sales, whose company had pulled out of Africa in the 1990s, is eager to expand in Sub-Saharan Africa: "If there is a bright spot for us it is Africa. The continent is the last chance to start at zero and generate high growth from there." Africa to the pharmaceutical giant Bayer is one of the remaining markets with special promise.

Hansgrohe (bathrooms, faucets) sees the market in hotels and airports and also private households as the middle class is growing and can afford expensive faucets.

Nevertheless, most German entrepreneurs are still on hold for investment in Africa. Comla Paka, ambassador to Germany, expressed his country's need for foreign investment in infrastructure, in roads and ports, but finds cooperation between the two countries rare. "Many African countries find access to European markets very difficult and in the end prefer to do business with countries like China and India." Germany's trade volume with the 53 countries of South Saharan Africa puts it in perspective: with 26.6 billion Euros it was one sixth of the trade volume with its small neighbor, the Netherlands.

Rising demands in all fields in emerging economies offer great opportunities for small and middle-size companies. A good example is Austria's company INTECO, specialized in steel melting technologies. Located in rural Bruck an der Mur, a small town of only 12,000 people, Dr Harald Holzgruber has turned INTECO into the worldwide leader in the fields of special metallurgy with an export rate of 90 percent.

For sure a sign that the West possesses all it takes, but its dysfunctional, self-interest driven thinking keeps getting in its own way. It is starving despite its generously filled serving plates.

Performing Under New Conditions

It can be imposed or chosen, but the tough farewell to Westerncentric thinking will come. In 2009, Barack Obama's "yes we can" raised new hope and thousands of supporters cheered him in a spirit of renewal. "Yes we can" can be the backbone of turning a game around. But, it remains the backbone without muscles as long as there is no strategy of how to do what. Coming back to our comparison with a company, which business could afford to have a board of directors who are split in opinion using half of their resources to prove each other wrong? Treading water and wasting its resources does not prevent the West it from holding on to yesterday's self-perceptions. How to interpret President Obama words at the beginning of his second term: "We have picked ourselves up, we have fought our way back and we know in our hearts that for the United States of America the best is yet to come."

Is America's best time necessarily linked to global dominance? Would America be better off stripping the obligations that come with it and harnessing the benefits of a multicentric world? After all, Europe security policy has been a free rider on the security guarantees of the United States. Given America's exhausting wars in Afghanistan and Iraq, the United States is now no longer willing to play the role of the global police, forcing Europe to step up to greater self-responsibility mainly toward its eastern geopolitical neighborhood. The eroding hegemony can well be seen as a release and an opening to renewal and regrouping in the reformed world of the 21st century.

Nevertheless, this is not the picture the US paints of the future. A little more than a year ago 16 Intelligence Agencies of the US National Intelligence Council released an assessment on what the world will be like in two decades. In summary, it said that China will be the world's largest economy by 2030 but the United States will still remain "first among equals" in the international system. Europe, Japan, and Russia will continue to experience relative decline and Asia will dwarf the rest of the world in terms of economic and military power (which would make it hard for the United States to stay the first equal among equals).

The first among equals is certainly a new way of interpreting equality. And it seems hard to sell even in America. The country's once seemingly unshakeable optimism is giving increasing room to worries about its economic future.

Searching for National Game Makers

To most parents their own child is the greatest child on earth. But at the same time most parents know that other parents, who believe their child is the greatest, do not share this very personal view. The same in many cases is true for the way people see their home country. There is nothing wrong with it. If every American sees his country as "the greatest nation on earth" it is great for America. America just needs to take into account that Koreans might claim the same to be true for Korea, Brazilians for Brazil, and to a Chinese China is the greatest nation on earth.

There is also nothing wrong with America's aim to recover from years of economic and political stagnation to new glorious days. It gets different though when domestic goals expand to reinforcing America's role as hegemon and guardian of rules and norms in the global community. Even though many of Western norms and rules are worthwhile, the promise that America's best days are yet to come needs to be measured against the global conditions of the 21st century. But whether that goal can be realized, or not, precondition is to fix its present house first.

"The United States is drifting into a class society. Relative prosperity of the lower class is dissolving. Wages declining for decades, massive cutbacks and recession have scratched the myth of a meritocratic America," writes *Die Welt* in its March 13, 2014, issue. Increasing austerity measures led to mass protests in several states. Wal-Marts employees demand minimum wages of $15 an hour and employees of fast food chains go on strike.

Daily Beast, an American news and opinion website, founded by former *Vanity Fair* and *New Yorker* editor Tina Brown, writes about a new political generation which is much more to the left than previous democrats. Between 1989 and 2000 average wages for college graduates rose by 11 percent, while they were shrinking 8 percent from 2000 to 2012. Unpaid intern jobs have become the norm.

America's ability to rejuvenate should not be underestimated, but a social time bomb is ticking.

A nationally representative survey by the American Pew Institute said that "the share of American adults who identify with the middle class has never been lower, dropping to 44 percent from the latest survey (January 2014) from 53 percent in 2008 during the first months of the recession."

Adapting to Global Game Change

The economic picture of stagnation should not mislead one to believe the global influence of the West, especially of the United States, has disappeared. It is still omnipresent. In business, in cultural and private life Western thinking has permeated all countries. It became part of life in non-Western cultures although not always visible on the surface. In cultural influence, the United States will stay the "first among equals" for some time. To a certain degree Westernization is still accepted, even welcomed. But the West has to adapt to the changing global reality. And part of this is to leave space and not overrule the self-perception of other cultures, especially when national pride is revitalized by economic and social progress.

To drive a car needs a license, to vote for the direction of a country needs political education.

Every person who wants to drive a car has to pass a test. A driver's license gives a person the right to move freely on all accessible roads. But it comes with the responsibility to respect traffic signs and rules and to not intrude on the rights of others. Individual freedom of all drivers is assured as long as each driver respects the rights of all other drivers. There is a superior common interest that keeps traffic working as a whole.

In Western democracy every eligible citizen has a license to vote. But hardly any Western school system prepares its next generation for this responsible privilege. Democracy means the people are in charge. But if "we the people" are in charge "we the people" are also responsible for the quality of the system. It takes at least some basic education to make decisions about the future of a country involving matters that are often remarkably complex. To make it even more complex it now all takes place in the context of politics is local, economics is global.

Voters, who to a great degree have become tired of voting for future governments they will not trust anyway, give very low approval rates; in the United States around 26 percent. In Great Britain 62 percent of the voters think that "politicians tell lies all time" (YouGov opinion pol 2012). And it is not only that, while between 1999 and 2013 Britain's private service sector increased productivity by 14 percent, government service sector went the opposite way, it declined by 1 percent. People are disillusioned. But it is the same disillusioned "we the people" who as a majority demand government services "we" are not willing to pay for and exhort promises politicians cannot fulfill. The cat chases its own tail.

To attract the best people to go into politics needs the conditions to attract them.

Good governing requires mastering the economic challenges of the 21st century. It demands the capacity to govern in the context of global political and economic crisis, to domestically sell unpopular measures without endangering the stability of the system. Instead, anything that would endanger a candidate or a party from being elected is avoided.

In addition, today's politicians need the qualifications of multinational CEOs and receive the remuneration of mid-level management. That leads to the best people not going into politics but into their own much more profitable endeavors. The few remaining idealists are often frustrated. No wonder many of them understand their years in politics as preliminary investment to profitable subsequent endeavors.

China: A Model for the Global Southern Belt?

Economic problems are at the center of the crisis in Western democracy. Economic success brought China into the limelight of the global community. It shattered the theory of the 20th century that wealth is inseparably connected to Western style democracy.

It was not India, the most populated democracy that broke the West's monopoly on prosperity; it was of all nations, the People's Republic of China, run by the autocratic Communist Party of China. It could not have been worse for the West. While in the best times America doubled its living standards every 30 years, China has more than doubled the living standards of its people every decade from $150 in 1971 to $6,900 in 2013. The 2013 American Pew Survey of Global Attitudes reports 85 percent of the Chinese are "very satisfied" with their country's direction; even in the context of the government announcing the plan of setting necessary painful measures in order to stabilize the economy and to deal with environmental damage. In addition, growth is likely to stay at around 7 percent. In developing a new governing model China is walking its own path.

China's economic success keeps the debate about China as a governing model for emerging economies of the Global Southern Belt alive. Can China be a model? In our opinion the answer is yes and no. If we stay with our metaphor of half time, sports teams could think that what worked in some other team could be adopted one on one. Nonetheless, China does have strategies that could work in any governing model, and in fact in any endeavor: China adopted from other countries what worked and dropped what did not. It implemented change not nationwide, but in a trial-and-error process.

Does that make it a model as such? No. But it offers guidelines that might work in some cases if adapted to local conditions.

Can the Western model, which was embraced by China to push its economic and technological development, become a model for its political development? The answer lies not in judging China, but in understanding it.

China's Pillars of Change

No matter from which side we look at China, the most visible and most criticized of all pillars its system rest on is communism. But as much as this is apparent China and the West understand it differently. China's understanding of communism and membership in the CCP differs greatly from Western views. Engel's definition of a communist society was that of "methodical utilization … of enormous forces of production … also the means of life, and quality of living … are available equally and in constantly growing abundance." As Marx said, to each according to their needs, from each according to their abilities. Sino Marxism can be understood as a guide to recognize and solve problems on the path to a final goal. Simplified, a communist society is said to be a society in which all can live in a way that meets their basic needs. Paired with "all knowledge arouses out of practice" the definition of "socialism with Chinese characteristics" is the temporary definition of a society not yet fully evolved and therefore without final description. It is the "Chinese dream" to live in such a society. This understanding communicated in simple words should resonate deeply in the international community in which "the fight against inequality" has become the slogan of many governments.

To communicate the Chinese understanding of Marxism is a precondition to understand the role of the CCP and its structure. China's meritocracy within the party and the periodic political education as training for good governance is mostly interpreted by others as periodic brainwashing. There is no awareness of the basic difference in membership of the CCP. Western political parties have to court citizens, while China's party selects members from among the best petitioning to join.

China is different. And it builds on structures created over millennia. How different even young, modern Chinese are thinking became very obvious to us some years ago. We were in Shanghai and met a young student who was applying to become our daughter's au pair. She had brought a file filled with school reports, certificates, and other achievements. They were quite impressive.

At the end, with a little breath that announced something grand was coming, she said: "And this is my membership in the Communist Party." We were baffled.

The Communist Party of China (CPC) by 2013 had 86.69 million members from a population of over 1.3 billion people. The system is building on the tradition of the Chinese empire, in selecting "Mandarins," as scientists, judges, and administrators. The title Mandarin could only be accomplished after years of elite education. Strict and harsh examinations were guaranteeing that only the best made it into their ranks. Their performance was under strict control. The lowest ranking Mandarins were teachers, the highest advisers and scientists and messengers and diplomats for the emperor.

Becoming a member of China's Communist Party follows the same line. To be a CPC member can boost careers of any kind. But to be a member of the CPC is also prestigious because it is part of China's political meritocracy. The education process never stops. In all of China's provinces and cities we have visited, political leaders impressed us with solid education. Many in China's administration studied in American, British, and German Universities. Moving up the political ladder requires proven leadership qualities and a record of academic success.

We thought it was very interesting when Stephen Rhinesmith, who has studied and trained leaders throughout the world, said that in his experience China has one of the best private–public leadership development approaches. He told us about a meeting he had with a leading academic at Peking University, who told him that future business education in China will also include public administration. His words that "it is hard to be successful in the private sector unless one also understands how the government works," we can only underscore. Successful future business leaders will not only need to have an MBA, but also the basics of an MPA (Master's of Public Administration).

Democracy needs to be developed, not enacted.

Russia, Venezuela, Egypt, Iraq, Syria, and Libya, to name some, have proven that democracy does not grow naturally once its seed is planted. In many cultures democracy finds no cultural roots to build on. And on barren ground even the best seeds cannot sprout. It took Western democracy a long time to mature. A look back in history holds some surprises.

Before the 20th century voting, a basic right in Western democracy was often connected to assets, status, tax payments, education, and gender. At the time of declaring independence from England in 1776 in the young democracy of the 13 United States of America, more than 460,000 slaves, transported from Africa, contributed to the economy. And up to the mid-20th century African Americans did not share equal rights. Switzerland established women suffrage as late as 1971; Liechtenstein, one of the world's richest economies, in 1984!

To establish a sustainable democratic system takes a maturing process on each side, the citizens and those elected. Democratically elected leaders in Africa, Asia, and Europe have proven that power can corrupt. Mohamed Morsi in Egypt, Viktor Yanukovych in Ukraine, Vladimir Putin in Russia, Recep Tayyip Erdogan in Turkey, Paul Biya of Cameroon, and Robert Mugabe in Zimbabwe, Omar Al-Bashir of Sudan are some recent leaders who were partly democratically elected, but soon cut the constraints that limited their power.

An election does not automatically create a healthy democracy, often enough it becomes the footboard of corrupt leaders to establish a self-serving system, to cavalierly override constitutions and independent institutions. There is no formula about how to steer a country's development toward a fair and equal democratization process except to support every single component that contributes to the creation of political consciousness. Education in this regard plays as high as role in creating political awareness as it does in achieving economic goals. We will specify later in this chapter.

In most of its China reporting the West is waving the penalty card.

In the global search for new governing models, it is indispensable to look at China. It holds world records on major economic indicators of results. Nevertheless, when China looks toward the West, it is often facing the penalty card not for its economic policies, but its political process. Very few reports aim to communicate a better understanding of China, as did a two-page article under the headline "The China experiment" in Germany's influential newspaper *FAZ Sonntag* (*Frankfurter Allgemeine Sonntagszeitung*) on November 24, 2013:

> The West still has not understood China. The country is mastering the challenges of our time with an unusual political style making it innovative and agile … Socialist market economy links experimental discovery processes with national development programs. Goals and priorities are set. Creation of means and adaption of instruments up to decentralized initiatives and experimental mood. It allows a generally clumsy system to create unexpected dynamics. Chinese politics combines the chances of globalization with stamina and flexibility, which at the beginning of its opening politics no one would have expected … Are we witnessing the birth of a successful new social model?

In our research for *Innovation in China* we worked closely with Stephen Rhinesmith, who is also a Director of the Naisbitt China Institute. In his work as an executive coach and consultant for international companies, he has often experienced the difference between the group-oriented culture of a country such as China and other countries. In his experience: "the sense of hierarchy and willingness to give loyalty in return for security is very different from more individualistic Western cultures where everyone wants to be free to change their affiliations depending on their needs." Any approach to understanding China's political, cultural, and economic development has to take cultural differences into account.

E-democracy as today's door of Wittenberg Castle

As we have written in the introduction, the Internet today is what Wittenberg Castle's door was to Martin Luther: a medium to share discontent. In this context social informatics, which uses methods of informatics, sociology, economics, and psychology will be a field of increasing importance. New social developments communicated via software and a new generation of social networks. FireChat created in early 2014, is increasingly becoming a bottom-up instrument to connect, organize, and unite people. During the days of the protest in Hong Kong, 500,000 people signed up the app within days (*recode.net*, October 28, 2014).

We asked Dr Colin Rhinesmith, who teaches Social and Community Informatics at the University of Oklahoma School of Library and Information Studies, what role this relatively new curriculum will play in the future: "In the 16th century, when Luther nailed his theses on the door of Wittenberg Castle it was easy for authorities to take the paper off the door. Today it's closing a door. Governments can shut down the Internet and interrupt communication. That's what students feared in Hong Kong. But they quickly turned to a backdoor and adopted innovative mobile technologies, which allowed them to stay connected even without access to cellular or wireless networks."

Professor Rhinesmith is convinced that "social informatics will play a decisive role in understanding how information technology shapes our social interactions, but also how broader social, political, and economic forces shape the information systems that we use for work, school, or play. Events like the protests in Hong Kong remind us that we often tend to focus on the impacts of technology without recognizing how, what I call infrastructural developments shape the everyday tools that we use. Social informatics can help us to make sense of these often less visible aspects of technology. We can use this knowledge to hopefully gain a deeper awareness of and more control over the ways in which information technology impacts our lives."

We can expect that the use of new technologies such as FireChat is only one step in the technological maturing and sophistication of communication systems.

The Internet of course communicates in both directions, from the people to the government and from the government to the people. If handled smartly, it is an early indicator of the rising discontent and frustration among citizens. Establishing interactive websites from President Xi and Premier Li down to local government levels does not only allow people to let off steam and anger, but helps the government to get a sense of what is in the hearts and minds of ordinary people. As we wrote in *China's Megatrends*, "in such a highly decentralized society, the leadership frames a broad concept for the society as a whole that incorporates bottom-up ideas, initiatives and demands. Top-down and bottom up initiatives are established and encouraged to adjust in a flexible manner as conditions and circumstances require. All in the context of the overarching common goal set out by the leadership."

This pattern is part of the vertical structure, supporting a constant flow of ideas and experiences up and down the government hierarchy. Within this structure, China is in the early stages of creating a democratic model that fits Chinese history and thinking. While this vertical democratic process certainly has its weaknesses, its major strength is that it releases politicians from election-driven thinking, and permits long-term strategic planning which has enormous economic payoffs.

In the eyes of the West justification for governing a country stands or falls with being electable; in the eyes of the Chinese, justification for governance rests on the level of accomplishment achieved. Under this formula, the Chinese government has performed unquestionably well.

The Chinese leadership holds on to the Communist Party, but as much as the CPC holds on to its command and control in governing the country, the conception of what command and control means has changed radically over the last 30 years. The Party has moved from an arbitrary top-down autocracy to a functioning one-party leadership with strong bottom-up participation, a vertically organized society with increasing transparency in its decisions and implementation.

The West creates committees, China learns from trial and error.

Very different from many African, Asian, and Latin American countries the Chinese governing model is in a process of decentralizing power.

Already China's first steps of reform grew out of practice. Bottom-up when farmers themselves agreed to split up their commune's land into 18 individual plots and allocate them among its member households. It was a dangerous agreement against all rules of a system that had tied down farmers and farming for decades. The bold act was supported by the party secretary of Anhui province and, well known, later by Deng Xiaoping who believed that bottom-up initiatives and energy, once released, would support and implement the goals set and outlined by the Communist Party.

Looking back to the years since 1978, the Chinese author Wu Xiaobo's analysis is that "policy makers have found that their task was to understand how to go with the flow and enhance the end result. In addition to having the necessary courage and spirit, they simply have to figure out how to channel the people's own creativity along the correct path." Deng Xiaoping picked up on agricultural reforms initiated by simple people acting with the bravery of desperation. He received their act as a lecture for the country's reform and opening-up politics: China began to experiment in geographically limited trial and error zones.

FAZ/Sonntag describes it this way: "China applies techniques, which work well in dealing with uncertainty and non-linear developments. The Chinese system is adaptive not because of its authoritarian character and power of the central party but because of its special corrective mechanisms embedded in experimental techniques." It was "the start of a dynamic development the West still cannot understand. Every analysis by the West is connected with doubts whether a one party system can master the enormous challenges and be able to reform."

The West cannot afford to misinterpret China.

In times when it is foreseeable that the era in which the West is setting global rules is ending, it seems reasonable to understand the drivers of China's development, the special reform technique, which makes the country so dynamic. The West ignores especially the very special system of preparation of political decisions, because it simply does not fit into the picture of a static centralized system. "It is not easy," writes *FAZ*, "to describe the new system that China is creating. Partly because, as it is the case with other eras that have evolved, it takes a while before a new system finds its name. China's leadership most often calls its approach 'Socialism with Chinese Characteristics,' and others call it 'Chinese Capitalism,' or a 'Socialist market economy'."

We go with Thomas Kuhn: "You cannot understand a new paradigm by using the vocabulary of the old paradigm." The "more the new paradigm unfolds, the better defined the adequate vocabulary will be," we wrote in *China's Megatrends* in 2009.

Looking at China's governing model based on a principle of Western democracy as the ultimate government model can only lead to disappointment and unrealistic expectations. The real answer does not lie not in ideology, but performance. Gideon Rachman, chief foreign affairs commentator for the *Financial Times* quoted Deng Xiaoping's translator, Zhang Wei-Wei, who said: "The Chinese believe in performance legitimacy. If the government governs well, it is perceived as legitimate."

It is a reach to predict China's future political path. If we listen to Chinese in China the perspective reaches from President Xi within a decade to become the first elected President of China to a turn to a 21st century Cultural Revolution. Whatever plans circulate behind closed doors, which by the way no commentator knows, China's CCP and its Standing Committee is determined to stay in power. They are well aware that while China's new middle class is a great achievement, it is also a great challenge to their demand of absolute power.

In *China's Megatrends* we wrote that the sustainability of the government would depend on keeping equilibrium between bottom-up demands and top-down rules and regulations and restrictions. If either the political leadership crosses the line of tolerable force or bottom-up forces, the people exceed tolerable resistance, the construction of the Chinese model is in heavy danger to implode. Handling the protests in Hong Kong can be seen as an indicator for how mainland China is able to balance the gap between holding on to its course while respecting the will of the people.

Arab Spring

Disastrous social/economic conditions were the drivers of the outcry for reforms and democratization process in the Arab Spring. A majority of the people in the Arab Spring countries lived in poverty. In a population with an average age of 24, one-third of the population was illiterate. The absence of opportunities for young people, a mix of despair, lack of self-esteem, and methodical repression by governments lining their own pockets, created a climate of hopelessness.

In 2010, Spring was in the air. But no Arab summer followed the promising beginnings. The cold wind of reality brushed away the warm breath of hope that for a short time had nourished courage and ambition to fight for more equality and a better life. Syria is still drowning in civil war. In Libya militia are fighting for power and influence while Egypt is on a path to a military dictatorship.

The lack of education and consequently a lack of job opportunities are reasons a young Arab population stood up against their country's leadership. But there are two other important issues: dignity and meaning. The young generations of north Sahara countries have lost ground under their feet. The dilution of religious values and tribal tradition paired with poor economics created a vacuum that is now filled with the deceptive and alluring promises of radical fundamentalism. Self-announced leaders operate under the cover of a divine mission with the authority to empower the powerless to subdue whoever falls in their category of infidels. As in any other cases, emotion does not listen to reason. Such conditions cannot be changed overnight, nor be abolished by military power. Healthy social environments, affiliation to family and community are the bottom-up measures to avoid the emotional vacuum creating the receptive conditions for radical appeals.

The danger and scary part of ISIS is its attraction to the youth. Not very different from regimes in the past the pattern is the same: the promise of empowerment and acknowledgement. The blame against an enemy created with justification either by religion or by race. The images of an ISIS fighter against the sunset, his flag waving in the wind, his Kalashnikov casually thrown over the shoulder, pictures reminiscent of the Marlborough man riding into the sunset. It cleverly appeals to emotions and Western media as an unintended consequence of reporting, promotes such images.

The West, witness to the threat for years, has made many mistakes it has to pay for now. Johanna Mikl-Leitner, Austria's Minister of Internal Affairs, made that clear in an October 2014 TV discussion, "Children of the caliphate, it is our fault?" We talked to her next day and she reinforced: "Real integration should have begun 20 to 30 years ago [when immigration of Muslims to Austria increased rapidly]. We should have been aware that many of the people coming to our country suffered a lack of education and hardly spoke any German. Consequently they moved almost solely within their circles. This kind of isolation and a lack of opportunities to improve living conditions made them receptive to radical groups, which presented their message as a God-given mission. It is our comprehensive social duty to break through that circle and offer advice and guidance. And it cannot be limited to one ministry but must be coordinated among all relevant and responsible ministries. It must be a concern on national level with integration of communities, cities, and provinces."

We agree, and it is not only true for Austria. Condemnation and imprisonment will not solve the underlying social problems. In most cases there is a reason behind being attracted by radical thoughts, and even the call for killing fellow citizens. The fight against radicalization of all kinds cannot be won by punishment but by working to abolish environments supporting it. Minister Mikl-Leitner, who has been pushing for concerted plans of action, also warns of fear mongering: "We need prevention and we need rehabilitation. But while we have to admit the shortfall in the past, we cannot simply blame society and ignore the self-responsibility each person has for his or her acts."

This certainly includes the responsibility of the Islamic world to distance itself from radical pseudo religious criminal groups, something only very few Islamic leaders have done. If moderate Islam fails to distance itself rigorously, it will pay with further loss of status in the global community.

Religiously gilded groups such as ISIS, Al Qaeda, and the Taliban will remain disturbing and destructive elements, but they will not be able to stop the overall development to a more equal and participative world.

In the fight against radicalization and abuse of Islam, countries with a stable social/economic environment are rare in Northern Africa. But in the midst of this rather pessimistic outlook Tunisia despite all initial and continuous problems stands out.

A generation was growing up with little or no hope to live a good life they dreamed of. In Tunisia the situation finally escalated in the self-immolation of the fruit vendor Mohamed Bouazizi. Bouazizi set himself on fire in protest against confiscating his wares and being humiliated by municipal officials. It was the spark that ignited a larger fire. Starting in Tunisia it became a firestorm spreading quickly over northern Africa. It became known as Arab Spring, but as we know now, it will take a long time until the first sprouts will show.

All signs are pointing to Tunisia to be leading the way. It is a path into new territory toward peaceful coexistence of an ethnically diverse nation. And while the unification of liberal and fundamental groups in anger over the death of Bouazizi was a huge leap, the real battle for a modern Tunisia started after the victory over President Zine.

Tunisia builds on consensus instead of confrontation.

In the most remarkable achievement of the Arab Spring, Tunisia has made great progress toward a functional democracy. The foundation is a constitution uniting its population rather than (as in the other Arab nations) splitting it.

In January 2014, after two years of struggling for compromise between Islamists and secularists, Tunisia's new constitution was approved by 200 of the 216 deputies of the National Assembly. The new constitution is the most liberal in the Arab world, and supported by both the dominant Islamist party and the secular opposition. The document acknowledges that Islam is the religion of Tunisia, but also guarantees that Tunisia remains a civil state with separation of powers and ensures universal freedoms and rights, including special consideration for the young and parity for women in local political structures. The constitution also stipulates that future governments cannot amend it. The overwhelming support from both sides has proved Tunisia to be the most promising candidate for a transition into a democratic system.

In parliamentary elections held in October 2014 the secular Nidaa Tounes party led by 87-year-old Beji Caid Essebsi, won 85 of 215 seats, defeating Ennahda, the Islamic party. Nidaa Tounes will name a prime minister and lead a coalition government. The election of a new president was set for November 23, 2014. Tunisia's secularists and Islamists have managed the transition to democracy even though stormy times still lay ahead. It is a bright spot in the gloomy picture of Northern African countries.

Game Change in Political Systems Has to Arise Domestically

To try to impose Western democracy on countries with different cultures and histories is like speaking to someone in a language the person does not understand. While it is difficult enough to revitalize a country's economy, to bridge the gap between fundamentally religious and secularist groups in many countries has proven to be the highest hurdle in creating a government that is acceptable to all.

As said before, to most countries in Northern Africa and the Near East, Arab Spring brought no real change in political climate, but it has at least launched the search for new governing models. Education will be a key element in both achieving economic progress and opening up minds to take the responsibility in any form of democratic demands of its people. America's wars in Afghanistan and Iraq have demonstrated that even with the best intention (which can be questioned), it is neither possible nor desired to force Western democracy on countries with cultures and histories that have little in common with the culture and history of their self-appointed Western lecturers.

In the demand for democratic governing models evolutionary change is the path.

"The people still want a bigger say," was the headline in an article on Middle East and Africa in the *Economist* in its November 18, 2013, issue. Saudi Arabia and United Arab Emirates are no exception. There is a shift in relations between the leaders and the people. A demand for change is inspired by the Arab Spring. Arab Gulf monarchs are not likely to drop their claim of power, but it seems that there is a process of improving their performance to legitimize ruling their countries.

Meritocracy is a key word when it comes to governing without drawing legitimacy from being elected. The controlling function is not played by mostly government controlled media, but by social media. YouTube, Facebook, Twitter, and other networks provide vast uncontrolled space for exchange of opinions, judgments on political leaders, and developing ideas. Saudi Arabia, rather closed as a society, has one of the most active social media in the world. In Arab countries, just as in China, the misbehavior of leaders can no longer be brushed under the carpet, but is spread via Internet to the upset or amusement of all. Whether it is a government official in the Arab Emirates who was caught when he beat up the driver of a car, with which his car had collided, or a princeling in China causing an accident with his Ferrari, the omnipresence of cell phones reveals it all.

The Internet has opened the door to another world and young Arabs want to join it just as young Chinese and Brazilians do. When young people ask us how to bring change into their country our advice is to push as far as possible without crossing the red line to revolution. In most cases evolutionary change is the way to go.

The increasing global connectedness forces autocratic systems to allow stronger participation of the people.

The *National*, a government-owned newspaper of the United Arab Emirates, in its editorial on December 4, 2013 reported a once unthinkable act. Sheik Mohammed Bin Rashid, vice president and ruler of Dubai, prime minister of the UAE, and the father of modern architecture of Dubai, in preparing his country for post-oil era is building up Dubai as a tourist destination, finance, and industrial center. In his tweet on twitter, read by millions of followers, he called on: "every man, woman (!) and child to join us in the biggest ever national brainstorm session to find new ideas for health and education."

A meritocracy that allows greater transparency and holds political leaders accountable seems one way to go. Innovation is not limited to technological innovation and is being expanded to social and cultural innovation. The more it is performance that justifies rulership the more it is necessary to look for new approaches to stay competitive over market opponents. Improvements in education are the basic tools. To measure progress and failure governments in Dubai and the UAE have set up Key Performance Indicators (KPIs).

In Dubai the government set a goal for 2021. Every ministry has to meet KPI demands, whether it is education or improving the business environment, giving the annual reports to the public plus monthly reports to Sheik Mohammed bin Rashid. None of the 46 ministries and regulatory agencies wants to be at the bottom of the list.

While the UAE is ranked as one of the least corrupt countries in the Middle East, it will in the longer run have to build a bridge between old traditional top-down governing to more participation of the people.

Chronicle of an Experiment

It is possible to act with boldness. And of all countries it was the second poorest country in Central America, Honduras, which in 2011 was on course to surprise the world with an experiment. A city built from scratch, with its own government, own laws, courts, police and tax system, free of corruption, and organized crime. It would become a source for wealth and progress, a shining example, an inspiration for countries with economic potential but not capable of changing obsolete national governing structures.

Two men independently became the godfathers of the project—Octavio Sánchez, a member of Honduras's National Party, and Paul Romer, an American economist. Sanchez dreamed of education reform, a flourishing economy, and liberation of women. Honduras's problems, he believed, were not caused by too much capitalism, but by politicians who are not able to organize society in a way that enables people to create wealth.

Thousands of miles north of Honduras, in Colorado, Paul Romer was convinced most developing models have failed so far. The solution to him is Hong Kong, where British norms and institutions successfully created an environment for economic growth. So much that it later became one of the models for economic reforms in China under Deng Xiaoping. When in 2010 Romer presented his concept in a TED talk millions started to watch him online, one of them Octavio Sánchez. All Romer needed was a country willing to apply his idea. He found it in Honduras.

When you hit rock bottom you have reached solid ground.

The starting point was simple. It could not get much worse in Honduras. The murder rate was the highest in the world. Almost every second person lived on less than $1.25 a day. Only 250,000 of its 7.9 million inhabitants were paying taxes, and yet some trade was booming, 95 percent of drugs smuggled to the United

States were passing through Honduras. Octavio Sánchez and Paul Romer, each in his own way, had been dreaming the same dream, to bring wealth to a run-down country following the Hong Kong model. The same day Sanchez listened to Paul Romer's TED talk he got the permission to contact him. The beginning of a bold experiment based on a simple principle: take a piece of uninhabited land big enough for a city of several million, govern it by well-trained rules and let those who like the idea move there.

In December 2011 the *Economist* wrote: "Hong Kong in Honduras. An ambitious development project aims to pull a Central American country out of its economic misery. Can it work?" to starting over, unburdened by frozen structures and overseen by foreign experts running the city. Wealth created strategically in what Romer called a "charter city." Built from scratch, with its own government, own laws and own currency, autocratically governed until matured enough to hold elections. The project of "special development regions" passed a constitutional amendment and it approved "constitutional statute" allowing the creation of autonomous legal frameworks. On January 19, 2011, the Honduras parliament voted 124 Yes against one No to changing the constitution accordingly. On December 6, 2011, President Porfirio Lobo appointed the first members of the "transparent commission" whose duty was to oversee the new entity's integrity and make sure to keep it clean of corruption.

Step by step the project gained momentum. International media, the *New York Times,* the *Wall Street Journal,* and the *Economist,* reported an experiment never seen before. Romer became the hero. International attention grew, and frictions rose locally. Romer fought for a solitude piece of land northeast, far away from Honduras's crime scene and corruption. Sanchez wanted to build the city near Puerto Cortes, Honduras's most modern harbor, backed by the interest of the New York entrepreneur Michael Strong, who had been waiting for an opportunity to invest in Latin America. Within 10 years Strong planned to invest a billion dollars in the city. And he was well connected with US entrepreneurs who are interested in outsourcing their production. China is cheap but far away. Honduras is next door.

Honduras at that point was about to start the most radical experiment against poverty and underdevelopment ever.

Journalists wrote about Romer as the hero of the story. Hondurans saw it a little differently. At the brink of realization, as success can almost be smelled, it turned into a fight for prestige and egos. Romer called the project "Charter City," Sanchez prefers RED (Spanish initials of special development regions). Romer talked to the Canadian government as mandate power for the city. Canada's premier was supposed to appoint a governor for the city. Sanchez did not want to hand over sovereignty to a foreign nation. Within half a year collaboration between Romer and the Honduras's government turned sour. Economist Romer wanted to bend realty toward his concept. Sanchez, the politician, wanted to adapt Romer's concept to reality.

Criticism of the project rose in Honduras. The left called it pure neocolonialism making the rich richer. A group of lawyers called it unconstitutional and brought the case to the high court. The opposition, which had been supporting the project at first, made a U-turn and joined the protest groups. A breakthrough experiment turned into politics as usual. Honduras's high court in Tegucigalpa declared the project to be unconstitutional.

The death stroke to the original idea came with the announcement that Honduras signed a memorandum of understanding with Michael Strong. Romer, who was taken by surprise, pulled out of the project. Strong began with a small pilot infrastructure project. Octavio Sánchez wanted to hold on to the idea, "but we need to create the right conditions in the midst of political turbulences. The possibility of a foreign country ruling didn't fit, everything else did."

"It was a mistake to get Romer on board. We should have realized the project by ourselves. As we will do it now." With more control of the state, less independence for the city, and the guidance of a new commission of 21 experts, Sánchez still hopes his dream for Honduras, written in 1991 when he was 15 years old, will come true. There is still time. In his dream, the story ended in 2050, when a flourishing Honduras is host to the soccer world championship.

Whether Honduras in 2050 will be where Sanchez wishes it to be is uncertain (*Die Zeit*, "The Re-start," October 31, 2013; *The Economist*, "Hong Kong in Honduras," December 10, 2011; *The New York Times*, "Plan for Charter City to fight Honduras poverty loses its initiator," September 30, 2012).

Singapore: Economic Transition in One Generation

In a simple comparison we often say that the West is a lecturing society and Asia is a learning society. "What can we learn?" seems to be the question in any given situation. We were reminded that it was this principle that has helped Singapore and China to get out of economic disaster when we visited Suzhou's Industrial Park. Its museum shows the history and the early beginnings of a modern industrial township in 1992, when China learned from Singapore.

Learning and making necessary changes was certainly a guideline in the life of China's first teacher, Lee Kuan Yew, who went from a star pupil of colonial Singapore by way of elite higher education in Britain to be its leader. In the 1970s he had made up his mind that socialism did not make any sense and was even causing the decline of the British economy. "Lee took Western menu for a modern state—and tinkered with two parts Hobbes [1588–1679, English philosopher, founder of the theory of modern absolutism for the sovereign], one part Mills [1806–1873, British philosopher and one of the most influential liberal thinkers of his time], with a dash of Asian values," wrote John Micklethwait and Adrian Wooldridge in their book *The Fourth Revolution*.

It was not by chance that Deng Xiaoping's first foreign visit as leader early on in China's opening-up was to Singapore. And it was not by chance that Xi Jinping when anointed as China's next leader "wanted to jump in the queue to meet the senior who has our respect." And to "meet the man who according to Margaret Thatcher 'was never wrong': Lee Kuan Yew" (John Micklethwait and Adrian Wooldridge, *The Fourth Revolution*).

Singapore is an example that it is possible to turn around an economy harnessing the efficiency of autocracy and at the same time win high acceptance of the people. The formula: Smart long-term strategies, a meritocracy in results-driven politics. Singapore GDP per capita rose from $511 in 1965 to $51,709 in 2013 (World Bank).

Building on the Efficiency of Autocracy

Singapore, only 712 square km, started its rise under the authoritarian rule of the Lee Kuan Yew family clan, which turned swampy soil into a flourishing economy. When Lee Kuan Yew became prime minister of Singapore in 1959, he faced mass unemployment, a lack of housing, arable land, and absolutely no natural recourses. Within only one generation Singapore turned from a developing to a developed nation. Singapore's People's Action Party has won every election since 1959. In 2004, Lee Hsien Loong, Lee's his eldest son, became his successor.

Singapore today ranks number six of the countries with least corruption. In the 2012 PISA global education survey Singapore ranked number 2 on mathematics and literary skills, number 3 on reading literacy, and number 3 in science literacy skills. In computer-based mathematics and computer-based reading literacy skills, Singapore holds number 1 in the global ranking. In per capita income Singapore ranks between number 3 (IMF), number 4 (World Bank), number 6 (CIA), and it holds number 2 in the Global Competitive Index. With one out of six households, Singapore has the world's largest percentage of millionaires. It hosts more than 7,000 multinational corporations; its economy is ranked as one of the freest, most innovative most competitive and most business friendly. World Bank called it "A top paradise for business."

Singapore has beaten its former colonial master Great Britain living standards, quality of schools and hospitals. It expects high engagement and pays teachers and administration personnel very well, around $4,500 per month.

Even though acute poverty is rare in Singapore, it ranks number three in income inequality of developed countries following

China's Hong Kong and the United States. Nevertheless, unemployment of active people above 15 is only 2 percent.

Sitting at the Fullerton Hotel's outdoor restaurant a parade of nationalities can be watched strolling along the Singapore River. Singapore's ethnic picture is as colorful as its cuisine. Western Chinese and Confucianism, Malay, Islamic, and Indian culture have not led to social cultural frictions but to an intriguing, multinational, multicultural picture.

Even though Singapore does not match many criteria of Western democracy, we found citizens content with their government's performance. In our many visits to Singapore, and according to what Singaporean friends and expats tell us, there is little reason to protest. "Once in a while some might call for protest, but who would show up?"

According to Micklethwait and Wooldridge, Lee's model is "elitist and stingy, even bossy when it comes to state-directed capitalism, unashamedly elitist and even royalist, looking like Leviathan personified." But it "provides people with the opportunities that they need to rise and then leaves them to sort out their own welfare." The roadmap from dirt poor to filthy rich was drawn in Lee's chamber. As he is said to have once said: "We decide what is right, never mind what the people think." As long as Singaporeans do well, no one seems to mind.

Africa, Economically Getting Back on Its Feet, Politically Still in Its Early Development

The West is starving in front of a full plate we wrote a few pages earlier. This is, in a very different way, even truer for Africa. What a continent that could be! Lee Kuan Yew sent opponents to prison, ruled Singapore as an autocrat for almost 30 years, but how many African people would gladly pay that price for leaders with the determination and ability to turn African nations around.

Corruption, misgovernance, unemployment, and a strong gap between urban and rural areas put a hold on Africa's advancement in previous years. Infrastructure and education in many African countries was worse than at the end of colonial times when the first euphoria expected the fastest growth to be in Africa. Instead of Africa, Asia, led by Japan and South Korea, made the big leaps toward wealth, while Africa's GDP is still only three percent of global GDP. But now the global context has fundamentally changed. And that is Africa's chance.

To create sustainable growth, African countries need political reforms. There is still a lack of good governing. "Kleptrocrats" and autocratic governments are in charge, transparency and the rule of law is in short supply, corruption is spread in abundance. Zimbabwe, ruled by President Mugabe, created a world record of 60 million percent inflation in 2009, the miracle of 63 districts that have more voters than inhabitants. With an average life expectancy of 37 years for men and 34 for women, it can be proud of its 74,000 hundred-year-old voters. Before the catastrophic land revolution, which expropriated 4,000 white farmers, Zimbabwe once was the breadbaskets of Africa, now the country has to import corn.

That all sounds grim, but what once was a fertile and prosperous agriculture can be restored again. The Mugabe era in one way or another will end and there can be a new beginning. After all, at the end of the cold war, writes German magazine *Der Spiegel*, in December 2013, in a three-part essay on Africa, only 3 out of 53 African nations were half decent democracies. Today, it is 25 out of 54.

Dealing with Africa's problems is the first step to leveraging its potential.

Africa's current postcolonial borders are hardly a reflection of historically grown ethnic diversities, ethic divisions, or economic bundles. Much more are they the result of negotiations among former colonial powers, set at the end of the 19th century. Africa's maps, not much different from Latin American maps, are relics of its colonial past. Arbitrarily drawn nation states became the only organization models, their borders were often seen as one of the basic maladies of Africa. They separated extended tribal families, cut trade routes, and exacerbated exchange of food and other resources. Artificially created national borders around territories reversed the process of nation building. Searching for a common identity and national awareness and pride as a consequence of shared identity of ethnic descent, religion traditions, and languages are one of the main challenges of African countries.

People are bound together economically, but their desire to manifest their distinctiveness is growing. African nations are opening up to the world, and deal with the paradox that the more global they become the more local they want to act. The more tied to other ethnic groups and tribes, the more they insist on what makes them different. And that can manifest itself in violent ways. In the search for new governing models fitting African history, economic, cultural, and ethical hurdles are blocking the way. Many African countries still face the problem of creating a system providing political order, protection from physical violence, rule of law, basic social security, infrastructure, water, energy, and food supply.

Many African countries are still among the world's poorest nations with an average income lower than $1,036 per year. In Somalia, according to the UN, almost 3 million people need life-saving assistance. Philippe Lazzarini, UN aid chief for Somalia said "50,000 children are at the doorstep of death because of severe malnutrition." UN AIDS operation is asking for donations of $933 million to cover the most urgent help projects in 2014.

According to a Reuters Report international donors have cut down on their donations in Somalia due to urgent needs in Syria, South Sudan, and Central African Republic. There are still large insufficiencies in creating legitimate political and legal order and basic welfare systems services in many African countries. Judges and courts are often corrupt and there is a lack of equality in front of court. Vocational training of police forces is as bad as their wages, so many of them are taking part in criminal activities.

Nevertheless, in many African countries governing is undergoing a transition period.

No Honeymoon for India's New Prime Minister Narendra Modi

Some so-called democracies are serving the countries ruling class and international capital rather than its people. While this is the case in many African "Kleptocracies," it has also been the case in a different way in India. India is praised as the world's largest democracy and often awarded with a way too optimistic outlook. In 2007, a McKinsey report anticipated India's middle class as "the next big spenders" but by 2014 average incomes have not risen high enough to match the prognosis. Many Indians blame India's long-ruling socialist party and the Gandhi family.

But now change is in the air, at least rhetorically. On the ground the congress has already been criticizing Prime Minister Modi for not holding on to "his election rhetoric phrase." Congress members lampooned his blog and said the PM needed to come out of election rhetoric. India's leading business newspaper the *Economist Times*, quotes Modi's personal blog on June 27, 2014, when he wrote after one month in office: "Previous governments had the luxury of extending this honeymoon up to a hundred days and even beyond. I don't have such luxury. Forget hundred days, the series of allegations began in less than hundred hours."

Wall Street Journal (June 16, 2014) reports about Prime Minister Modi's first foreign visit in early June to Bhutan, building on inaugural outreach, when he had invited all regional leaders. And quotes P.D. Rai, a lawmaker in Sikkim, which shares the border with Bhutan. "Although India would like to have a greater say in South Asian matters beyond trade, so far we have not been able to exercise substantial political clout. In the longer term, Modi's government aims to make India the dominant foreign investor across South Asia as well as the main provider of infrastructure loans, the same way China has done in much of the rest of Asia and Africa."

At least India's business community is very optimistic about PM Modi's future achievements. According to a June 2014 *McKinsey* study, 96 percent of executives in India believe that their country's economy will improve in the next six months and 75 percent believe that conditions have improved already. However, in June

2009, after the last election won by Manmohan Singh and his Congress party 72 percent of the executives said the same.

Will It Be India or China? A Joke

India still has a long way to go. And the election of Premier Modi in the best case brings a U-turn just as Deng Xiaoping's did for China. Nonetheless, we still hear the question "will it be China or India?" While some commentators never took the question seriously, it has faded as China's dominance has clearly been established. India's layers of regulations and taxes will hold it down for years to come.

India's bureaucracy weighs heavily on its possible race to catch up with China; it could use its quite younger population to its advantage. While the average age in China is around 38 years, and will grow older in the next decades, India's average age is around 28 years. India's more than half a billion young people are an enormous potential if they find the support and environment to leverage it. But without better education there is no opening-up to the opportunities that the global economy offers. India needs a sharp U-turn in its position toward women and dalits, the untouchables.

A headline in *Gulfnews.com* February 25, 2014, reads: "India's disrupted democracy." While the author, Shashi Tharoor (India's former Minister of State for Human Resource Development) praises India's democracy as "an extraordinary instrument for transforming an ancient country into a 21st century success story," he also writes that the "temple of democracy, as Indians have long hailed their parliament, has been soiled by its own priests, and is now in desperate need of reform."

India's 15th Lok Sabha (the lower house of parliament) passed into history ignominiously on February 14. "India's parliament," *Gulfnews* writes, has had the "least productive five years in its six decades of functioning democracy with entire sessions lost to opposition disruptions and with frequent adjournments depriving legislators of time for deliberation. The MPs elected in May

2009 passed fewer bills and spent fewer hours in debate than any of their predecessors."

What are people to do but protest if people elected to run the country "shout slogans, wave placards, scream abuse, and provoke adjournments—indeed, do almost anything but what they were elected to do."

What about China *and* India?

"Just like the emerging tip of a buried treasure that awaits your discovery, or a huge volcano that is preparing itself for a billow eruption, much is to be expected from the cooperation between our two countries." Strong words spoken softly by China's foreign minister Wang Yi. Different from political rhetoric in many countries, China has proven announcements of economic strategies are not just talk.

During his visit to India in early June 2014, Chinese foreign minister Wang Yi called Sino–Indian relationship the "most dynamic bilateral relationship with the largest potential in the 21st century." It could be quite an economic storm sweeping over Asia if the two nations would accomplish what is obviously China's plan: cooperation instead of confrontation. Wait and see is the tactic in the border issue between the two countries, that could become a hurdle in harnessing the "vast potential yet to be tapped" as Wang put it in a written interview in the *Hindu* newspaper on June 8, 2014.

China Daily (June 9, 2014) quotes Saibal Dasgupta, veteran correspondent for the *Times of India:* "Modi makes quick decisions and is building a smooth connection between his new leadership and Beijing." According to media reports Prime Minister Modi is said to have earlier visited China four times to get inspiration for upgrading India's industry, which with 15 percent of India's economy is half of China's 31 percent. China's Premier Li had underscored the role of India in China's Asia strategy when visiting India in his first overseas tour and President Xi is expected to pay an official visit to India before this year is over. China–India bilateral trade has grown 20-fold since the 2000 but "given our 2.5 billion populations, such cooperation is still far from the scale and level that it needs to be," said Wang. The volcano is rumbling.

Russia: Dancing on the Sidelines

"Russia goes from fake democracy to faux dictatorship" was the headline in *Bloomberg View* by Leonid Bershidsky, Moscow and Kiev correspondent. Vladimir Putin, Russia's former and current president, has signed restrictive regulations on freedom of assembly and free speech. He has limited the field of nongovernmental organizations and cut down on the rights of gays and foreign adoptions. But, writes Bershidsky, "so far no one is bothering to enforce most of the rules."

Leadership of a Different Kind

Russia certainly has become unpredictable. After the fall of the Soviet Union, Russia and Europe founded a new partnership with a degree of reliability. Uncertainty and volatility do not go with partnerships. NATO deputy chief Alexander Vershbow in October 2014 in remarks to a group of journalists: "Clearly, the Russians have declared NATO as an adversary, so we have to begin to view Russia no longer as a partner but more of an adversary than a partner." recently called Russia an enemy rather than a partner (*cbsnews.com*, April 24, 2014).

Huge amounts of money were invested in 2009 by the then President Medvedev to bring international experts to Yaroslavl, a 1,000-year-old city about 160 km east of Moscow. Medvedev's *Global Policy Forum* showed similarities to Putin's Valdai International Discussion Club, which was launched in 2004 at Lake Valdai, north of Moscow. The goal was to change perception of Russia by soft power. Despite all criticisms of Moscow's intelligentsia that most participants "were useful idiots who have the wool pulled over their eyes and go home parroting the propaganda that was served up to them with lobster terrine and fine wine," as one participant put it, it said a lot about Russia's political reality.

At one of the three *Global Policy Forums* we attended in Yaroslavl, the theme of a discussion with the then Russian President Medvedev was whether democratization or economic growth is essential to a country's development. Can poverty and democracy go hand in hand? Is a certain degree of wealth the precondition for establishing sustainable democratic systems? Russia is lacking both real economic progress and political reforms.

Powerhouse or Cipher?

To some countries, natural resources are as much a curse as a blessing. It shields the need for economic reform and growth supported by good governing. A gas deal, which in the context of the global economy Steve Forbes in an editorial calls "not worth a footnote," will have little influence on solving Russia's basic problems.

Steve Forbes is convinced that Russia, "despite its immense resources and highly educated population, which includes a considerable number of capable scientists and mathematicians, has a shockingly small economy that is amazingly depending on the export of oil, gas, and a few other natural resources. In our high-tech era Russia should be a powerhouse instead of a cipher" (*Forbes Asia*, June 2014).

President Putin certainly has a different view. He admits Russia, now the eighth largest economy of the world (World Bank), has a lot to do before "reaching the top." In an interview with French *FT1* TV and Radio *Europe 1* on June 4, 2014, Putin was asked how he would like to be remembered: "I would like to be remembered as a person who did his best for the happiness and prosperity of his country and his people."

"A lot to do" before trust and hope is built among Russia's youth

---

In spring 2010 we attended a meeting in the run-up for Skolkovo Innovation Center, a technology business area to be built near Moscow as a platform for innovation in science and technology. After the official part we had the opportunity to discuss the plan with students who should be the beneficiaries of support given to start-ups and young entrepreneurs. None of the students trusted the project. At the end, the tenor of their opinions was that it will not be them who receive support but political favorites. Our most significant observation was the lack of trust and hope among Russia's youth.

In the meantime Russia flexes its muscles. From most countries' view, it occupied and annexed Crimea and fear rose that the whole of Ukraine would be next. Many Russians applaud Putin's goal to gain back global power. Russia has a special position. It shares a long boarder and an ideological past with China. But also has a foot in Europe, to which it is the third biggest trading partner. Russia's democratization process had a short life. One can call Putin a postmodern czar, an autocrat or the strong man Russia needs.

Our colleague, Stephen Rhinesmith, who was also a former special US Ambassador to Russia, believes that: "Putin's main concern is re-establishing Russia as a geopolitical global player." He cannot do it economically except through threatening to withhold its gas and oil. But this is not an economic policy: it is using economics for political purposes. The long-term gas deal that Putin finalized with Xi Jinping can be seen as use of Russia's natural resources not only as a stick, but also as a carrot. In both cases Putin's concern is not the economic development of Russia but the use of Russia's resources for global influence. After the Crimea annexation President Obama said in a press conference that Russia was "just a regional, not a global player. In some ways, this is the greatest insult one can hurl at Putin, because it goes to the very core of his desired legacy to be the leader who brought Russia back to the geopolitical influence it had as the Soviet Union."

To Europe Putin's invasion of Crimea was as a wake-up call on the attempt to reestablish Russia's position as a global power. It is somewhat ironic that in Crimea people died for the dream of an independent European Ukraine while in Europe Europe-skepticism is rising. The treaty to establish the Eurasian Economic Union among Russia, Belarus, Kazakhstan, and Armenia (and possibly Kyrgyzstan) as a single economic market of 171 million people and a GDP of around $3 billion is supposed to come into force on January first 2015. Its goal, to become a powerful bloc with high influence on the global stage, fits right into Putin's imperial plans.

In our opinion, feeling put down by the Europeans, Russia is turning toward the Global Southern Belt, living door to door with its main player, China, this should not come as a surprise. More sanctions from the side of the EU and the United States, whether justified or not, will only speed up the process. Tsar Vladimir IV certainly offers what the vast majority of the Russian population wants: an iron hand, a strong backbone, and the vision of a revitalized Russian Empire.

Game Changers and Enablers: The Two Big "E's"

In the introduction we wrote, "throughout human history our perception of the world has been greatly influenced by time, location and environment." We have to add education. Education is one of the lenses through which we look at the world and our life in it. The ways millions of uneducated people in poor countries judge their chances in life differ greatly from those lucky enough to have had a good education. Educated people are most likely to spot the opportunities globalization offers to the country where they live. And they are less susceptible to being recruited by religious fundamentalist or guerilla groups.

"Words define the borders of our world."

—*Ludwig Wittgenstein, Austrian/British philosopher*

How true this is. A recent EU study on literacy says that every fourth child in Europe has significant deficits in reading ability.

Understanding what is read is so marginal that it is not enough to pass professional training. Androulla Vassiliou, EU commissioner for education, said: "We are in a paradox situation. In our digitalized world, reading and writing is more important and more relevant than ever but our reading and writing ability does not hold up with this development. We urgently need to work against that. Investments to improve reading and writing competence are economically meaningful at any age—they create practical advantages for the individual and for the society which in the longer run add up to billions.

> It is not by coincidence that we are still holding on to the wisdom of ancient Greek philosophers. Education in a gymnasium (training facility educating for competing in public games, socializing and intellectual goals) was a premise for participation in the Greek culture. Rhetoric was part of a formal teaching. Aristotle called it "the art of finding the available means of persuasion."

One of the most famous women in history, Egyptian queen Cleopatra VII, is commonly praised for her beauty. Stacy Schiff's biography *Cleopatra: A Life* corrected that picture. "Cleopatra," she writes, was "a shrewd strategist and ingenious negotiator who shaped the contours of the ancient world." Hardly any of the Romans who preserved her story raved about her beauty. The most remarkable thing about her was not outstanding beauty, but her outstanding eloquence. Egypt's education was based on Greek philosophy, and eloquent speaking was a skill with very high value also in the Egyptian society. Cleopatra's education began with vocabulary lists of the Greek language, poetry, and stories. She could write verses, and was familiar with the tangled genealogies of the gods; she would know the stories backwards and forward. Learning was a serious business, involving endless drills, infinite rules, and long hours. To develop artful speaking took much effort, continuous studies and various exercises. Only experience and wisdom would lead to an unfailing strategic sense. When Cleopatra graduated from the studies of rhetoric and public speaking at 13 or 14 in Alexandria, she truly knew how to talk.

An approach familiar in China in the centuries between 700 and 200 BC the "Hundred Schools of Thought" also led to significant intellectual and cultural developments. During this era major philosophies such as Confucianism, Legalism, and Taoism, arose. The most famous Chinese philosopher Confucius emphasized the use of eloquence in speaking.

Education was of high concern in the Reformation movement in the 16th century. Martin Luther's theses were his most distinguished act, but Martin Luther was as much a strong advocate of establishing compulsory schooling, unheard of at the time. He believed, access to education should enable every parishioner to be able to read the Bible.

The reformation was tightly connected with humanism and its education reform. It was Johann I, ruling the German dukedom Pfalz-Zweibrücken, who after converting to Calvinism, established mandatory education for girls and boys in 1592 in his territory. It was the first mandatory education in the world. In the United States compulsory school attendance was first established in the state of Massachusetts in 1852.

The purpose of education is to learn how to learn.

In China, Shi Shi high school in Chengdu was the first public secondary school in the world, created 2,150 years ago by Wen Weng, the magistrate of Shu, during the Han Dynasty. Shi Shi has been operating uninterrupted ever since. Today, it is a modern complex and is one of China's experimental schools in education reform. Two years ago we joined a class at Shi Shi where the subject and English were simultaneously being taught: climate change with lecture and Q and A in English.

In one of our trips to Hamburg, where our daughter Nora lives, we got to know Stephan Sachse. In the midst of writing this book, very soon we were in a discussion about education systems, and the role digital education will play in the future. It was interesting to learn that Stephan is dealing with the very matter as the CEO of Datenlotsen, a company that provides innovative technology solutions to the higher education sector.

Our question was how to use digitalization as a tool to improve education, especially when it comes to higher education. How much digitalization has infiltrated all spheres of life from a very early age we of course realize when our grandchildren can hardly believe that we grew up in a world without smartphones, ipads, and laptops. Many executives, teachers, and administrative personnel have not been prepared and educated to successfully implement digitalization into schools and universities. That, we learned is where Stephan jumps in as a provider for digital education solutions for business education and corporate universities.

Stephan Sachse:

Digitalization of education is only in its infancy, but it is of enormous impact. It reaches a generation that has grown up with mobile devices, social media and digital content and adapts, they conceptualise and share extremely quickly. That supports disruptive business models in education that displace existing technologies, products or services.

Only six years after the start of iTunes U the platform recorded 575 million active users and 315 million mobile devices that actively use the learning material on offer (lectures as an audio or video file, scripts, etc.). "No back row" is the approach of Start-Up 2U.com, a US company founded in 2008. Their goal is no smaller than to design the best online course programs. Online students will no longer be separated from their fellow students, but actively integrated in on-the-job training and local classroom-based learning. The average class size is 10.4 students and there are 97,000 instructor-led live class sessions on offer. In October 2014 stock market value of 2U.com had reached $720 million.

Of course, such companies are a challenge to traditional structures in education. In Europe, education markets are not commercialized. The concept of a competitive educational environment does not exist and often faces heavy resistance from governments and educational organizations. In France the system for universities to supply themselves with IT systems was liberalized only recently. By contrast, to be able to supply themselves with software universities in Germany formed a cooperative in 2014. The failed introduction of a central nationwide standardized university authorization system illustrates by way of example the efficiency of such structures. The country of poets and thinkers is running the risk of losing its international connection.

Life-long Learning

Investments to improve reading and writing competence are economically meaningful. They create practical advantages for the individual and the society. Mandatory education does not automatically translate into a better life or economic growth. Nevertheless, many countries are announcing proudly to have added a year or two to mandatory education. But quantity does not raise quality. OECD's Programme for International Student Assessment (PISA), which is evaluating education systems worldwide, proves that every year. In a study on *Education and Economic Growth* Eric A. Hanushek, Stanford University and L. Woessmann, University of Munich, observe that "what people know matters, but policy today simplifies and distorts this message. It recognizes that education matters, but focuses most attention on ensuring that everybody is in school, regardless of the learning that goes on." They come to the shocking conclusion: "By reasonable calculations, many countries have fewer than 10 percent of youth currently reaching minimum literacy and numeracy levels, even when school attainment data look considerably better."

In any governing model, education has to be the number one economic priority.

Reform of education has become a must in almost every government program on the globe. In the 21st century competitiveness of human resources will play the decisive role. Despite wide consensus about this not much has happened. As with any reform, to create something new something the old has to go. Governments are defending their monopoly-like position on education resulting in higher costs and lower quality.

A ranking of South Sahara countries showed clearly that the more a country spends on health, education, and agriculture, the better equipped it is to reach the UN millennium goal to reduce the number of people living in extreme poverty in half by 2015. In the past decades mandatory education in African countries has been extended. But education of teachers is poor and curriculums far from up-to-date. In many countries classes have to take place in open air. There are too few teachers and therefore many pupils are squeezed into one class. Many developing countries are struggling with the same problem. To move upward economically they need a well-trained workforce. But especially in rural areas this is a huge challenge.

It was one of China's problems when it started its "Go West" strategy, and it found a good solution.

If you cannot get to a good school, a good school will get to you.

This motto could be written over Chengdu's comprehensive efforts to bring equal education to urban and rural areas. The program's goal is to establish a network of distant learning and urban–rural sister schools. Shi Shi Middle School and Baima Middle School are examples of such a sharing of the high-quality education resources in urban and rural areas.

On one of our research trips to rural areas in Chengdu we visited Huaikou. It was hard to imagine that this modern town we drove through had been a dirt poor village only a few years before. Factories had settled in the area bringing jobs to people who up to then could only live hand to mouth working in their small plots of land. For the next generation of this town life will be different. All the children attend school in a brand new building, several buildings, to be precise.

When we visited we were welcome by scores of boys and girls standing on the balconies, yelling hello and how are you, waving as if we were rock singers. It was a heartwarming reception we will never forget. But it was not only the excitement and obvious upbeat mood of the students that impressed us. Even with all the investment going to rural areas, financial resources are limited. To offer those students the best education possible, teachers from the best high schools in urban Chengdu teach certain curriculums via video. We attended such a class.

The image on a huge screen suggested that the distant teacher was right in the room. Communication was direct and easy. The students were very serious; it seemed they were very much aware that only one generation ago such an opportunity would have been unthinkable. Later on, two girls came up to us and asked for an interview in their student newspaper. Their English was fluent. This was even more impressive when we learned that quite a number of the parents of the students have very modest, if at all, reading and writing skills. But no matter how poor the parents might still be, the town's education supporting program aims to guarantee that no student in Chengdu would have to drop out of school because of family financial difficulties.

Education and training will be one of the major business sectors of the 21st century, and the new sector of competitiveness among nations.

A comprehensive reform of education holds enormous economic opportunities. *Forbes* has predicted that disruptive education technology will be "the next $1 trillion opportunity." Early pioneers such as Massachusetts Institute of Technology (MIT) have been putting courses online for more than a decade. Its free open coursework has accumulated 100 million students, now increasing by a million a month.

It is a paradox that unemployment in Europe continues to rise (22 straight months of increasing unemployment) while jobs for trained technicians and managers in new high-tech industries are beyond present availability to fill them. In Germany alone, more than 50,000 engineers and natural scientists are needed to fill this gap. On one hand there is a lack of German students, on the other hand the hurdles to study in Germany are rather high and many foreign studies are not recognized. It does not fit to the picture that Germany is bidding for foreign students as low-birth age groups are kicking in.

Almost 24,000 Chinese have chosen one of Germany's universities; not least because of the very good reputation German engineering has in China. Still only around 8 percent of the Germany's 300,000 foreign students (including people living in Germany but have no citizenship) are Chinese. The goal is to increase this number to 350,000.

The United States still is the most attractive country with the highest number of foreign students, where more than 250,000 Chinese students are holding student visas. In the years 2012 and 2013, 819,644 foreign students, undergraduate and graduate, enrolled to US colleges and universities. (*US World Report Education*, November 11, 2013). The highest ever number in history with relatively few supported by US scholarships and 49 percent coming from China, India, and Korea. China hosts the most students from Korea, almost 65,000, followed by 18,500 students from the United States and 15,000 Japanese students. Almost 500,000 students from 200 nations chose a British university or college for their studies. In addition, 600,000 come to do an English language course (*British Council*, October 2014).

"If we consider," said Stephan Sachse in our conversation, "that in 2013, 2.7 billion people had access to the Internet and that the Internet keeps growing by 16.1 percent on average each year we get an idea about the advancements in access to knowledge. In addition mobile devices are becoming cheaper. China alone produces more than 10 different smart phones at less than $100.00 and prices keep falling."

We were not too astonished when Stephan told us that according to the GSV Education Report 68 percent of US college students believe they can study more efficiently with a smartphone or tablet device and in 2013, 38 percent of all US college students owned a tablet computer. But we had not been aware of the announcement of Mehmet Zafer Çağlayan, the Turkish Minister of Industry who after a visit to Apple in Silicon Valley in summer of 2011 announced that Turkey would purchase a total of 15 million tablet computers for $15 million to support education in the coming years. Çağlayan's goal was that each Turkish student would own a tablet by 2015.

Despite all talk about the urgency to reform of education the reality is that in many cases education is not holding up with the demands in professional life. Consequently, this opens business opportunities, and Datenlotsen is one of companies that harnessing them. In 2012, 3,000 companies in Europe and start-up directory Crunchbase recorded 2,300 start-ups in the education field, mostly in the United States disruptive business models made possible by easy availability of information any time anywhere reaching a larger and larger numbers of teachers and pupils.

Kroton Educational, Brazil, has the largest education company in the world. With a net income of $98.5 million (2012) it is also highly profitable. It was founded in 1966 in Belo Horizonte and offers education from preschool to postgraduate education. Koron has around 520,000 students and 15,000 employees.

Personalized education or education is one size fits all?

Today, digitalization makes it possible: merchandise not only sells to the masses and for a low price, but is also personalized. Comparable to iTunes, where people do not have to buy a CD with all songs of a certain singer, you can choose and create your own music list. And just as digitalization revolutionized the music industry, it will revolutionize education. A system existing in the same way for centuries is about to transform.

The forerunners are MOOCs, Massive Open Online Courses, education videos, which deliver knowledge around the globe in short sequences. Instead of a few hundred students in an auditorium, hundreds of thousands can follow Internet seminars. The Californian MOOC platform is used by 5 million people. That is twice the number of all students studying in Germany. Vocational college Potsdam attracts 75,000 online students.

It is a fascinating idea to be able to study with the most engaging professors for free. Stanford professor Sebastian Thrun in 2011 put his lecture about artificial intelligence online and got

160,000 followers. His own students were obliged to subscribe to his course. The surprise was that of 600 best graduates of the course none were Stanford students. Many of them came from emerging nations and would otherwise not have had access to academic education as there are too few college places in their country and they could not afford studying abroad (*Die Zeit*, November 21, 2013).

MOOCs are only the beginning and not yet the real transition. Still all are learning the same way even though all have different starting points and goals. The future is not massive, but personalized education, POOCs instead of MOOCs.

Ideally, the professor creates a program for each student. Detached from any standard textbook he can recommend fitting material. The student is under constant surveillance, the teacher recognizes boredom as much as excessive demand. In a seminar for 150 this is not possible. Digital education can create what otherwise is only doable in small groups. Intelligent software adapts to speed and ability of the single student, and guides to relevant content.

US start-up *Knewton* recognizes various learning levels and adapts the program accordingly. All get to their goal, albeit at a different speed, but without overburdening or boredom. In New York's school *New Classroom* a computer calculates each night the student's material for the next day. Pedagogues have time to care about the student. An MIT Lab in Boston, USA, offers help when students get stuck. A program detects if a student is losing attention and concentration via a camera installed in the laptop or smartphone of the student and it reacts accordingly. A pilot project in Berkeley managed within one week to predict the grade of the students' graduation work by analyzing their e-mails.

Global competition for talent points to a global concept of foreign studies and student exchange.

A preview of how global competition for talent will play out can be seen in European football. Premier teams choose the best players in the world, independent of their nationality. In the competition among teams talent is the transcending consideration. However, in the World Cup Championship, a competition between national teams, it reverts back to nationality and players play only for their own country.

In sports there are no basic rules for accepting a player in certain clubs. Outstanding talent does not always follow norms. In the competition to get the best students innovative thinking should go further than installing testing centers in a country's foreign embassy. Opening up educational institutions to foreign students is not only culturally desirable but also economically beneficial.

Closing the Gap Between What Is Taught and What Is Needed

Given Datenlotsen's experience in dealing with more than a hundred universities and educational institutions in designing and delivering digital support we asked CEO Stephan Sachse for his opinion on the widening gap between what is taught in universities and what is needed in the corporate world.

This is his take:

> The path of a student into industry is certainly no longer unidirectional. Given the increasing shortage of qualified specialists industries are starting to apply new methods for acquiring qualified personnel. The tool is Digital networking. It enables companies to actively support students from the time they enrol and it gives access to advice on what to specialise in early on.

Harnessing Synergies: Dual Education

The first companies have already started to design their own curriculum which enables them qualify junior staff selectively. In addition, certain universities are paid to conduct master's degree courses on behalf of companies in line with designed study program. The university becomes the content provider.

An example is the Dual University Baden-Württemberg, founded in 2009. With 34,000 students it has become one of the biggest universities in Germany. Currently, more than 10,000 partner companies send their staff to the university to receive dual university education. The practical relevance of the various courses and the continuous exchange between the university and the partner companies ensures graduates find work quickly. The system of a university covering several locations was designed based on the US university system.

Students are able to make the best use of networking opportunities and find new ways of financing study and explore new ways for career planning. The visibility of qualifications will improve and become much broader, not only in social networks. A database of qualifications and certification will be available to a selected group of interested parties.

Learning is a social process. Online universities connect students: American with Chinese, Brazilians with Koreans, work via Skype and other social chats that can help each other 24 hours a day. Around the global someone is always online and able to answer questions. This is a service no college professor can offer. Peer grading, an evaluation by fellow students, shows a surprising equivalence to the evaluation of professors and supports active engagement. Colleges have to develop strategies for the digitalization of education. Politics has to create data protection and adapt legal conditions for high schools. The place to invest is not in mass education, but personalized education.

CHAPTER 5

Cities

The Global Game Makers

Two hundred years ago, only 2 percent of the world's population lived in cities. By the end of World War I the percentage had risen to 16 percent. Today, more than half of the world's population lives in cities. In the coming two decades, the world's urban population will rise to about 70 percent. Historically, cities have been the centers of power and the drivers of change. Fasten your seatbelts.

Cities, as everything in nature, are either growing or dying. The declining process might be a very slow one, as with the old city of Leipzig, once one of Europe's centers of education and Germany's publishing industry. The University of Leipzig was founded in 1409. The weakening process might be as fast as in Detroit, once the center of America's automobile industry, hitting rock bottom with the bankruptcy of General Motors followed by the financial bankruptcy of the city in 2013.

Even a short look back in history shows the importance of cities in economic, political, intellectual, and social development: Athens, Rome, Alexandria, Luoyang, Peshawar, Pergamum, Kaifeng, Angkor, Bagdad, Peking, Paris, Hangzhou, London, Venice, New York, Vienna, Tokyo, Bombay, Istanbul, Shanghai, just to name some of them.

City–states stood at the beginning of civilization: first in Mesopotamia, followed by Phoenicia and Greece. Rome transformed from a city–state to a global empire. High cultures such as Mayas and Aztecs in South America organized their cultures in city–states. In the dark ages Florence, Venice, Pisa, and Genoa were important sea-republics.

Cities are the incubators of culture, politics, economics, innovation and even decline.

From the storming of the Bastille at the beginning of the French revolution to protests at the Lincoln memorial in Washington DC when Martin Luther King gave his famous "I have a Dream" speech. Central locations in metropolises have been utilized for political purposes of governments as well citizens protesting about economic or political grievances.

In the year 1989 protests did not only upset China at Tiananmen Square; demonstrations in Augustus Square in Leipzig, in Alexander Square, in Berlin, and Wencenslas Square in Prague in the same year were milestones in changing Europe's geopolitical landscape.

More than 1,000,000 people protested on Teheran's Azadi Square against Ahmadinejad in 2009. Half a million demonstrated at the Tahrir Plaza in Cairo in 2011, which led to the fall of Egypt's President Mubarak. More than 200,000 demonstrated in Kiev's Maidan Nezalezhnosti, the central square of Kiev in 2013, after Ukraine's government turned down an association agreement with the EU. Compared with these figures, Occupy Wall Street protests with 2,000 Americans protesting against the dominance of the financial world in Zucotti Park in New York City in 2011 seems quite a small crowd.

Cities: Game Makers in the Most Dramatic Population Shift in History

The world's economic, social, cultural, and political processes are increasingly being played out within and between the world's cities. According to the UN, by 2050 the world population will increase to 9.1 billion; of which 6.3 billion will live in cities. Cities will absorb all global population growth.

"By 2050, urban dwellers will likely account for 86 percent of the world's population in the more developed regions and 64 percent in the less developed regions with a global urban population of 67 percent." (UN World Urbanization prospects, 2011 Revision) "Population growth is therefore becoming largely an urban phenomenon concentrated in the developing world," (UN Water Developing Report, 2012). Chinese cities will have 7 million more children in 2025 than they have today while in all of China the number of children is declining (McKinsey).

Urbanization is expected to continue in the developed and underdeveloped regions. Asia's urban population is estimated to rise by 1.4 billion, Latin America and the Caribbean by 200 million, and Africa by 900 million. According to the World Bank, urbanization has reached 51 percent globally (2011); the average rate of urbanization is 1.97 percent (2010–2015). African countries such as Mali, Malawi, and Niger hit an average urbanization of almost 5 percent with Burkina Faso passing 6 percent.

The competition in the great global opening-up will not take place among the countries of the world, but among the cities of the world. Enterprises looking for new consumer markets, the best growth opportunities, best infrastructure, qualified workforce, and service-oriented local governments will find them in cities. As blue-collar work is increasingly disappearing in ever more divisions of production, cities of the future are not competing with low wages but with high-tech centers creating a nourishing environment for innovation to support industries in the run-up to the next growth revolution.

Cities will generate 80 percent of the global GDP.

"Urban world: Mapping the economic power of cities" is a study in which McKinsey identifies 600 cities that today generate 60 percent of the global GDP. Generally speaking, cities generate 80 percent of the global GDP. According to this study, by 2025 the top 600 cities "will still account for 60 percent of the GDP, but the cities will not be the same. In 2025 emerging economies will have 435 million households with an annual income of more than $20,000 at purchasing power, which is 10 percent higher than in similar cities in developed markets." The geographical location of the cities will reflect the shifts in economic importance in the global economy.

As growth rates will be much higher in the emerging economies of the Global Southern Belt than in saturated markets, cities with high economic growth are most likely to increase revenues. The mix in population and the growing middles class will add significantly to the chance to outperform competition. It is no big surprise that a large number of the top 600 cities, as McKinsey estimates, will be located in China. Already today, cities such as Chengdu, Chongqing, Hangzhou, Tianjin, Harbin, Suzhou, Shenzhen, Guangzhou, and Wuhan to name a few, surprise visitors with a rapidly changing face and enormous drive. And still many of those cities are hardly known in the West.

China is currently undergoing the largest scale urbanization in history. At least 100 million rural inhabitants will become urbanites by 2020. Thirty years ago only 20 percent of China's population lived in cities. Today it is 57 percent. Chinese cities will grow most among global metropolises in the next 16 years, according to Oxford Economics. By 2030, nine Chinese cities will join the world's biggest municipal economies, while eight in Europe will drop off. In 2013 Shanghai's GDP grew 7.7 percent to $353.9 billion (*China Daily*, January 27, 2014). Shenzhen's GDP increased 10.5 percent to $237 billion during the same period with a foreign trade volume of $537 billion (*deltabridges. com*, February 12, 2014).

The leader in urbanization in the Global Southern Belt is Latin America.

Learning from each other was the goal at a forum on urbanization cooperation between China and Latin America during the

July 2014 BRICS Summit in Lima. With around 80 percent of its population living in urban areas, Latin America needs to make cities sustainable and keep a balance between economic development and environmental considerations.

The 2011 McKinsey study "Building globally competitive cities" calls Latin American cities "The key to Latin American growth." The large 198 (population 200,000 or more) Latin American cities host 260 million people and are estimated to generate 65 percent of Latin America's growth. Their GDP per capital will rise to $23,000 and the population will grow to 315 million by 2025. In this process, Latin America's relatively young population will need adequate jobs to create the wealth for future investment and sustainable growth. To implement necessary reforms and create a nourishing environment for entrepreneurs will be a huge challenge for Latin America governments. Cities will play the deceive role in the process.

In the top 25 ranking of the McKinsey list 16 cities are Chinese, 4 are other Asian, 2 are American and 2 are European. America's urban landscape, once far ahead on practically every measure, is represented by only one city, New York. Nevertheless, also in the United States, urban centers are the engines of development and growth. Edward Glaeser, professor at Harvard and author of *Triumph of the City*, tells us that about 18 percent of America's output comes from its three largest metropolitan areas. In comparison, Greater London is more than 50 percent more productive than the rest of the United Kingdom. Glaeser talks about the economics of "agglomeration," the reason why people and businesses become more innovative and productive in dense areas where proximity allows for the free flow of goods, services and ideas that power collaboration.

Glaeser says "our cities are productive because they magnify humankind's greatest asset: our ability to learn from people around us."

In the United States 80 percent of the people live in cities, in Europe it is 60 percent. The average income in US cities is almost 35 percent higher than the income in rural areas and small cities. In Europe the decline from urban to rural is 30 percent. McKinsey

(June 2014) estimates New York to remain the second largest city by GDP behind Tokyo by 2025.

Oxford Economics estimates that "by 2030, nine Chinese cities will join the world's 50 biggest municipal economies, while eight in Europe will drop off the list. Of the 10 forecast to grow the most by GDP seven are in China, including Tianjin, Beijing, Guangzhou, Shenzhen and Suzhou." We would encourage having an eye on cities less known in the West, despite their importance in China. Cities are Chengdu, Wuhan, and Hangzhou, to name some. News about the tallest building in the world Wuhan wants to finish in 2018 will quickly bring it into the limelight of international press. With a height of exactly one km Wuhan's Phoenix Towers are planned to be not only the tallest building, but also set new ecological standards.

India Is among the Slowest in Urbanization

India shows a very low urbanization, which underscores the huge gap in development rural India has even among emerging economies. Nevertheless, McKinsey estimates that by 2030 590 million Indians will live in cities, but to achieve that "700 to 900 million square meters of commercial and residential space needs to be built—or a new Chicago every year." In addition, 2.5 billion square meters of road "are waiting to be paved." A lot of work for new Prime Minister Modi whose party will have to create the conditions under which that can happen (McKinsey Global Institute Analysis, UN Populations Division). Moody's look into India's future is not too optimistic. It estimates that: "the Indian economy is unlikely to return to previous growth rates of around 7–8 percent in the near future even if the new government pursues a strong reform agenda due to the depth of the issues to be addressed." Modi's challenge in fighting bureaucracy, corruption, cast system, lack of education, and infrastructure cannot be overestimated.

Janaagraha, an India nongovernmental organization (NGO), published a survey in June 2014, which concludes: "Indian cities do not have the money or expertise to deal with the rapid urbanization sweeping the country" (although compared with other emerging economies it is not all that sweeping). In the survey, it came as a surprise that Calcutta, often judged as crumbling, ranked number one and Chandigarh, considered one of India's best-planned cities, ranked at the bottom," based on four parameters: urban capacities and resources, urban planning and design, transparency, accountability and participation, plus empowered and legitimate political representation (McKinsey Global Institute Analysis, UN Populations Division, *Wall Street Journal*, June 6, 2014).

In its October 2014 report on "Understanding India's economic geography" McKinsey advises companies "to consider a granular pan-India play" targeting metropolitan clusters. They expect 49 clusters "to account for about 77 percent of India's incremental GDP, 72 percent of its consuming households, and 73 percent of its income pool from 2012 to 2025."

Charles Correa, India's greatest architect, in interview with the *Financial Times* architecture critic Edwin Heathcote, said: "Despite their problems, people are in the cities because once you've experienced that density of life, you can't move back to the country." Actually, he said, "most of us live in very ugly cities yet are happy. A hundred years ago Gandhi said the villages were important and he was right. But today it is the cities, which have become places of hope where people are much freer. The cities are India's greatest wealth. Cities aren't the problem, they are the solution."

Mayors: National Game Makers?

The economic shift from the world as a collection of nations to a world as a collection of cities is well under way. In this context, the words of former New York mayor Michael Blumberg are gaining weight: "I have my own army in the NYPD (New York Police Department), my own State Department, much to Foggy Bottom's (Washington) annoyance. New York has every kind of people of every part of the world and every kind of problem." When asked if Washington does not like it, he said: "Well, I don't listen to Washington very much." The difference to Bloomberg between "my level of government and other levels of government is that action takes place at city level."

"By expanding and diversifying the networks through which cities are already cooperating, cities are proving they can do things together that states cannot," writes Benjamin Barber in his book *If Mayors Ruled the World: Dysfunctional Nations, Rising Cities.*

National governments have often become too cumbersome to be active players on the contemporary competitive global arena. Governments with long decision-making processes are not very well equipped for what is needed: international collaboration. City leaders, in general, have proved to be more pragmatic and less ideological. International city networks are being formed to deal with some of the global problems that are basically unattended by international organizations.

As said before, cities have become great staging areas for protests for change. "At their core, all are great urban dramas, with the city and its spaces as chief protagonist. This unrest should be seen as a wake-up call to all of us: politics is this, the first truly urban century, will largely take place in cities and will largely be about them," says John Rossant, chairman of the New Cities Foundation.

A New Job Specification: Managing Social Economics

Benjamin Barber argues that our best hope of meeting the challenges of the 21st century, global pandemics, crime and terrorism lies in a global system of networked cities, a "global parliament of mayors." (A parliament of mayors sounds fanciful, but do expect many more associations and alliances of cities.) When it comes to fixing the American economy, Bruce Katz and Jennifer Bradley in their book *The Metropolitan Revolution*, put their hope on cities and argue that American cities and metropolis are "fixing our broken economy, while the federal government and many state legislatures are stuck in partisan gridlock."

Edward Luce plays the same horn. On January 20, 2014, he writes in the *Financial Times* that at a time when the US federal government is largely paralyzed, it is the cities where America's future is being played out. A rising generation of city leaders across the United States is pushing ahead with their agendas.

Luce too blames the political gridlock paralyzing the country at national and state level and believes "it is in the cities where Americas most significant 21st century trends are most vividly on display, and where the most interesting politics is taking place." And he quotes Bruce Katz of the Brookings Institute who also believes that Washington is less and less relevant.

Luce also attributes a rising share of economic action to cities. Even in the high-tech sector, which is traditionally suburban, capital is following talent to the city. "San Francisco beat Silicon Valley when Pinterest, Twitter and Zygna all chose the city as their headquarters."

In his book *City: A Guidebook for the Urban Age*, P.D. Smith says that the buzz of urban life, and the opportunities it offers for cooperation and collaboration, is what attracts people to the city, which in turn "makes cities into the engines of art, commerce, science and progress," a summary of widespread similar observations, now to be experienced by more and more people.

Jim O'Neill, former Goldman Sachs economist, now chairman of the City Growth Commission: "If you look at some of the most successful economies in the world, where many cities play a critical role, they enjoy some degree of independence over their finances and policy choices, China, Germany and the US, all being good examples."

Compressed Energy

Ryan Avent, an economic correspondent for *The Economist* and author of *The Gated City*, puts it just right: "Cities have long been incubators and transmitters of ideas, and correspondingly, engines of economic growth." Cities have their annoying problems, but, Avent says, what makes a city a city is the fact that a city is dense, and when it comes to economic growth and the creation of jobs, "the denser the city the better."

Avent goes so far as to say, "Put workers with similar skills in cities of different densities and the one in the denser place will be more productive. Density facilitates interaction" He creates a simple restaurant example: Suppose that within a population one person in 100 develops a taste for Vietnamese cuisine, and suppose that a Vietnamese restaurant needs a customer base of 1000 people to operate profitable.

> In a city with 10,000 residents, there are not enough people to support a Vietnamese restaurant. A city of one million people, by contrast, can support multiple Vietnamese restaurants. Not only will this larger city enjoy a specialty cuisine available in less populous places, but its ability to support multiple producers of this cuisine allows for competition, improving the price and quality. The result is a stronger, more productive, and higher microeconomic than in the city of 100,000, where only one Vietnamese restaurant can survive or in the town of 10,000 where none at all.

Density of course does not work without talent. And, as Avent says, density is not magic, but a facilitator of interaction. That plus a larger and larger mix with talent as part of the blend, can produce a kind of magic, especially in growth and productivity.

"A quick scan across the world reveals that where growth and innovation have been most successful, a hybrid public private, domestic-foreign nexus lies beneath the miracle. These aren't states, they're 'para-states'—or, in common parlance, 'special economic zones'" (Parag Khanna in *New York Times*, October 12, 2013). Today many cities work like "special economic zones."

China established its first four special economic zones (SEZ) in 1979, among them Shenzhen, which was transformed from a 126-sqare mile village to a busting metropolis and today one of China's richest cities. Eight years later, in 1986, there were 179 SEZs in 46 countries. By 2013 their number had grown to more than 3,000 in 135 countries. The largest special economic zone in Latin America is the Brazilian city Manaus, with a population of 2 million. The Arab world has 300 SEZ, half of them, like Jebel Ali Free Zone, one of the world's largest and most efficient ports, are located in Dubai. Parag Khanna in an op-ed quotes Blumberg saying that he does not care about Washington and adds: "But it's clear that Washington listens to him. The same is true for mayors elsewhere in the world, which is why at least eight former mayors are now heads of states."

"Around the world, mayors take charge" is the headline in an article in the *Atlantic*, which says: "A pattern is emerging in national elections around the world: across regions and continents, mayors are increasingly becoming federal leaders and have also become leading voices in some of the most important global debates." Not always with glorious results, as the example of Francois Hollande, former mayor of Tulle, or Teheran's former mayor Mahmoud Ahmadinejad who became President of the Iran.

China of course has a long tradition of politicians moving up the party ladder by achievements in various positions, including being a mayor and party secretary of first a city, then a province before reaching the top stage as a member of the Standing Committee.

Game Makers in Global Relations

Chicago Mayor Rahm Emanuel is on the go. In his second trip in two months paid by the city's economic development agency, he visited China in December 2013 to promote business opportunities with China. He was accompanied by Chicago-based representatives from Caterpillar, Motorola Solutions, and Hyatt International. Emanuel believes "this will further advance Chicago as a destination for tourism, business and transportation, and demonstrates this administration's commitment to being the most China friendly city in the world."

It was not lip service. During Rahm's Beijing visit economic partnership agreements between eight Chinese cities and Chicago were signed. "We hope that the cooperation between the Chinese cities and Chicago can change the structure of trade, taking the next chapter to areas such as manufacturing, science and technology, new energy and healthcare rather than just soybeans and cotton" said Commerce Minister Gao Hucheng and he pointed out that bilateral trade between China and the United States will total more than $500 billion in 2013. At the beginning of China's opening-up in 1979 it had only been $2.45 billion.

Chicago's Mayor does not limit his activities to China. His first international trip in November 2013 was to Mexico. Behind Los Angeles with 1.5 million Chicago has the second largest Mexicans population of all US cities. On this first trip to Mexico City, with which Chicago has been linked as a sister city since 1991, Rahm Emanuel signed a Global Economic Partnership with Mexico's Mayor Miguel Angel Mancera. The agreements support trade, industry specializations, strong research institutions, exchange, and learning while developing global trade and investment strategies.

Mexico's government has increased funding for innovation in private sectors up to $230 million in 2013, quite an increase from 2012's $150 million. Rapid progress in science and technology is essential in both private and public sectors.

In 2012, The Competitiveness Institute (TCI), the global practitioners network for competitiveness, held its conference in Monterrey, one of Mexico's cities with high growth potential. With its focus on cluster and innovation, TCI is pushing strategic collaboration forward and supports Clusters in Latin American cities based on three pillars: collaboration, sectorial strategies, and innovation. Monterey presented itself as a model of successful economic transformation to one of Mexico's most important cities for cluster and business development.

Boosting competitiveness has become a necessary measure for Africa to stabilize its growing role in the global economy. Maputo, Mozambique, hosted the 5th Pan African Competitiveness Forum, which was focusing on "Innovative Clusters and Innovation systems …for the accelerated Industrial Development in Africa." The Forum was established in 2008 in Addis Ababa with the support of the African Union, the Swedish International Development Cooperation and TCI. The 6th Forum in Tanzania was held in August 2014 and aims to enhance Africa's social and economic development through innovation and cluster-based integration and inter Africa trade" (Pan African Competitiveness Forum website).

Game Makers in Harnessing Synergies

City-to-city matchups had an early start with the "Sister Cities" program created by President Eisenhower in 1955. While its original purpose was citizen exchanges rather than economic link-ups, cities in different countries began to exchange visits with each other, some lead to longer term relationships. Many of China's cities were frontrunners in this city-networking field.

Wuhan, together with Chongqing and Nanjing, is one of China's so called "three furnace cities" because of their summer heat along the Yangtze River Valley.

Wuhan started its sister city project in the very early days of China's opening-up, in 1979. And of all places reaching out to other cities, the city of Oita was chosen. Oita is the most populated city in the island of Kyushu, Japan, China's fiercest enemy between 1937 and 1945. In the 1970s the city became a major production place for electronic products, among them the new companies Toshiba and Canon, which built and expanded their plants in the city. And new technologies were one of the focuses of China in its early stage of opening-up.

Wuhan was not looking back, but looking for bonding with other cities in order to learn and benefit. Only a few years later, in 1982, Wuhan signed agreements with Duisburg, Germany. A significant industry at the time was manufacturing of iron and steel mills. The partnership with Duisburg opened access to qualified German engineers helping to build a Chinese workforce, which then helped the city to build a cold-rolling mill.

Since its first sister city agreement, Wuhan has signed agreements with 18 cities in Europe, USA, Asia, and Latin America.

Cities face tough competition for industry settlements, foreign investment, high schools and universities, a well-trained workforce, affordable housing, and decent living conditions.

Global cooperation and competition to attract investments, trade, and talent is changing from nation to nation, to city to city. With Chengdu doing business directly with San Jose, the relationship between China and Costa Rico is becoming almost incidental.

Cities: Playground for Trial and Error Politics

The Chinese leadership has vowed to put urbanization at the core of his economic and social agenda, which means moving 100 million rural Chinese into cities during the next decade. It is a dramatic shift. Just a generation ago, China's urban population was only 20 percent.

Centralization and globalization are the frame in which China is building clusters to create synergies that boost competitiveness. McKinsey divides China into 22 city clusters, each with its own characteristics and strength. It always again astonishes how fast such clusters develop and also how much China's "Go West" strategy, the economic opening of 12 western Chinese Provinces and Inner Mongolia, is bringing economic growth into former poor, agricultural regions.

In 2011, we published *Innovation in China, The Chengdu Triangle*. The city mostly known for its Panda breeding is a model city when it comes to attracting investment, creating jobs, and combining it with a leisurely lifestyle. Dell, the US Computer Technology Company, alone is investing $100 billion between 210 and 2020.

Even by Chinese standard, small cities such as Suining, with four million people, are jumping on the growth train. In its so-called logistic haven, which in 2013 when we were there was half finished, investment according to *Suining Daily* has reached 6 billion Yuan.

It is important to emphasize that the implementation of Chinese central government reforms is the responsibility of local jurisdictions. For example, cities and provinces will carry out the relaxation in the one-child policy, not the central government, and of course some local jurisdictions will do a better job than others. The same is true of the long list of reforms that were dealt with in the "Third Plenum."

And, it should be no surprise that there is a great disparity in the efficacy of China's thousands of cities. One city that has been very aggressive in implementing economic reforms is Forshan, a city of seven million people in the southern province of Guangdong.

Forshan was already a standout of economic development and is embracing the new reforms of the Plenum. The *Economist* singled out Forshan as one of China's model economic development cities.

To begin with, Forshan's GDP per capital was almost $15,000 in 2012, higher, the *Economist* points out, than some member states of the EU—a manufacturing powerhouse, with some of China's most successful private companies, including household appliance maker Midea, which had 135,000 employees and revenues of more than $16 billion in 2012.

The city of Forshan now has one private enterprise for every 20 residents. In 2012 they grew twice as fast as the remaining state-owned companies. The Third Plenum highlighted that the market should play a more decisive role in China's economy. Clearly, the city of Forshan has already experienced the positive result of its embracing a market economy.

Creating Livable Cities

What is criticized in the Janaagraha study of India is the lack of coordinated urban planning. This of course is gaining importance in all parts of the world, including emerging economies. Once basic needs are covered, the quality of living is gaining importance.

The challenge of global rapid urbanization is the need of economic drivers. But, integrated high-tech clusters without creating sleeping ghettos and high transportation costs need a holistic view and strategic development. One answer we experienced in China is institutional strategic city planning to create a solid ground for coordinated urban and rural development.

China's cities, which are dealing with dangerous and very visible pollution, are experiencing a change in mindset. Instead of solely competing for the highest GDP cities are also rivals in becoming the "most livable city."

Chengdu, where we spent a lot of time in research for China's urbanization, reached its goal and was voted as China's most livable city in 2014. In many visits to other cities, like Hangzhou, Wuhan, Changchun, Suining, and Suzhou we heard the same plan, cities do not only compete in GDP, but also in a newly propagandized happiness index.

We spend much of our time in China, but our home is Vienna, which in the index of most livable cities is ranking number two behind Melbourne. We believe that Vienna is a great city, but we could name a lot of cities, which to us are great places to live as well. At the end it is an individual decision. It may be the drive and energy of a city, its business opportunities, its climate, its living costs, or its culture that makes the difference.

In April, we had the opportunity to speak at a conference in Changwon, Korea. It was the time when the cherry trees blossom. Many of them had been planted in the days of Japanese occupation. After the Japanese had left, the people of Changwon did not tear them out, but added to them, turning a relic of terrible times into a symbol for renewal and growth. Hundreds of thousands of cherry trees are bordering roads; they grow along the tracks of trains, they are blanketing the hills, and embellishing parks and gardens, all advertising the city's attempt to be as livable as innovative.

Epilogue

In our first conceptual thoughts the working title of this book was *Half Time*. Similar to the half time of a football game, when the players are looking back at what was achieved and what mistakes made and forward to create a strategy for the best performance in the continuing game.

Half time is the time to anticipate and get aligned to changes. We are holding on to the familiar conditions of the 20th century and hesitating to embrace the new arrangements of the 21st century. As we describe, new players are pushing themselves into the global economic and political playing field, hungry for success. It is the West that labels them emerging economies, so why are we surprised about their goal to leverage their full potential and work toward a much stronger influence on how the global game is played? After 200 years of dominance the West will have to warm up to giving greater room to its fellow players.

The emerging economies of the Global Southern Belt are no longer acting as subordinated players to the hierarchies of a Westerncentric world. Moreover, they are uniting their voices and building new alliances to create more balanced interactions within the global community. It will take flexibility to handle the ambiguity of the transition period. It is a time of questioning, of developing new strategies and goals.

Embracing the global game change from a Westerncentric to a multicentric world is resisted by another 20th century mindset. When China gradually gained ground against the only superpower, the United States, Western media were quick to put the new picture into an old frame, replacing the Soviet Union and America with the new bipolar couple, the United States and

China. But, China is not going to play the bipolar game. Instead its strategy is to build alliances. To be good partners on equal eye level with African, Asian, and Latin American countries are within the pattern of the Chinese thinking in networks. Chinese believe in connections—guanxi—built over a long period of time. China is taking guanxi to a global level.

Why not connect multicentric with multiprospects? What is a smart move for China is a smart concept for all of us. Our guanxi, our networks of influence, have to be built on thinking in a global context as the game change takes place across-the-board: in economics, in politics, in social developments, and in cultural development. The economic awakening of more than two-thirds of the world's population will change trade routes and consumption patterns, and lead to new monetary frameworks. It is like shuffling the cards for a new game. The difference is that in a game of cards we have no influence over the cards we get. In the global game change we do.

Game change has already entered our working life. Incumbent enterprises are facing competition from new types of competitors. Workers are caught in transition. Our children will have to find their position in a global market for talent, yet most education systems are trailing behind future demands. The rise of the West was built on strong work ethics, diligence and ambition, but they are losing ground fighting for fewer working hours, greater social benefits while ignoring the rising competition of a well-educated, forceful, and hardworking youth in emerging economies, especially in Asia.

There is a lot of talk today about inequality and redistribution. The arguments are as populist as unrealistic. There will never be total equality in income, but there can be equality in education as the foundation for best opportunities in the job markets, nevertheless connected to talent, diligence, and ambition. It is education not redistribution that creates a sustainable foundation for economic progress. Furthermore, corporations are increasingly recruiting knowledge and skills from a worldwide talent pool operating in a gradually borderless business world. More than 200 million international workers were part of the global migration in 2010.

And yet worldwide migration remains a neglected matter in global institutions. Increasing mobility and economic interconnectedness demands cooperation in international law and institutions dealing with these aspects on a global level. More so as in the longer time frame we will see one economy for the whole world.

America led the world as a country of immigrants. Around 50 percent of US innovation has been achieved by the country's 12 percent migrants. Highly skilled migrants fill gaps where native labor falls short. Demographic shifts in advanced economies especially in Europe will demand an increasing number of migrants to return to a sustainable ratio of working to nonworking citizens. We have to open our doors instead of closing them. The great spirit of Western democracy needs to be revitalized. The West needs leaders with long-term strategies instead of a self-serving political class with a short-term election-driven mindset. And only education in governing can avoid a majority falling into the trap of short-term election benefits.

Global access to the Internet and digitalization is changing production in macro and microeconomics with decreasing numbers of blue-collar workers. The next stage of Internet development allows companies, entrepreneurs, and individuals in emerging economies to participate in the global economy, as more and more consumers spend their money online. China's knowledge-intensive products such as pharmaceuticals and semiconductors have become the world's second largest. Virtual collaboration, web-meeting software, and file-sharing sites support globally minded people. It opens countless doors for those who make swift moves but creates barriers for those who still live with the picture of 20th century labor markets.

Decentralization and rapid urbanization is creating a more accessible matrix. The goal to create livable cities, garden cities, and green cities is increasingly replacing the sole focus on economic growth.

The future is in our hands. Change does not just come about. It is the summary of thousands and thousands of single actions. It is in the hands of citizens and governments. It is half time. Global Game Change is not just a foggy picture any more. It is taking shape and we can see the contours of new arrangements. Our country, our region, and city may lag behind in adapting to the global game change. We may or may not like what the transition will bring, but the direction is set and hanging on to the pictures and mindsets of the past will neither change reality nor serve us.

We are optimistic. The Global Game Change represents unlimited opportunities to reinvent our economic and social relationships as we shape the new world of the 21st century.

Appendix

China

A Closer Look into China's Roadmap

The 2013 Role of the Third Plenum

Every culture has its own language. But even though hardly anyone would contradict that, when it comes to translating it into practice we have our problems. We sometimes remind ourselves that the Chinese mind is as different from Western thinking as are Chinese characters to Latin letters. And it is not just the wording. Holistic thinking and strategies that go way beyond current legislative periods while at the same time leaving room for flexibility are seen differently looking at it through Western lenses. A Western mindset creates Western pictures, which often lead to misinterpretations of China's official language. Such was the case when China announced the results of the Third Plenum. Was it a declaration of intent or ambitious reform package for the next decade?

The Third Plenum is held every five years and deals with China's economic roadmap.

It is the third time China's new leaders have led a plenary session of the Central Committee, a forum where traditionally important reforms are announced. There are many voices in China saying that China's new leader Xi Jinping and the 2013 Third Plenum will play in the same league as Deng Xiaoping's 1978 announcement of China's reform and opening up.

In the 2013 Third Plenum 370 top Party officials met for four days to outline and approve China's economic plans for the next 10 years. The resulting report is important because:

1. China will increasingly claim a role that matches its new economic and geo-political position in the global community.
2. There is a strong and growing consensus in China that Xi Jinping is the most powerful leader since Deng Xiaoping.

Deng Xiaoping's reform and opening-up of China and his call for "emancipating the mind" of the Chinese people led to a remarkable unprecedented turnaround of China and its rise to be the workshop of the world. "President Xi echoed Deng's earlier speeches, saying it would be a 'dead end' if the country failed to reform and it should waste no more time in implementing 'deeper reforms'," wrote *South China Morning Post*, March 14, 2014. The article called Xi and Deng "both practical men whose reforms were designed to tackle the social and economic problems facing the country."

Deng Xiaoping's reform and opening up led to the domestic revitalization of China.

Xi Jinping will rejuvenate China in the context of China as a global power.

Deng Xiaoping's reforms played out relatively unobserved by the global community.

Xi Jinping's reforms will play out under the close observation of the global community.

Deng Xiaoping's reforms applied success models of advanced economies to China.

Xi Jinping's reforms will themselves become a model for the Global Southern Belt.

In his speech to the 18th National Congress of The Communist Party of China on November 14, 2013, President Xi Jinping made it clear that China is entering a new stage in its development. He called for "standing rock firm with completely new image in the family of nations."

President Xi Jinping and Premier Li Keqiang are preparing to unleash market forces as never before.

To judge the reliability of the announcements of the Third Plenum needs to be examined against China's history. It was the first time the government has promised to open up protected industries, including finance and energy, to more private capital, giving entrepreneurs the opportunities they lacked before. Although these openings are initially expected to be modest, China will also move to market-determined pricing for necessities such as fuel, food, and pharmaceuticals. China's opening-up to global markets will demand a constant surge in productivity, efficiency, and innovation that the leadership believes will enhance and drive the overall economy.

This includes China's state-owned enterprises (SOEs), which through the headwinds of global competition will be forced to develop corrective mechanisms. Ruchar Sharma, Canadian lawyer, and bestselling author and head of emerging markets at Morgan Stanley Investment Management estimates that over the past five years, the value of private companies in emerging economies has remained broadly stable, while the value of state-owned companies dropped more than 40 percent. He said investors have once again come to see state companies as "slow-witted giants, prone to overinvest and overbuild. Government-run companies are valued at about half the price of private firms in the same industry, from banking to telecoms."

The more crucial part of President Xi's push is to make existing SOEs more like private companies in their operations (if not in their ultimate ownership). There is a go-ahead to create new, privately held banks. It seems the president and the premier are preparing to unleash market forces as never before. In a November 2013 ad in the *Wall Street Journal* China presented itself as "embracing evolutionary change ... and as a country moving towards a market driven system powered by the private sector."

It was an interesting experience in 2006, when we spoke to a meeting of 400 CEO's of Chinese state-owned companies. We were asked how many of China's state-owned companies should be privatized? We answered "almost all of them." Instead of the shock we expected the response was broad applause.

A Blueprint for China's Future

The formal Chinese language and relatively clumsy English translations should not mislead one to discount the importance of the Third Plenum documents. They are a blue print for China's future development, setting broad policy directions for deepening reform and further opening-up. By all accounts the worldwide response to the plan to continue the overhaul the Chinese economy has been overwhelmingly positive. The Third Plenum presented the most comprehensive and most ambitious national reform program since Zhu Rongji.

FAZ Sonntagszeitung on November 13, 2014, reflects this view: "China on the Third Plenum has presented the most comprehensive and most ambitious reform package of this decade. In most parts of Western population this is not taken seriously but declared as a declaration of intent. What a misjudgment!"

Forbes, November 24, 2013: "The market was apparently pleased, rallying across multiple sectors, including bank stocks. The plan appears to be a crowd pleaser, possibly because it appeared to be detailed enough to be credible." Forbes does see low points in the Plenum, but the article closes "With appropriate, market-friendly reforms, China still has decades of robust growth ahead of it."

International Business Forum, November 15, 2013 wrote that President Xi Jinping's sweeping changes reaffirms the leadership's commitment to social and economic reforms. It quotes *Capital Economics* opinion: "Questions will remain over implementation, but this is the most impressive statement of reform intentions that we've seen this century."

The *Economist* was cautiously optimistic about the party's new blueprint: "The rhetoric (of the Plenum) is very positive. But Mr Xi will have to battle a deep resistance to change among state-owned enterprises, local governments, and even an urban middle class that likes his notion of 'social fairness' but does not want to see its own privileges eroded by the granting of equal access to health care and education to migrants from the countryside. As the resolution rightly said, reforms have entered deep water."

Financial Times wrote: "This meeting did not disappoint, as Mr Xi's administration published a sweeping blueprint for social and economic reforms" But it adds, "For those with a finely tuned ear for Chinese pronouncements, the meeting was far more about domestic reforms than encouraging more foreign investments through further opening up ... Further market-oriented reforms aimed at removing government control over the prices of key inputs such as water, energy and land were also clearly aimed at reinvigorating the economy ... Global companies that have had rough time saw few clues that their fortunes were about to improve. Some observers," *Financial Times* wrote "had hoped the plenum would announce concrete measures to rein in China's state-owned enterprises, which dominate vast swaths of the economy, while also unveiling land and residency reforms to better the lot of the 260m migrant workers."

The *New York Times* believes that "there are two reasons to believe that the leadership's latest promises are credible, and that reforms will be momentous, maybe even historic. First because of President Xi's very solid power base and second because China's imperative for change is greater today than at any point after the Cultural Revolution." The author of the article in the NYT, Stephen S. Roach, senior fellow at the Jackson Institute of Global Affairs at Yale University and former chairman of Morgan Stanley Asia, concludes: "Thirty-five years ago, an earlier Third Plenum gave Deng Xiaoping an opportunity for China to unleash the most powerful economic development story of modern history. America needs its own Third Plenum moment."

Excerpts from the *China Daily*: Summary of the Third Plenum Reforms

From a Western point of view, a vague formulation such as upgrading the market from a "basic role" to a "decisive role" is not too exciting. From a Chinese point of view it means more room for adapting the economic approach to be globally competitive. In our opinion, the character and range of reforms are well defined with a strong emphasis on decentralization, transparency, and a stronger role for the individual. In March 2013, *China Daily* dedicated a series of reports on details of the reforms. The list below is a short excerpt of the wide range of China's reform package for the next decade:

Deeper reforms: Streamlining the administration, delegating more power to lower levels, government reform of fiscal and tax system, transparent budget system, general transfer payments, reform of banking modernizing of the SOE sector, mixed ownership of economic entities.

Wider opening: Bilateral, multilateral, and regional opening-up to a new open economic system, embracing global markets, upgrading export and foreign trade, leveraging the Shanghai Pilot Free Trade Zone, opening inland border areas into hotspots, investment agreements with such key partners as the United States, EU, South Korea, Australia, and the Gulf Cooperation Council.

Domestic demand: Boosting domestic demand, removing barriers to a nationwide unified market, cutting distribution costs. Raising government spending.

Rural development: setting a minimum of sustaining 120 million hectares arable land, increasing the quality and productivity in agriculture. Setting a minimum purchase price for wheat and rice, dealing with social issues of the rural population.

Urbanization: Further industrialization with greater consideration of citizens, urban residency for migrant workers, reform of the hukou system, improving infrastructure and water conservancy, energy and municipal services.

Economic reform: Science and technology management systems, a trial reform policy of science parks, support cutting edge and key technologies, strengthening property rights, full IT integration in industrialization.

Egalitarian society: Coordinate social economic development. Raise the quality of education, support underprivileged students in poorer regions, greater power of universities on enrollments, develop vocational education and establish private schools. Medical reform and health insurance.

People's well-being: Social security system, increasing employment opportunities, public housing, support of start-ups, collective wage bargaining, loosening the one child policy.

Environmental protection: Fighting pollution by improving industrial structures, raising energy efficiency, reduce car emissions, reducing PM10 and PM2.5 emissions. Raise proportion of non-fossil fuel, push hydropower and nuclear projects, implement major ecological projects, protect forests, conserve water, and reverse the expansion of deserts.

Between Two Worlds

In most Western comments, all acknowledgement of economic progress of China fades away when it comes to touch politically sensitive matters. Everybody has an opinion, but not too much of it is built on real background information. In the past years several Chinese officials and private people have encouraged us to write about China's most controversial regions, Tibet and Xingjiang province with its capital Urumqi. We have refused so far because of the complexity of the situation. There are too many ways to look at it, too many historical facts that are not yet clear to us, and most of all, a lot of emotion.

Having been to Lhasa for a week, we got a mixed picture of modernity and spirituality, of Tibetans who want to become integrated in China's economic progress and those who feel overrun by Han Chinese, with their ambitions, their aggressive will to move on. In addition, there is the role of the government that, depending on who you talk to, is either supportive or suppressing. Whether you call it good or bad, Tibet is in transition. Not much different from the change most places in the world have or are undergoing on their path to industrialization and in this case, to leapfrog into the digital age.

We have met young ethnic Tibetan entrepreneurs, fiercely embracing modernity. We have met people who want the Chinese out by tomorrow. We have visited farmers who welcomed the support of Beijing and proudly showed their new homes and their cows. They are proud of their children and grandchildren who now have higher education, make a better living with much less hard work. We have heard about corruption and assaults of Chinese police and we learned of monks whose life in a monastery means security and a good income. There are so many facets and certainly there is not only one truth except one: whether they are Han or Tibetans, those who are the most ambitious and the most persistent are on the side of modernization and feel its benefits.

The same is true for Urumqi. And the grim picture painted in Western media is, if all true, only one side of the coin. We have been invited to come and make our own picture of the region, even in times of turbulence, but so far we could not make it. There might be a number of business reports that show the other side of life in Urumqi, but the only one of the kind we came across appeared in *Forbes Asia* in June 2014. It tells the story about Kudret Yakup a young Uighur entrepreneur, who founded Erqal Capital, by his estimate one of 300 to 500 companies controlled by ethnic minorities, which have "a three to five year plan, a growth strategy, a proper team and a steady cash flow." Erqal Capital, with its office in downtown Urumqi, is an investment firm but also clubhouse for homegrown entrepreneurs. Erqal Capital currently has five investors and six deals worth $25 million. "Kudret Yakup," writes *Forbes*, "is a pioneer. Brought up in Han Chinese schools, he is the only one of Xinjiang's 13 million minority ethnics—mostly Uighurs, like him—to sport a Harvard undergraduate degree. Four years after graduation he has circled back to his roots to tap into what can be surprising deep pockets."

We can look for confirmation of our opinion or be open to learn something new.

Aikebaier Abudula, co-founder with Yakup, has invested $14 million in cash into the company not counting undisclosed additional assets. Abudula made his money as a recognized jade trader when he got into mining in early 2000, before the trade rush. He and his two illiterate brothers have been trading jade all around the country and have now also invested in real estate, pharmaceuticals, and hospitals. They are well connected to the east of China, another asset of the new company. Abudula values Kudret's knowledge in finance and of the US market. "I have been to many places," he said, "and seen all kinds of entrepreneurs. I have a deep understanding of the gap between us and those (outside of Xinjiang) …Without a good grasp of joint capital our enterprise will not grow big nor pass wealth to the next generation."

Marika Viciziany, professor of Australia's Monash University who conducted the first research on Xinjian's private entrepreneurs, believes that there are many more wealthy minority families than we imagine. She recalls a visit to a small town north of Kashgar, on China's western edge, "where a family owned a handful of luxury cars and a huge, atrium style, multistoried house with a large tree at its center."

Yakup's view on where "enterprising ethnic minorities might best entertain hopes" is not far from what is true all over China, whether you are Han or a minority: if you insist on going into real estate, insist on getting the mines that are not supposed to belong to you, then you will have to rely on the government. But if you open a restaurant, for example, you can have tens of thousands of branches all over China—and nobody will restrain you" (based on *Forbes Asia*, June 2014).

About the Authors

John Naisbitt, Chairman of Naisbitt China Institute, has been in the limelight of the publishing world since 1982, when his book *Megatrends* was published. As a *New York Times* number one bestseller for almost two years, it was one of the publishing's greatest success stories, selling more than 14 million copies in 57 countries. The *Wall Street Journal* called his work "triumphantly useful … taking bearings in all directions and giving us the courage to do the same."

Megatrends was followed by international bestsellers including *Re-inventing the Corporation* in 1985, *Megatrends 2000* in 1990, *Global Paradox* in 1992, *Megatrends Asia* in 1995, *High Tech High Touch* in 1999, and *MindSet!* in 2006.

John Naisbitt holds 21 honorary doctorate degrees from and professorships at American, Chinese, and Russian universities and South Korea's Pukyong National University.

In his early career, John Naisbitt has been an executive at Kodak and IBM. At the age of 34, he was appointed as the assistant secretary of education to President John F. Kennedy. After the president's assassination he became a special assistant to President Lyndon Johnson. Urged by the social and racial turbulences in America's cities, John Naisbitt began analysis of social, economic, and political developments in the United States, which led to the publication of *Megatrends* in 1982.

Doris Naisbitt, an observer of global social, economic, and political trends, is the Director of the Naisbitt China Institute. She is also the President of the John Naisbitt University, Belgrade, the largest private university in Europe. She is a co-author of the bestseller *Megatrends China: Eight Pillars of a New Society*, *The China Model*, and *Innovation in China: The Chengdu Triangle* and the author of *Mai-Lin My China*. She holds professorships at Nankai, Yunnan, and Yunnan Normal Universities in China and Skolkovo Open University in Russia.

Doris Naisbitt entered the publishing world at the age of 39, after working in the production of television documentaries for Walter Davy, an award-winning director. She has a distinguished career in publishing, serving as the head of the Austrian publishing house, SignumVerlag. During her tenure, she upgraded the company by acquiring internationally known authors and establishing SignumVerlag as a player in the broader German language market, including Germany and Switzerland. Other international authors whom she has brought to the German language market include Peter Senge, the author of the world-acclaimed *Fifth Discipline*, and Don Tapscott, the author of the ground-breaking new book *Wikinomics*.